A Gift
from
Our Daughter Lou~
on my Birthda

FINDING A FLAME LILY

A teenager in Africa

Judy Rawlinson

First Published 2015

Published by Rawlinson Publications
Neighbrook, Gloucestershire, GL56 9QP

Designed by Loose Chippings
The Paddocks, Chipping Campden, Gloucestershire, GL55 6AU
www.loosechippings.org

Front cover and back cover photographs by kind permission of Melanie Bousfield.

Printed and bound in England by CPI Antony Rowe, Chippenham, Wiltshire.

Paperback ISBN 978-1-907991-13-4
eBook ISBN 978-1-907991-14-1

For Bob and my family

Remember the dust and the termites, the happy faces and friendship.

Megan Landless

(Photo: Robert Chisanga)

CONTENTS

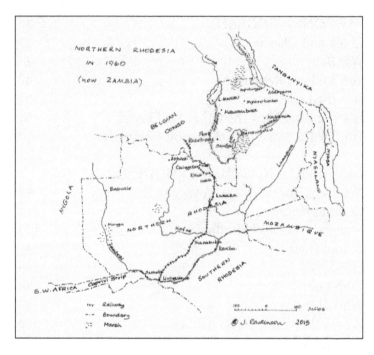

Maps showing the location of Northern Rhodesia

FOREWORD

Finding a Flame Lily continues a long and venerable tradition of British memoir writing set both at home and abroad. What makes this memoir stand out, however, is that the story is told through the eyes of a young, working class girl.

Still untarnished by the prejudices of the time, and recounting events with the candour of which only children are capable, our narrator gives a strikingly honest account of the people and places she encounters. Naïve and unworldly she may be, but young Judy proves to be an unexpectedly inquisitive, intelligent and perceptive observer.

Written over a period of ten years, the memoir is based on vivid personal recollection, original documents and private letters, as well as extensive background reading and research. Sources range from contemporary guidebooks and travel narratives to academic books and treatises.

The result is a fresh, engaging memoir on one level. On another, it's a well-written and well-crafted narrative, interwoven with enduring themes – adolescence, first love, first loss and sense of identity – as well as a ready, whimsical sense of humour. It's also a searching portrait of two countries during an important period of adjustment: the social reordering of postwar Britain and the first stirrings of independence in Northern Rhodesia.

The story is also coloured by unusually well-observed characters – from 'barfly Nina', a bored housewife, to Simon, the aspirational Bemba cook. Judy also shows an acute ear for dialogue, whether recalling the Cockney brogue of her East End father or the Afrikaner slang of her school mates, as well as the evocative noises and notes of the African bush.

The book is a charming memoir and an entertaining and satisfying read but is also a beautifully-observed piece of historical, political and socio-economic commentary. Rather like the eponymous flower, *Finding a Flame Lily* may beguile you in more ways than one.

Frances Linzee-Gordon
Travel writer and photographer

PREFACE

This is a story about a childhood spent in postwar London and Northern Rhodesia (now Zambia) during the last days of colonial rule in the late 1950s. It is also about my ordinary yet remarkable family, including a father from the east end of London and a mother who grew up in the Burmese jungle. My parents uprooted themselves from dreary postwar Britain to seek a new life in Africa in a country about which we knew very little. There followed the happiest years of their lives.

This period of my life, until I left the continent to continue my education, changed my perception of the world. I discovered a new environment and myself. It was happy and sad, colourful, sometimes monotonous and intensely irritating but also magical, one I shall never forget. Africa is like the bite of the tsetse fly – it gets into the blood – and it instilled in me a love of the natural world and wild places. When I disembark from a plane anywhere in the continent south of the Sahara I feel as though I am coming home.

My memories are vivid but I apologise for any inaccuracies; all the events actually happened but I have altered some people's names. Times and attitudes have changed and I know that some of the events, words and phrases recorded in the book may seem politically incorrect – but I tell it how it was.

This book took a while to complete – I wrote the first draft in 2005 – and I hope that everyone with a love of Africa, its wildlife and people will enjoy it.

Neighbrook, Gloucestershire, 2015

All the events in this book actually happened but names have been changed, in some instances. You may recognise yourself if you were especially nice, naughty or both.

PART ONE

LONDON

Chapter 1
CHALK & CHEESE

Mum and Dad, with Gran, on their wedding day.
Maymyo, 1936

It wasn't until Dad was demobbed in 1946 and home for good that it struck me how different my parents were in almost every way. I wondered how they had ever married?

A good looking man, my father, Jack, was fair, with a mop of floppy, light brown hair. His intensely blue eyes were almond-shaped and turned into slits when he laughed. A true cockney, his face was long, with high cheekbones, softened by a wide grin and a good line of chat, which he used to some effect on the ladies. By nature he was talkative, impulsive but generous, practical, gregarious and naïve. Dulce, my mother, was as dark as Dad was fair, with soft, almost black hair with a slight natural wave and bright, dark brown eyes. She was intelligent, musical, cultured, quick on the uptake and unassuming. Whereas Dad tended to rush around in an energetic fashion, Mum seldomy appeared to hurry yet she achieved a tremendous amount in a day. She rarely lost her temper but could rule us with a quiet word and a look, being mistress of the caustic comment. Dad loved gardening, Mum didn't, though she adored the scented sweet peas and old-fashioned roses that Dad grew. Dad was a flash in the pan, Mum was a dark horse.

My father Jack was a true East Ender, born within the sound of Bow Bells in 1911. His earliest memory is of his sister running into the street to grab his hand and drag him inside: bombs were falling, being dropped by Zeppelins. He had grown up as the youngest child in a poor, highly dysfunctional family: alcoholic mother, absent father, three sisters and a brother who had died in a motorcycle accident. Despite the fact that he was intelligent and anxious to go further, his mother had forced him to leave school at the age of 14 to help support the family. His jobs had included making tomato boxes for Spitalfields Market (for wholesale fruit and vegetables), working as a timber man on the docks and making barrels in a cooper's, where he also drove a brewer's dray. He had tried to join the army in Woolwich, the Royal Horse Artillery, but had lied about his age – he was only 16. His mother found out and notified the army so he was yanked off home unceremoniously, to help provide for the family. He tried again when he was 18 and this time successfully joined the King's Royal Rifles, the KRR, in Winchester. His spell in the army was a solid

Dad in India, 1942 – 1943

foundation for the rest of his working life and made full use of his practical nature and mathematical ability.

By the mid 1930s my father had been stationed in various parts of India and reached Rangoon, Burma, where he met my mother at a church dance.

While my father's origins were simple my mother's were unclear: she had been born south of Rangoon to a police inspector and his half-Spanish wife but there was a dash of Indian blood in our ancestry, which my mother was always careful to conceal. When my parents met, Mum had progressed from working for the Harbour Board to become the private secretary to Sir Kenneth Harper, Managing Director of the Burmah Oil Company in Rangoon. She had trained as a secretary in the 1920s, unusual in that country as at that time most clerical workers were male. She lived with her widowed mother in an apartment with their faithful Indian retainer, Ramsamy, who had followed them around the country for many years. Every night he guarded my grandmother by lying across her bedroom door to go to sleep! An anonymous donor had offered to sponsor Mum at university some years earlier but she had declined because her older brother, Eric, had not been given the same opportunity. Despite their being among the top three students in the Higher School Certificate results for the Indian sub-continent, my grandfather had died young and there were not enough funds to ensure a university education for the children: work was the only option and Mum had her own mother to support.

Mum was 32 by the time she married my father – almost consigned to being on the shelf by the standards of the day. She had received proposals of marriage before, but told me that she had turned them down as she had stipulated that my grandmother be part of the package – Mum refused to abandon her. My father had to ask the army's permission for him to marry my mother, a fact that was only revealed to my brother, John, when Dad was in his seventies.

John was in the garden of my parents' house in Farnborough with Dad, who was steamed up about something. He had not been at all well and had just argued with my mother.

"Honestly, John, she treats me as though I was Ramsamy sometimes!" he exclaimed. "It wasn't always like that. She wasn't bossy when we were young – quite the reverse. And you know, I had to get permission from my commanding officer to marry your mum. And he refused."

"Why?" said John.

"Because she was Anglo-Indian."

"What?!"

"I got round it, though."

"I got her pregnant. Then, of course, I was allowed to marry her. But I had to leave the army."

That earth-shattering conversation explained so much about our family. Why we were different from those around us, always on the move, why my mother was obsessed with our having a good education and behaving well. I can't blame my mother for being vague about her

Top: *Mum on train to Maymyo, 1936*
Centre: *Mum's apartment, Rangoon, 1936*
Bottom: *Mum, far left. Anyone for tennis?*

origins. In those postwar days, any suggestion of Asian blood would have been frowned upon, whereas today it is celebrated, as my children point out.

None of this was apparent to my brother and me as children, however. The fact that my father was a cockney sparrer, my grandmother's voice was faintly accented and my mother's pronunciation pure BBC did not strike me as at all odd. I just knew that Mum had high standards, in speech, language, education, manners – and expected us to follow her example. I adored her. We were aware that we did live a little differently to our London neighbours. They did not eke out their wartime rations with spicy lentils, potato curry or crispy noodles, use table napkins, call elevenses tiffin or attend private schools, as John and I did. How my parents afforded it was due to Mum's talents as a money manager, her secretarial work and the continuing presence of Gran as a live-in babysitter. Dad's army wage and his postwar jobs in sales and the building trade in no way matched Mum's, something which irked him and would later provide the spur for seeking a better job and a new life abroad.

Although Mum and Dad had met in Rangoon they were married in Maymyo, named after one Colonel May, a favourite place of respite from the heat of the plains in colonial days. It has been called the most beautiful hill station in the Far East, and was the summer capital of colonial Burma. The town was very British in character, with half-timbered mansions, roses growing in beautiful gardens and quiet, tree-shaded roads, surrounded by teak and bamboo forests.

In the 1920s George Orwell had taken the train to Maymyo. He wrote:

19

You start off in the typical atmosphere of an Eastern city – the scorching sunlight, the dusty palms, the smell of fish and spices and garlic, the squashy tropical fruits, the swarming dark-faced human beings – and because you are so used to it you carry this atmosphere intact, so to speak, in your railway carriage. Mentally, you are still in Mandalay when the train stops at Maymyo, four thousand feet above sea level. But in stepping out of the carriage, you step into a different hemisphere. Suddenly you are breathing cool sweet air that might be that of England, and all around you are green grass, bracken, fir trees and hill-women with pink cheeks selling baskets of strawberries.

Gran went to my parents' wedding, of course and is included in some of the photos. Dulce and her mother Irene had been through hard times together and there would be more in the Old Country.

Mum had started work straight after leaving school – no chance of any further academic education for her, although she took a secretarial course. She continued to work full time until the age of 68. Having had such a prestigious job in Rangoon, the money saved from her salary ensured that she had enough money to help pay for the family's fares to England and the rental of Lavender Cottage, in Grayshott, Hampshire. John was born there and I was to appear some years later, in North London. Our lives there would bear little comparison to the more leisurely, social times my parents had enjoyed in tropical Burma.

Chapter 2
WAR BABY: London, 1941-1946

Photo taken for Dad whilst in India, 1944

I was born early on the in the war, in a hospital in Kingsbury, Middlesex on Honeypot Lane. I always thought this address sounded romantic until I later found out it was also the home of Zenith Carburettors: yes, I had opened my eyes to the world on a future industrial estate. My father was abroad at the time and Gran would catch a bus to see my exhausted mother with her new baby. After the birth Mum was given a cup of tea then, a few hours later, one sausage and a spoonful of grey, lumpy mashed potato. As she surveyed this none too sumptuous repast, the mother in the next bed raised an eyebrow and commented, laconically "'Ere, that mash is just crying out for a bit of gravy, innit?"

Until I went to school at the age of 4, Gran and Sally – the first in a long line of family spaniels – were my constant daytime companions. Our little family lived crammed into the rented ground floor of an end terraced house. The kitchen was really just a scullery. We spent most of our time in the tiny living/dining room, sandwiched between two bedrooms in the front and back of the flat. The lavatory was freezing cold because you had to go outside under the lean-to to reach it, was but its wooden seat warmed up quickly before you grabbed two statutory leaves of scratchy Bronco off the toilet roll. The only bathroom in the house was part of the flat above so when we were tiny a tin bath was used in front of the fire, where we sheltered behind a clothes horse draped with towels as we were vigorously dried. We were allowed two "proper" baths a week, with no more than the prescribed four inches of water ("even the King abides by the rules", said Gran), heated by an Ascot geyser. The blue pilot light burned with a wavering flame. To spark the whole thing up involved matches and great care, until the gas ignited with a frightening WHUMP. A trickle of water spluttered out of its long tap, clouding the whole bathroom with steam of a searing temperature.

To climb the stairs to the bathroom was an unnerving experience as we had to run the gauntlet of Mrs. Williams, the upstairs occupant and the other tenant, a loud Irishwoman with the dramatic good looks of a young Maureen O'Hara. There was no Mr. Williams. Dad, in his guileless fashion, charmed her, but Mum was wary of her volatile temperament.

Many of our neighbours were Irish, working on one of the light industrial estates on the Edgware and North Circular roads or in the building trade. Some had emigrated from Ireland during The Troubles of the 1930s, when discrimination had been a problem. "No Irish" posters were put up in many a lace-curtained front window in boarding houses, as they struggled to find work and a roof over their heads, and there had been high levels of alcoholism and homelessness. They filled the Galtymore Dance Club at night, the notes of the band's manic fiddles and flutes spilling out through the doors on to the Broadway. They patronised the pubs, staggering out at closing time, accompanied by a rank smell of stale beer and fag smoke wafting on to the pavement. The maudlin drinkers' chosen music would be a soulful ditty such as "I'll Take You Home Again, Kathleeen" or "Danny Boy" and we gave them a wide berth on the bus.

To relieve our cramped living quarters we at least had the run of a garden. During the war it supplied many of our vegetables to supplement a frugal diet. Mum managed to grow plenty of runner beans and peas in Dad's absence. Wartime rations dictated one egg a week, very little meat or fish and miniscule amounts of dairy products, meat and sugar. We were healthy but thin. My mother, skinniest of all, sacrificed her portions for the rest of us and consequently collapsed in the street one day, anaemic and malnourished.

"I know what, Dulce, I'll find some stuff to make a henhouse," said Dad, home on leave. "It's stupid, you giving the kids all the best food. You need to look after yourself, girl. An egg a day, that's what you need."

Dad scrounged some rusty air raid shelter mesh and scraps of wood to make a henhouse and chicken run. He walked to the station early one morning and came back with some day-old chicks, Rhode Island Reds, which grew into beautiful, glossy hens.

Christmas, 1941, just after I was born, had been the first one to be subject to food rationing.

The weekly allowances per head were:

4oz bacon
6oz butter
2oz tea
8oz sugar
2oz cooking fats
3oz cheese
4oz jam
2 pints milk

Oh yes, and three eggs – a month!

I was going through a ballet craze at the time. Mum had forked out for dancing lessons to improve my non-existent co-ordination and correct my flat feet. I adored my pink satin ballet shoes (secondhand), special concert tutu (lovingly stitched by my mother) and romantic music. Mum must have struggled to provide special dresses as clothing was still rationed. I did try hard but I wasn't cut out to be the next Margot Fonteyn. My only redeeming features were the long toes on my narrow feet, the first two equal in length, so I could stand *en point*.

Mum was a talented dancer and had a chest full of her pre-war glad rags from her ballroom dancing days with Dad. It included a grey silk gown with thin straps cut on the bias, a peach-coloured chiffon number with fine multicoloured stripes and a beaded black crêpe de chine, plus numerous silk camisoles and petticoats she had sewn by hand herself. Occasionally she had a chance to wear one of the dresses to an office dance, when she would come to kiss me goodnight smelling deliciously of Coty L'Aimant. The drawers in her little tallboy contained her selection of chiffon scarves, all smelling of this perfume, and neat piles of lambswool jerseys. Dad liked to dress up too and his claim to fame was that he had once danced with Merle Oberon, the film actress, in his army days out east. As I subsequently found out, she was Anglo-Indian, a fact she had taken great pains to conceal during her life.

In homage to my favourite ballet character, I christened our largest hen Odette, after the heroine of Swan Lake. She was glossy, plump and totally spoilt. I carried her everywhere, even to bed if possible, and provided her with the most succulent worms I could find, although I couldn't understand why the worms died when I put them on the rockery to dry out.

The hens provided us with large brown eggs, which Mum cooked in a number of ways. I was put off coddled eggs for life, which Mum baked in brown ramekins. These emerged from the oven looking set but, in reality, were sickeningly soft in the centre, with some of the whites still clear.

The shed and the lean-to were other special places when the weather got cold. We had one climbable tree in the garden, a pear which was covered in white blossom each spring. To Mum's disgust, Dad cut it down one year because it "wasn't producing any pears".

"Have you no soul, Jack?" asked Mum.

My grandmother cooked up the hens' layers mash and collected their eggs, a task she delegated to me when I was on holiday. She was housekeeper, provider of our high tea after school, childminder, nursery school teacher, confidante, seamstress and surrogate mother rolled into one. Gran also did most of the grocery shopping, which involved managing the ration books and eking out food for the month, standing for hours in endless queues in all weathers and wheedling extra bits and pieces out of shopkeepers and market traders. Her haggling skills were considerable and she was both cheerful and charming, even in the face of adversity.

Mum was working as a secretary in an office at the Ministry of Information, which had taken over Senate House, Gower Street. She had worked throughout the terrible Blitz and watched the Battle of Britain dogfights from the rooftop in 1940, the year before I was born, saying it was too much of an effort to keep going down to the basement air raid shelter. I think she enjoyed the excitement in an otherwise dull existence. Dad was abroad with the army, probably on the Indian subcontinent but exactly where we weren't sure. He had set sail on a troopship, the P & O *Orion* and posed for a photo taken on shore leave in Durban, South Africa. My brother, John, five years older than me, must have been at school. He might even have been evacuated to a boarding school, an experiment in pastoral care and education which was to prove unsuccessful. Gran was relieved not to be looking after him for a while. She'd spent many anxious moments chasing one small, lively boy around the streets when air raids threatened as he was either off on his bike or playing marbles in the gutter. He paid no attention to boring, external interruptions such as air raid sirens and became extremely irritated at being hauled indoors.

My fiery half-Spanish grandmother, Irene Florence Mendieta, was born in 1883 in Calcutta. When her mother moved to Rangoon, Burma, she was sent to La Martiniere school in Calcutta as a "Foundationer". It had a good scholastic reputation and discipline was very strict – cold baths at 6.00am, summer and winter. My mother noted:

Mother was always something of a rebel and was once put in solitary on a diet of bread and water for speaking out of turn. She had a fine soprano voice and was in the School Cantata – they allowed her out to sing her part and then returned her to her "cell"!

La Martiniere, founded in 1836, still exists and was rated the top girls' school in India in 2014.

Gran left school at 16 to join her mother and married Henry two years later. He was the son of a Sergeant Major in the Buffs (the Royal East Kent Regiment) and was born in Toungou, Lower Burma as Upper Burma had not yet been annexed by the British. Mum said:

He was extremely good looking. Being fond of outdoor activities – swimming, riding shooting – and there being few openings to choose from, I suppose he naturally gravitated towards the Police, which he joined as a cadet. He was soon posted out to the districts and this proved his undoing, although he himself preferred the life to a desk job. He contracted malaria, which plagued him for the rest of his life, and he eventually died of pernicious anaemia brought on by unrelenting bouts of malaria and sprue.

The births of my mother and uncle were attended by the doctor (drunk, on one occasion) and Karen tribeswomen near the Siamese border. Henry, known as Hal, Irene and their two children Eric and Dulce were constantly on the move and lived camp-fashion in wooden government bungalows. Away from the line of rail, Hal had to tour by country boat and bullock cart to deal with insurgency and was often away from home for weeks at a time, leaving his wife alone with two small children. On one occasion, when chasing dacoits (armed bandits) he had to travel by elephant over the Siamese boarder south of Moulmein. Mum told me that Gran was never afraid to be alone and

how she endured the life I can't imagine, because she was always a very sociable person and loved company. Her optimism and good spirits were fantastic in face of the really hard time she went through. I can still see her sitting at her hand sewing machine, making clothes for us children and singing her heart out. She was always warm and comforting and, though she didn't spare the rod, we always felt we were loved and safe with her around.

"No, I don't want to wear it!"

Gran was trying to truss me up in a liberty bodice, a harsh woollen vest which fastened down the front. The rubber buttons dug into my skin.

"But you must."

"Why?"

"Because it's cold outside."

I struggled.

4223. Calcutta.
La Martiniere.

Top: *La Martiniere school, Calcutta,
19th century*
Left: *Dad in Durban during the war*
Above: *Mum, Dad and my godmother
Grace*

"Jud-eee Iren-eee! Come on, darling, please."

When someone addressed me by my full name I knew they meant business and were on the verge of being cross.

I gave in. Gran added leggings, a blouse and flannel skirt, hand-knitted cardigan, coat, gloves and my favourite raspberry Fair Isle beret. Finally, she put on my shoes with the bar and buttons – I couldn't manage those.

"Where's your hankie?"

It had dropped down the side of a chair. Gran fastened it to my coat with a lamb brooch as it had no pockets. She patted her hair, tied neatly in a bun, checked her highly polished shoes and took down her coat from its hook, along with the dog's lead. We walked out of the front door, which Gran locked, down the little path of black and white chequered tiles and through the front gate.

We were ready to face the world. Three of us walked slowly down the road, towards the shops: a little old lady, a toddler and a dog.

Our part of north London was not a slum or posh but somewhere in between. It was the best my parents could afford. We lived on an ordinary North London street, with Edwardian terraced houses of red or buff London brick, long triple sash windows up and down, tiny front gardens bordered by low walls and privet hedges. A few householders had made an effort to plant shrubs – a lilac bush, laburnum, forsythia or sooty spotted laurel – but this was wartime. There were no cars parked in the road but the pavement was punctuated by plane trees, bare at this time of year, their leprous bark designed to filter the city smog laden with pollutants. Everything was sepia-tinted, monochrome – buildings, clothes, gardens, sky. Even the pram my grandmother was pushing was an unfashionable brown. The only flashes of colour were the famous red double-decker buses and a scarlet pillar box on the corner.

An air raid siren pierced the air, rose to a shrieking crescendo then intensified as it swooped up and down the scale. Flinching, I edged closer to Gran and clutched her coat as we walked down Cricklewood Broadway. The dog put her ears back and tugged on the lead.

We must have looked strange. Gran was pushing our scruffy pram, well past its youth, now containing a basket into which she would later pop our purchases, along with Sally. On command, she would jump in with one graceful bound and stand guard while we went inside the shops. She was big for a cocker spaniel, with a glossy black coat and luxuriant, curly ears.

"Sit, Sally. Stay," said Gran.

The dog sat. She waited obediently and patiently in the pram, looking as imperious as Charles I in his wig. Woe betide anyone who went near. Her expression said "Don't muck about with me!"

The siren was deafening and I felt a knot forming in my stomach. The roads started to empty as people found shelter. It was the era of buzz bombs, some 9,000 of these being launched in 1944, mostly aimed at London. Calmly, Gran ushered us into Garland's, the newsagent's next to The Crown, and we clattered down a rickety staircase into their basement. Sally's claws clicked on the threadbare lino. We were the only people there, the other occupant being a huge, claw-footed Victorian bath.

"Don't be scared, Jude," said Gran, giving me a cuddle.

I didn't like the look of that bath. At least there weren't gas masks hanging on the wall, as there were under the stairs at home. I'd had hysterics when Mum had tried to put one on my head as a practice drill.

Finally, the all clear sounded – a continuous wail – and we emerged into the sunlight. A few early drinkers dived into The Crown next door. No doodlebugs, the V1 flying bombs, hit North London that day. A number 16 bus spluttered into life, ready for its journey down the Edgware Road towards Marble Arch and Victoria.

Cricklewood was a village which had sprung up on the Broadway, the old Watling Street, a Roman road which ran straight up to the north-west and Holyhead. After the First World War layers of migration had settled there to man the light industry factories and provide labour for the building boom of the 1930s. It was even documented in a ditty called McAlpine's Fusiliers (McAlpine being the name of a large construction company):

'Twas in the year of '39, when the sky was full of lead,
And Hitler was heading for Poland, and Paddy for Holyhead.

Come all you pincher ladies, and you long-distance men,
Don't ever work for McAlpine, for Wimpey or John Laing.

You'll stand behind a mixer, and your skin is turned to tan,
And they'll say, good on you, Paddy, with your boat-fare in your hand.

The craic was good in Cricklewood and they wouldn't leave the Crown,
With glasses flying and biddies crying, cause Paddy was going to town.

I used to think that the name Cricklewood was romantic but the reality was anything but. Our little family had arrived there shortly before my birth and we were one of a succession of immigrants to settle in this part of the city, certainly not the last.

Despite this sobering encounter with the bathtub in the basement, Garland's would become one of my favourite destinations, for comics and sweets. In later years, when we arrived home for tea after school, Gran tried her best to get a word out of us and failed. We were immersed in our copies of the Dandy, Hotspur, the Beano and Girl.

The newsagent was our second port of call after Joe and the boys, with their barrows parked outside the Express Dairy. They sold fruit and veg at knock-down prices to Gran, always an expert at negotiating a bargain. Next on her list was the ironmonger, where she bought bran for layers' mash. Here smells of linseed oil mingled with the subtler aromas of paraffin and bonemeal fertilizer. Our final stop was the bakery, where Sally's nose twitched at the wonderful smells emerging as people swung in and out of the glass doors.

We weren't going to the butcher today. Thank goodness. I didn't like its pungent whiff of raw meat on the turn and a sawdust-strewn floor to mop up blood. Listless women queued interminably for their chops or meagre ration of mince at the counter while I admired the wall tiles picturing cows, lambs and pigs in happier times. The fishmonger's was even more odoriferous but offered the bonus of seeing live eels sinuously wriggling in a cast iron bath outside. I was sent there on my own when I got older, told to check on the catch of the day written on the blackboard and given strict instructions to buy a nice bit of cod or haddock and some scraps for the cats.

"'Ere, give us a pound of pussy's pieces for the little girl," the jolly fishmonger would yell, beaming under his straw boater, to the titters of the queue. The double entendre was lost to one of such tender years.

There were no chain stores on the Broadway at that time, apart from Woolworth's and Burton's, The Fifty Shilling Tailor with the snooker hall above, opposite the Queen's cinema. The chemist, optician, dentist, hairdressing salon which reeked of permanent wave solution, Lyons café, photographer and a second café cum ice cream shop completed the range of goods and services available, plus the inevitable pawnbroker with the three golden balls hanging outside.

During the war life was a struggle but we never considered our lives to be deprived. Our four-room existence was no different to that of our neighbours. We considered it normal to sleep three in a room, Gran, John and I, with a small light on behind the blackout curtains. We froze in winter, roasted in summer. Mum fought a continual battle with coal fires, sooty curtains and damp, keeping us warm, fed and safe. I sat in the Morrison shelter in the dining room during air raids and played with my friend Mary Mulhern. Mum was frantic that we wouldn't wear our gas masks in the event of an attack: these hung ominously in the cupboard under the stairs, looking like ghoulish horses' heads. There was a large air raid shelter in the street outside our house which nobody used. It was full of rubbish and smelled of pee.

I was excited when a bomb exploded in the next street. Mary and I were huddled in the Morrison shelter, a strengthened metal table in the living room, in effect an iron cage, under which we could sit for protection if the house was hit. Mum was at work, Mary and I were playing cards and John was in another room, I think.

John says:

I was just seven years old but I knew three things about buzz bombs: that first the light went out (when the motor ran out of fuel), then the buzzing ceased (sound travelling more slowly than light) and finally the V1 would crash and explode.

On this particular day, I could see out of the window. I saw the V1 flying by, then saw the light go out; the sound stopped and then, after a second or two, there was an enormous explosion which blew out all our windows. But we were spared.

The next day I walked down to gawp at the wreckage – this was a regular recreation for kids at that time. The V1 had destroyed half a dozen terraced houses on a neighbouring street, two on one side of the road, four on the other. In among the wreckage of the blown-up buildings I saw a Morrison shelter. It was completely flattened by the collapsed bricks – not much protection there. I still remember my reaction to that sight. I also remember missing in succeeding days two rosy-cheeked brothers who used to walk by our house to school every day.

The noise was deafening. The tremendous draught before the explosion, or the impact itself, had caused our front windows to shatter. Luckily, these had been crisscrossed with tape to prevent too much damage. Afterwards we could smell explosives and burnt brick on the dusty air, something I shall never forget. The smell of war.

I was too young to realize the implications of the incident and was merely excited. However, from the back windows we could see searchlights rake the sky from Hendon Aerodrome, the RAF base, and grew accustomed to the sounds of aircraft droning overhead, ours and the enemy's. Every night Gran and my mother made sure that our blackout precautions were secure, but they always left a table light on while the sound of anti-aircraft guns and explosions thumped around us. For years I could not sleep without a light burning, was terrified by loud noises and even now hate to be in a bedroom with the door closed. We were self-contained, even secretive for, as we were told, Careless Talk Costs Lives. John and I became attuned to the sound of doodlebugs, the first guided missiles. We could also distinguish between the sound of the various aircraft – Mosquitoes, Spitfires, Wellington bombers, Messerschmitts. Our entertainment consisted of playing with the few toys we had, me with my teddy (which John had given an experimental shave), Ming the panda and used ration books, John with his precious Meccano.

When I was old enough I was given the laundry list to pencil in and check as Mum couldn't cope with the weekday wash. Our scullery had a huge copper for heating water, and washday involved heaving wet linen around with tongs, putting it though a mangle in the lean-to and draping it from the kitchen airer, hauled up to the ceiling by a pulley. Wet sheets and towels slapped us in the face as we walked through the kitchen door. After the ritual of hanging it out and wrestling with the clothes prop on the washing line, the penultimate stage of this process was the folding of bed linen in the lean-to. However, Mum washed our smalls with Lux flakes in our ancient, back-breaking Belfast sink.

Dad was long-suffering. He shaved himself with great care, squinting with cornflower blue eyes into the cracked mirror on the scullery wall. He brushed a lock of light brown hair off his forehead and smiled at his reflection, for he was conscious of his looks. I was fascinated to see him like this, in vest and trousers, because I could take a good look at his tattoos. His left arm was adorned with a pair of legs surmounted by a pith helmet at thigh height, depicting a soldier melting in the heat beside a palm tree, while the noonday sun blazed overhead. I thought this was quite witty but Mum hated it. Dad also had a cross faintly marked on one wrist, which I thought was a shame as he had beautiful hands, shapely, with neatly trimmed nails.

The scullery was where we cooked, washed, walked out to the lean-to and garden, and where I drew. I covered the walls in scribble. Luckily the gloss eau-de-nil paint was eminently washable. I think Dad must have found a job lot of eau-de-nil because everything that wasn't wallpapered was painted in it. Cold linoleum covered the floor, giving way to varnished floorboards in the hall. It was a relief to get to the warm carpet underfoot in the dining room.

I was besotted by horses. As a substitute for the real thing, Dad made me two beautiful hobby horses, one brown, one white, which I galloped to death in a jumping ring I constructed in the garden using Dad's bean poles. Being a clumsy child, I fell frequently on the crazy paving until eventually Mum made my father dig it up.

I was delighted to learn that he had driven two horses pulling a brewer's dray in his youth. Maybe I could do that one day, too! I loved seeing police horses in the streets or the glossy animals on Horse Guards Parade but generally had to make do with trailing the milk float horse when he came down Cedar Road. I shot out when I heard the clink and rattle of milk bottles and the clip-clop of hooves to feed the shaggy creature with carrots. All too often his blinkered head was stuck in a nose bag, munching oats, while he stood at ease, bending one hind leg to rest a weary hoof.

The rag and bone man was easier to catch, shouting "Rag-a-Bone" at the top of his voice to signal his approach. I'd try and find something to give him – old clothes, a lamb bone, old newspapers, pots, anything – to make him stay a bit longer outside our house so that I could pat the piebald pony, who was friendlier than the milkman's horse. One day Mum was out and I frantically scoured the house for something to give him. Yes, my baby blanket would do – curly wool with a large "B" embroidered on it in red. I was too big for that now. His eyes widened as I gave it to him. Mum came in later and was not pleased. I had given him an expensive blanket, one that Mum's boss had given her, besides which it had sentimental value. No wonder the rag and bone man couldn't believe his luck.

"Never talk to tradesmen without telling me or Gran," Mum scolded.

"If you're so keen on horses, you can collect some of the manure," said Dad, handing me a bucket and shovel. "It'll go a treat on my roses."

The street was also our playground – cricket in summer, football in winter, skipping and hopscotch for the girls and sorties on a fairy cycle. Plane trees lined our road and caused some nasty ricochets for fast bowlers. On summer evenings I leaped around with a net to help John catch moths flying round the street lamps, or butterflies from the park's buddleia bushes during the day. After the war Dad got an allotment in Gladstone Park and I was ferried on a seat behind my mother's bike saddle, queen of all I surveyed. I would put my arms round her waist and enjoy the sensation of speed, with Mum's soft, fine hair blowing in my face. I was eventually given my very own fairy cycle – a red letter day.

Our next door neighbour had a sign by his front door saying "No hawkers or circulars". This must have included the knife man, who would set up his grindstone on the front path and sharpen our knives and shears, gypsies with clothes pegs and bunches of heather in their baskets and the French onion seller, on his bicycle. Gran would engage them all in long conversations: she was not banned from consorting with hawkers.

Gran was a sociable soul and chatted to all and sundry on her perambulations. Joe and the boys would save her tasty fruit from their barrows. They knew we didn't have much money. The look of the old girl wheeling the shabby pram and the spaniel told them that, even if she did "speak proper". True to her colonial roots, Gran didn't cook, clean or do the laundry. She did, however, walk me to and from school, wash the dishes, tidy our flat, mend our clothes, provide us with tea and sandwiches after school, crack jokes, teach me how to read and sing in a faltering but pleasant alto voice. She taught me to read and introduced us to old tunes – Lily of Laguna, Daisy Daisy, If You Were the Only Girl in the World – but disapproved of Vera Lynn, the Forces Sweetheart, whose songs she pronounced cheesy and cloying. Another colonial hangover was her fondness for an afternoon nap, when she fell asleep next to our enormous radio to the murmurings of a drama, music on the Light Programme or Woman's Hour. She encouraged me to do the same, so I obligingly curled up in an ancient armchair in front of the coal fire. Then she woke up and tackled a few light chores, including darning and knitting, often using wool from unravelled garments. I held the skein of wool while she deftly wound it into a ball. Thus energised, Gran could then stay up until midnight and sit in the bosom of the family, ensuring that my parents got no privacy when they came home from work. This was her time to enjoy company, with some adult conversation and she made the most of it.

The war dragged on. My father, stationed abroad, brought rare treats when he came home on leave: bananas, chocolate, stockings, cigarettes. Gran perched next to the wireless, listening to the news. Suddenly it was VE Day and there was a street party in Heber Road with bunting, paper hats, jelly, fairy cakes and ice cream. Fireworks exploded in the sky. Women linked arms and danced to The Lambeth Walk and the Hokey-Cokey. London went wild with excitement and crowds gathered in front of Buckingham Palace to watch the King and Queen and their two daughters appear on the balcony. Even my father, deeply suspicious, admitted that because the royal family had stood firm, remaining in London for the duration and Princess Elizabeth joining the ATS, the country's wartime morale had been given a tremendous boost.

Dad still didn't come home – he was in the Far East and had to wait for VJ day in August, 1945, when the atom bombs dropped on Hiroshima and Nagasaki broke Japan's will and forced the country to surrender. Japan had entered the war in 1941, sensing that the Allies were busy elsewhere and had neglected their defences in the Far East. They wished to annexe the strategic port of Singapore, the East Indies occupied by the Dutch and Burma, with its teak forests, oil and untapped mineral wealth. The consequences of Japanese occupation are well documented and some of my mother's friends had not survived. After VJ day, the USA ceased to help Britain with food aid and substituted a long term Lend-Lease scheme. It was clear that years of austerity lay ahead.

Chapter 3
THE SOLDIER'S RETURN

Metropolitan Police Horse

I had been used to having Mum to myself to cuddle up to. Even though Dad was now home from the army, I still squeezed into the parental bed on weekend mornings between the two of them for a cuddle. I couldn't understand why Dad got so grumpy. I was a little pest.

It was time for me to start my education, at St Helen's, a small private school in Blenheim Gardens, Willesden Green. Gran walked me there in the morning, collected me for a return journey at lunchtime and again in the evening.

Four years old, I set off in an unfamiliar school uniform. This was underpinned by the infamous liberty bodice and navy blue knickers. Gran deposited me in the cloakroom, which smelled of wet wool and sweaty shoes. I wept as I battled with the first unfamiliar task, tying and untying my shoelaces. We had to wear soft house-shoes so that we didn't damage the polished wooden floorboards inside what was a converted Victorian house, with a large garden. The pupils were mainly the children of the Jewish community, though you wouldn't have known it from the surnames. Goldstern had been changed to Goldstar, Herschfeld to Horsfield, Rosberg to Roxburgh. These were children whose parents had arrived after the First World War, when there was strong antipathy to all things German. Even my nice class teacher, Mrs Laing, was Jewish, not Scottish. My close friend, Juliet Wittman, lived nearby with her widowed mother.

The private school girls were more sophisticated than I, from the wrong side of the tracks. One had a permanent wave and another girl's mother must have spent ages tying her hair in papers in every night to produce bouncing corkscrew ringlets. One day a teacher asked the class whose mother worked: I was the only one to put my hand up.

The tuition was quirky but effective and we were receptive. I could already read, thanks to my mother and Gran, but sums remained a mystery. Thank goodness for the tables, weights and measures from the list on the back of my blue exercise book.

Miss Hutchinson, the headmistress, was scary: a formidable lady with black, permed hair who favoured grey, checked tweed suits and blood red nail varnish. Her crimson talons clacked impatiently on the desk as she waited for some hapless pupil (frequently me) to answer a question in her arithmetic lessons. Miss Best, who taught English and music, was a gentler soul stuck in a 1920s time warp. She wore brown jersey dresses which clung to her ample figure and kitten heeled shoes, pointy-toed with a bar fastened by a button. Her greying, brown hair was very short and shingled. We stood in a semicircle behind her and sang "Where E'er You Walk", "The Ash Grove" and "Nymphs and Shepherds", doing our best to emulate the Manchester Children's Choir we'd heard on the radio. It was hard to hold the tune when the girl next to me , sang in such ear-splitting tones (she later turned professional) but I concentrated hard, staring at Miss Best's pale, shaved neck.

The school was in a converted house, with a large garden – our playground. In the summer we sat in a semicircle on the lawn for some of our lessons and played rounders. This was the first time I saw a person wearing callipers; Esther had suffered from polio and couldn't play games, although I was told she was a strong swimmer. PT classes were held in the music room, also the venue for our annual sports day in wet weather. One year, true to my usual uncoordinated form, I managed to plunge spectacularly into the French windows during the sack race, poking my wrist through the glass. I dripped blood all over the floor.

"Quick, get a towel," said Miss Hutchinson. "You silly girl. Mrs. Laing, ring for a taxi."

In the taxi my teacher was more sympathetic and I quite enjoyed this unexpected trip, even if it was for medical reasons.

"Mm, Judy, you're lucky. Just missed the artery," said Dr. Thompson, our brisk but kindly Scottish doctor, peering at the gash on the inside of my left wrist. He bandaged it neatly and put my arm in a sling. I still have the scar.

After a year or two I was allowed to walk to school on my own. My pal Rosemary Plaster lived nearby so I usually had company down the leafy roads. We sometimes took short cuts down the alleyways but were chased by some nasty boys. If you got cornered there was no way out, so we only took these routes if there was a gang of us.

I loved going to Rosemary's house. She lived in a 1930s semi-detached house in the next street, which I considered a step up from ours, and her mother looked as though she had just swept in from the country. Mrs. Plaster's curly hair was braided in a plait coiled round her head and she always smiled. She baked bread, brown and speckled, kept a garden with a neat rockery, trees and a real fish pond, put polish on her furniture and quilts on the beds. Pretty china adorned the Welsh dresser in the dining room. Her two daughters played with dolls who lived in a wooden dolls' house and had their own cribs, decorated with hand-sewn, dainty bed linen and frills. Best of all, Rosemary's mum was there to greet her daughters when they came home from school and had her husband's supper ready when he returned from work. She was a proper mum, not like mine, who had a full-time job, threw a hasty evening meal together then collapsed in a chair, exhausted, for a smoke. I felt guilty for thinking this. The family included me in their holidays to Jaywick Sands, on the Essex coast, where we stayed in a damp bungalow, its walls tide-marked by the floods which sometimes surged over the salt marsh. There are photos of us shivering on the beach while Rosemary's cheery

45

mum wraps us in a towel. We are wearing shapeless, knitted swimsuits which sag unbecomingly when wet.

Rosemary was a Baptist and I accompanied her to church, even joining the Girls' Life Brigade. I enjoyed marching, singing rousing hymns, the games and being given the occasional honour of carrying the colours at church parade. Dad had trained me well for marching practice and taught me how to present arms on the hearthrug at home. I was less sure about the huge bath used for baptisms – was I developing tub phobia? I found the stained glass windows in the church hall absorbing, each one depicting a parable – The Good Samaritan, The Sower. I think Mum feared I was turning into a religious nutter but I preferred the theatrical aspects of the Baptist church to our earnest, often boring Anglican Sunday school. I also joined the choir when I was a little older. Rosemary was a good, sweet-natured person, more obedient than I. Even her hair behaved itself in its neat plaits, a few escaping tendrils curling round her neck, unlike mine, straight and fine, which stuck out in wisps no matter how much Gran strained to confine it. Ribbons simply slid off my hair and I was always losing them so rubber bands had to be used. I tried desperately to be more like my kind-hearted friend.

I adored my brother John, four and a half years older. I shadowed him wherever possible and was his willing slave, as were Mum and Gran, to a certain extent. He loved taking things apart, such as a clock which belonged to one of my aunt's friends in North Wales. She returned to find the innards all over the floor – he wasn't so good at putting it back together again.

John had already been sent to a prep school in the country, which he had hated. A report written by an unidentified master showed that he was focused, fascinated by those subjects which interested him and dismissive of all others. My parents decided to move him to Burgess Hill, Hampstead, a progressive establishment. He enjoyed himself but didn't do much work. John told me that one day he managed to climb up on to the roof for a lark and walk around the parapet, admiring the views over Hampstead Heath. Unfortunately, he walked past the window of the staff room, where the masters had assembled for a meeting, and he was spotted! He was told off for this particular prank, as Burgess Hill did not practice corporal punishment. This was in contrast to his secondary school, Marylebone Grammar, where the art teacher maintained discipline by whacking naughty boys with a T-square.

This report about John was written by an unidentified person. A teacher? A mentor? My mother? Who knows. Anyway, it refers to his time at Burgess Hill as being academically unproductive!

The weather being generally good, John was able to spend a great deal of time out of doors during the holidays..... He divided his time between cycling and walking, playing in the park and fishing on one or two occasions. When indoors he read a great deal..... He also made sundry articles with the aid of a knife, such as bows and arrows, daggers, canoes etc. and his enthusiasm in the use of pointed weapons far exceeds his discretion.

When he is engrossed in a book or a radio play he is so very much in a world of his own that he just doesn't hear when spoken to.

His biggest problem is a disinclination to get ready for bed and a greater disinclination to get up in the morning – I am not exactly a martinet but I try to make it no later than 8.30 in the evening, and I would like him to rise no later than 7.30..... as we have to all be out of the house fairly early his dilatory habits do very definitely upset the rest of the household..... He is untidy and careless about his clothes and shows little consideration for other people's possessions once they have served his purpose.

I appreciate Chile's endeavour to get him moving with his Arithmetic. Two years ago he knew up to his 10 times table and now he tells me he just knows his 7! His handwriting too seems to have deteriorated. I am glad he has taken up swimming this term and would like him to be interested in all games.

No change there with his handwriting, then – I am sure John will agree – or a lack of interest in games.

I longed to have a pet. Sally, the spaniel, had survived distemper as a pup and had developed a cranky temperament. One day I cuddled her when she was sleeping and she snapped, biting me on the forehead.

"That's it," Mum decided. "I can't trust her with the children any more. We'll have to find her another home."

John and I wept when Sally was taken away to her new owners, who lived on a farm in the country. I longed for a little sister but had a feeling that this wasn't going to happen.

I pottered around with the hens and noticed a timid stray cat hanging around the chicken run. She became part of the family, to be followed by another rescue cat, Toddy the tortoise and Gran's blue budgie, Joey, who twittered incessantly when everyone was talking but shut up when we did. Toddy didn't do much but loved having his chin tickled. I lay flat on my stomach on the lawn, eye-balling him as he overdosed on lettuce leaves and wandered into the aromatic shade of Dad's alyssum plants. Dozing on the grass, I gave him choice morsels and he gave my finger an enthusiastic bite – tortoises have sharp lips. He hibernated in a box in the airing cupboard for some years until, inevitably, he failed to wake up one spring.

"Cats, chickens, tropical fish, a tortoise and a budgie. Bloody menagerie," muttered Dad. "That cat keeps peeing everywhere, too," he said, referring to Kitty, who had a weak bladder and had to be shoved out of the back door the minute she had finished her saucer of milk.

John was immersed in hobbies. After the war, his ceiling was festooned with model aeroplanes which he had constructed, suspended from the ceiling. Work in progress was accompanied by a strong smell of dope. He loved radio comedies and other programmes such as The Goon Show and Journey Into Space, making things (at one stage cathode ray tubes littered the floor) and his music, mainly modern jazz. He amassed an amazing collection of tropical fish and when I was a bit older I was allowed to tag along on expeditions to Padbourne Aquariums in Praed Street, Marylebone. We gazed at the illuminated underwater world before us, at guppies, neon tetras, zebra fish and cichlids weaving in and out of water weed forests. The angel fish were stately and graceful and, when John could afford to have six heated fish tanks in his bedroom, he was able to breed these successfully in one special place. I was sometimes allowed to hold a mirror in front of the tank, to dupe the magenta Siamese fighting fish into thinking he was facing an enemy. Fins fiercely raised, he went crackers trying to attack his reflection. John moved up a gear by collecting insects, snakes and lizards and managed a takeover bid for one of Dad's sheds to house his little zoo a few years later. Dad patiently emptied the shed and paid the increased electricity bills.

We performed our ablutions in the kitchen and Dad was not impressed when he found two wash-bowls full of John's daphnia (water fleas) and tubifex, a nest of red worms used for feeding the fish in his aquarium.

"Bloody hell, John, what's this?"

"Fish food, Dad. They have to be kept under running water or they'll die."

"How am I supposed to shave, then?"

Chapter 4
JACK THE LAD

My new bike, 1949

Life was marginally better after the war but still a grind for my parents. London was grey and dingy, with soot-blackened buildings, peeling paint and streets with gaps where houses had been bombed, like missing teeth. Dad took me on a bus ride through the City one day and I was shocked to see the shattered buildings, gaping holes and rubble around St Paul's Cathedral. The city and its people were exhausted. Slowly, the bomb damage sites were clothed in greenery and blazed pinkly with rosebay willow herb and ragwort each summer. Willow herb germinated readily on burnt ground, hence its other name, fireweed. Its seeds spread easily and soon London's patches of waste ground and railway embankments became covered, in addition to the bomb sites. Though it was supposed to be out of bounds, we made dens in the site on Ivy Road, which was pockmarked with bomb craters and full of rusty wire and other debris. It was now overgrown with hawthorn, goat willow and elderberry bushes as well as fireweed and becoming swathed in brambles. We played for hours in our secret place. A few years later the site was cleared and houses were built, to our disgust.

Winters were freezing and we got dressed for school like lightning before racing into dining/living room. I had been at school for two years when we suffered the worst winter so far – the big freeze of 1947. Schools closed, long icicles hung from our lean-to, there were power cuts and coal shortages. We put on as many layers of clothing as we could to keep warm. Getting into icy sheets at night was agony and one lay immobile until a column of body warmth was created. Snow fell and remained for a long time. The cats hated it and would pee or worse in the footstep holes left by Dad's boots as he went to the coal shed. We grew bored, confined to our flat, and squabbled. Gran's budgie warbled on. Eventually the snow melted, turned into grey slush and finally to grimy puddles.

In the winter of 1952 we were confined to the house once more when smog descended on the city, killing 4,000 people. Filthy, greenish yellow fog thickened with the smoke from a million coal fires, industrial and traffic fumes swirled round our faces as soon as we stepped outside. Buses stopped running but the taxis kept going. Even street lights were barely visible through the murk. One afternoon I had to go out, to be taken to the dentist by Dad for a tooth extraction. I fought with the gas as the mask was clamped over my face and felt as though I was going into a tunnel in the Tube. Just as I thought I was going to suffocate a disembodied voice said "Judy, Judy, you can sit up now" and the dentist's face swam in front of mine. I ran my tongue gingerly over the unfamiliar filling where once there had been a jagged hole.

Dad decided I needed a treat so he took me to the nearest Lyons for a hot drink and – luxury – a toasted teacake. I had to drink lopsidedly, as my mouth was still numb but greed made me tackle the teacake, somewhat messily. Because of the smog, we were two customers among a handful of others. Dad engaged the waitress in conversation. They giggled together and talked animatedly. When we went up to the cash desk and Dad paid, she dimpled and said "Thank you, young man."

"She called you Young Man, Dad!" I said, amazed.

Dad smirked. As we walked home with scarves over our mouths and noses, I pondered on this. Young – what, my dad? I suppose it was my first inkling that my father was still relatively young – seven years younger than Mum – and attractive to the opposite sex.

When the smog finally lifted Mum was in despair. The window sills and paintwork were filthy, inside and out and the net curtains hung like thin, grey dishcloths.

"This climate!" she exclaimed, "It's dreadful. Even when I wash those curtains they still look horrible. I wish we didn't have to put them up." Lace or net curtains were considered essential for privacy.

I felt sorry for the children who lived a few doors away. Their father was a coal-man whose face was ingrained with black dust: he never looked clean, and nor did they. We would see him setting off with his coal sack bound to his head. There were no curtains at the windows and the floors consisted of bare boards. The children always had smeared faces and runny noses and sometimes went barefoot. The little boys pee'd in the street, against the plane trees – maybe that was preferable to a smelly lavatory. We called them The Dirty Kids. We were cold and miserable but they were truly poor and must have been worse off, though perhaps the father got free coal and they kept warm. I didn't know.

In 1953 there was another natural disaster: a great storm and tidal wave which swept round Britain's coastline, killed 2,000 people, wrecked villages and breached coastal defences. Rosemary's holiday cottage at Jaywick was underwater and it was sad to think of the salt-marsh, which I had last seen studded with flowers, under silt and mud. Horrified, we watched scenes of devastation on the newsreels. At the time, I realized that the Thames estuary had been badly hit but the seaside devastation was nationwide.

It must have been at about this time that Dad went off the rails. Since leaving the army he had worked at the Ministry of Pensions, where he was bored to tears, then became a sales rep for Caxton's, a publishing company. We even had a little car for a while, our first – a company Ford Popular, black and shiny. We could get out to the country at weekends, to Cooper's Green in Hertfordshire, Box Hill in Surrey, even down to the coast. We could pick primroses in the woods and cowslips on Dunstable Downs, where we watched gliders soar lazily overhead. People came home with armfuls in those days, to make wine but it seemed sad to me – they hung limply so soon after picking.

I wasn't aware of it at the time but Dad had found another woman – or, more likely, she had found him on his travels.

Gran chronicled the course of events in her diary.

July 5th, 1950
Mr Gould came round to see me today and offered us the option of buying 36 Cedar Road for £1500 and promised to see about the mortgage etc. I phoned Dulce and Jack and told them about the news.

August 15th
Princess Elizabeth had a baby girl, born at 11.50am. Jack went for an interview with Caxtons Ltd.

August 21st
Jack got car from Caxtons.

August 22nd
Jack handed in resignation to the Ministry.

September 6th
Jack and Dulce received keys to the house... We moved up at once and are so pleased at the extra space we have now.
September 25th
Jack went on tour in connection with work.

October 6th
Jack came back for the weekend in a very quarrelsome mood. Has been acting funny for the past two weeks. Takes no interest in the house or his children. Is

mostly full of his own importance. I wonder "who" it is this time?

October 15th
Sold nine chickens to Syd Dangerfield for £2.05.00 shillings. Sorry they had to go.

October 17th
Dulce phoned telling me that Jack had phoned her from Colchester that he was going to leave her as he had got involved with another woman. Jack came home this evening at around 7.00pm, packed a suitcase and phoned Dulce at the rehearsals at M&S. He said he had told the commissioner to tell Dulce that he was coming to see her and talk things out.

October 18th
Jack returned home this afternoon for good and was sorry for what he had done. He and Dulce went out for dinner.

October 21st
That beastly woman kept phoning in the hope of speaking to Jack but no such luck, we saw to that.

October 26th
The telephone was moved into the dining room today.

I was totally unaware of all this at the time – I was only nine years old – but knew that there was some unexplained tension between my parents. Dad would fly off the handle for no reason and was away on the road for much of the time, selling books, a prey to temptation and feminine charms. I can now realise how he must have felt, confined in a crowded flat with his family, with little privacy and almost no social life, in a boring job. His new work as a travelling salesman probably provided a low salary in which much of his income might have come from a commission on sales – but the open road must have seemed like a real release. London life must have seemed such a comedown after the travel, excitement, danger and comradeship of life as a soldier during the war. He was still young and attractive, no doubt about that, and although his fall from grace was inexcusable it was also understandable.

Dad's lady friend was a glamour puss, all long fingernails, short skirts and high heels. He blurted out to Mum that he wanted to go away with his new love. Silly fool, he also asked if she would like to meet the "other woman" so they could all have a drink together and talk things over. I think they did meet and Mum put her straight. No more was said. I expect the removal of the telephone from hall to dining room made it more difficult for Dad to make clandestine calls. Although he was the one to blame there were contributing circumstances. He was back in jug again – on Cedar Road. Dad resigned from his job, the little Ford Pop disappeared and there were no more trips to the countryside.

Then came a glimmer of light at the end of the tunnel. My father found a job with a building firm not far from home, William Moss, at Staples Corner on the North

Circular Road. Things were looking up. I was even taken on some of Dad's trips outside London, to one of the new towns being built in the home counties, Basildon or Stevenage. Talk of purlins and roof trusses, four-by-twos, stopcocks and downpipes passed into my consciousness.

Mum had been promoted at work and was now private secretary to Dr Eric Kann, director of research at the head office of Marks and Spencer in Baker Street. She enjoyed her job, the new challenges and confidentiality of her work and her boss. She could have risen up the ladder with M&S as a buyer but this would have meant travel, something she couldn't undertake with her responsibilities at home. She ate good meals in the staff canteen, joined the choir and became its accompanist and also enjoyed other perks such as medical help. In her youth she had developed gingivitis and had to have her teeth extracted – the only remedy in those days – and have false teeth fitted. This explained her determination to have her children's own dental needs attended to and the hours I spent having my teeth straightened at the Eastman Dental Clinic by students (free treatment for which I had to wait a year!) The pain and boredom of this was softened by my having lunch in the canteen beforehand, travelling on the top deck of the bus and having my mother to myself, for once. I loved looking at the advertisements on the walls of buildings, especially Guinness Is Good For You with the toucan and Mr Therm Burns For You, the cheeky little gas flame man. The clippie in a navy serge trouser suit leapt up the stairs like a gazelle to dispense tickets with a clatter from the machine, full of banter for her customers.

Marks and Spencer looked after their staff so Mum sometimes came home loaded with fabrics from Cloth Buying, remnants, samples and even the odd unwanted bolt of fabric. These were recycled into clothes, curtains and tablecloths. Nothing was wasted. She was on a tight budget but she always looked good – suits and dresses for work, slacks at home, and wore very little make up – no mascara to adorn her dark eyelashes and deep brown eyes, just a dab of face powder on her clear complexion and a trace of lipstick. Mum was a talented pianist and a hard taskmaster. I could sit at the piano for hours, composing little tunes and picking out popular songs.

"You're strumming, Jude," Mum would call from another room. "Practise your finger exercises and scales, darling."

When Mum sat down to play I could listen to her for hours. She loved Chopin, Debussy and Rachmaninov and was a talented choral accompanist. She played popular songs of the time too, and Dad would sometimes dance with me while Mum played. "Balling the Jack", as sung by Danny Kaye, was one of my favourites. Music was a thread that ran through family life.

Mum's boss was a patron of the arts and sometimes gave her tickets to functions he couldn't attend – the ballet, an opera at Covent Garden, a musical. She would take John and me in turns and we were exposed to some wonderful performers at an early age: Margot Fonteyn, Robert Helpmann, Moira Shearer in Sadlers Wells ballets, Frankie Howerd creasing us up in revue singing silly songs like "The Three Little Fishes" and calling us "Ladies and GentleMEN", Margaret Lockwood glamorous in fishnet tights as Peter Pan. Dad told a fib to the school one day and said I had an appointment with the dentist – and took me to a matinée at the Gaumont State, Kilburn to see a ballet! Christmas time meant a treat, usually a panto at the Golders Green Hippodrome. I crawled under the seat in Jack and the Beanstalk when the giant came on stage. Peter Pan, Wendy and Nana the dog were more my style, as was seeing real tigers in Bertram Mills Circus or a water ballet at the Wembley Pool.

Chapter 5
HOLIDAYS AND HOW
THE OTHER HALF LIVED

John and Judy at Shanklin, Isle of Wight, 1946

After the war, we were taken to the seaside once a year for the annual week's holiday.

Mum was determined we should be able to swim, both for safety reasons and because she wanted us to love the water as much as she did. The Seymour Baths were a wonderful facility, close to the M&S offices and we were all to use them once we could swim. Mum had saved up and taken us to swimming classes at the Finchley Road Baths, where a sadistic instructor had lassoed us at the end of a pole and yanked his gasping little fishes to the side, exhorting us to doggy paddle. Just as you thought you were getting the hang of it he would stop pulling, the rope would go slack and we would do our best not to drown, arms flailing and mouths gulping in gallons of chlorinated water as well as air. He also had us plunging our faces into the water at the rail while we kicked our legs to stay afloat, urging us to breathe in, breathe out. Rosemary's little sister Janice, who was asthmatic, almost drowned. When I compare this to how children are taught nowadays, often to a musical accompaniment in warm water, with lots of encouragement, physical help and all sorts of swim aids, our instructor would have been hauled up by the NSPCC or reported on Childline.

My blocked ears couldn't always hear what bossy boots was saying and I couldn't get it right. Anyway, at the end of the course of lessons we could swim and I could go to the baths with Rosemary or Juliet. After a dip we emerged cold and damp from the chilly pool, red-eyed from the chlorine and were allowed a treat – one chocolate marshmallow and a cup of Ovaltine when we got home. Bliss. We could also handle a tennis racquet and play the piano (thanks to Mum, again), though I hated sight-reading and had never practised enough to satisfy my teacher.

The Isle of Wight was blissful, with horses on the beach, white cliffs, miles of sand, springy turf on the downs and pretty villages. John remembers finding a piece of aircraft cowling (this was just after the war) and using it as a float, paddling along with his arms. He was about 10 years old but had not yet learned to swim. Children were so free and unsupervised in those days. However, our holidays were usually in Westgate, on the Isle of Thanet, a resort which was closer and cheaper. Dad would get in a panic as he took us to Victoria Station to catch the train – in a taxi, a rare treat. He was in charge of buying the tickets, carrying the luggage and keeping us all together in the maelstrom of passengers. Mum sat as calm as a queen on one of the suitcases.

"Your father's windy," she said, disparagingly.

We stuffed our small suitcases into the netted luggage racks, sat on scratchy moquette in the railway carriage and rushed to find a window seat, trying to contain our excitement. Even the sepia photograph of a famous beauty spot below the luggage rack was riveting. The engine room funnel blew out a cloud of explosive steam then came that first thrilling chuff, followed by the creak and groan of carriage linkages being strained – we were off! I tried hard to sit still. The train was always packed in the school holidays. We grew hotter and hotter. It was a choice between opening the window with the leather strap, exposing us to fresh air, soot and the smell of rotten eggs from the engine, or sweltering behind hot glass and inhaling the smoke from Woodbines.

We stayed in a succession of chilly boarding houses, presided over by starchy landladies, which guests had to vacate during the day regardless of the weather. Linoleum on the floors, candlewick bedspreads, thin curtains, lists of rules everywhere. One year we rented a caravan, which was tiny, a disaster, not least because we were all tall and kept banging our heads. If the sun shone there were rock pools to explore, shrimps and crabs to catch, the English Channel to swim in, walks along the cliff-top and picnics, which Dad hated.

"Sand in the bloody sandwiches," he moaned, withdrawing into his deck chair with the Daily Express.

"You have to enter into the spirit of things, dear," said Mum. She had settled herself comfortably in the lee of a groyne with her book and a cigarette, a Thermos of tea and some squash for us at her feet.

"I remember going to Amherst before the war (a town on the Burmese coast) – gorgeous sand and you wouldn't believe the colour of the sea. My father had to visit the Andaman Islands, too as there was a prison there," Mum reminisced.

I have a photo of Dad with his friends on one such palm-fringed beach plus several of Mum with her pals, displaying her long, tanned legs. How they must have missed those hot, sunny days, diving into water of a decent temperature, eating jelly coconuts and taking a gin and tonic from a passing waiter at dusk.

Mum must have found the English Channel a bit of a let-down. There were still gun emplacements around and even the occasional roll of rusty barbed wire, remnants of the war. John and I ran in and out of the water, gasping as the cold waves hit us, jumping over them with our water wings until we had the confidence and ability to dive through. We would stay in as long as possible until we were forced to emerge, teeth chattering, and be swathed in towels to change into our clothes. Occasionally Mum would take the plunge in her Jantzen swimsuit, ploughing through the waves in a trudgen, a stroke like the crawl but with a breaststroke leg action. My parents were decorous and would disrobe under the cover of a cylindrical striped towel with a drawstring top, like a tent. The better-off families could hire beach huts but we could only manage a deck chair or two.

Investigating the rock pools was almost as good as a swim. Poking around under stones to find crabs, tiny fish and interesting shells, putting one's fingers into the heart of a sea anemone to test its powers of suction, climbing around the base of the cliffs, shrimping in the shallows. When the tide came in we made sandcastles. There was always something to do on the beach.

We ate breakfast and a tasteless supper in the boarding house, but the highlight of the week was tea in a café, with a Knickerbocker Glory as the *piece de resistance*, hauled up on a dumb waiter from the basement like a jack-in-the-box. Even Dad cheered up at the sight of fruit and jelly topped with luscious ice cream and drizzled with syrup over the whole lot in a sundae glass.

Thanks to Mum's senior position as private secretary to one of the M&S directors, she was given the opportunity of using a cottage for a holiday on the country estate belonging to another director, Mr Sacher. The company was well known for looking after its staff and it rewarded loyal, hardworking employees. My mother certainly fell into that category.

Berrydown, near Overton, was a beautiful estate situated in rolling chalk downland in Hampshire. We were to stay in one of the furnished farm bungalows, our first taste of proper countryside. On our first holiday, over Easter, Mum and I travelled by train but John cycled the sixty miles down from London on a wet, windy day. He eventually turned up looking like a drowned rat. We spent good times down there, picking cob nuts from the hedgerows and feasting on blackberries in the autumn. I communed with cows and we ate watercress from the River Test, where we leaned over the bridge to watch trout keeping station in the clear water below. They aligned themselves with the current, their speckled camouflage making them almost invisible above the gravel of this famous chalk stream. I swung on the farm gate and pretended I was riding a horse. We swam in a deep pool in the river, mocked by the local kids, who were brown as berries and spoke with a Hampshire burr. John answered back, of course, and refused to be intimidated. He got his comeuppance when he tried to face down some geese when we went to a circus and was chased off the field for his pains. Sometimes the butler at the Big House would pick us late strawberries and raspberries from the kitchen garden. We couldn't believe that one small family had this vast mansion all to themselves, were surrounded by beautiful gardens tended by other people, owned farms, cottages and woods. It was our first brush with the landed gentry. I could hardly believe we lived in the same country.

We were also taken down to Devon twice by our Hampstead relatives. My aunt had naval connections – her father had been an admiral – and a retired naval officer let the family use his seaside home, near Kingswear, for holidays. My uncle collected us from the station in his shooting brake (a half-timbered car!) and we drove past fuchsia hedges then down a steep drive, under huge pine trees, to the house. We unloaded our bags in the balmy, salty, pine-scented air, looking down a hillside covered in blazing gorse to the sandy cove below and a calm blue sea beyond. My cousins and I would run down the steep slope to swim off the tiny beach, usually ending up rolling downhill, head over heels until we collided painfully with a gorse bush. I had never seen anything so beautiful or peaceful. The house was modest but fascinating, full of ships in bottles on the plate rail which ran round the reception rooms. From our bedroom at night we could hear waves pounding the cliffs below and see the flashing beam of the Start Point lighthouse sweep around the bay.

My uncle Eric, Mum's brother, his wife Daphne and their three children lived in Hampstead and were part of the liberal intellectual set. Their neighbours included Christopher Heal (of the West End furniture shop), the Labour MP Douglas Jay, Roy Jenkins (also Labour, later SDP), Marie Stopes the contraceptive pioneer and Sigmund Freud. My uncle Eric was a journalist of some repute, working on the Daily Telegraph, then later the Sunday Times and the BBC Overseas News Desk. He and my mother had been among the three top students sitting the Higher School Certificate in the Indian subcontinent. He had been poised to go to university but my grandfather's early death in 1918 from pernicious anaemia, when he was only in his thirties, put paid to that: he had been forced to go to work and found a job on the The Statesman ("India's leading daily newspaper") in Calcutta. My cousin tells me that he remained bitter about this curtailment of his education for the whole of his life.

In 1921 Eric was in Rangoon and he wrote to my mother at her boarding school, St Mary's, Fort Dufferin, Mandalay:

Top left: *38 Well Walk, Hampstead*
Top right: *Keeping warm by the seaside*
Centre and bottom: *Bere Mill, River Test and the cottage at Overton, Hampshire*

Top: *Devon, with Eric, Daphne and family*
Centre: *Westgate, 1948*
Bottom: *Shanklin, 1946*

26th January, 1921

Well, my dear old kid, what did I tell you! Hasn't yours truly covered himself with glory? I'm sending you the results and by them you'll see that out of the 11 scholarships Maymyo has nabbed 5, St. Paul's 4 and one of the other two has gone to the Moulmein Convent and the other to the Diocesan Girls'..... Mother wants me to go to College but I don't think that would do. Things are in an awfully unsettled state here just now and nothing seems certain. At any rate, I intend seeing Mr Kamen and will enquire about the possibilities of a Government stipend for the Medical College at Bombay. But all this is in the clouds just now; I'll write and let you all know for certain later on.

Rangoon is beastly warm just now and it is anything but pleasant strolling around during the day.

Absolutely "nahpoo" for further now.

With love to the mater and self
Eric

Eric had met his second wife, Daphne, an artist, on board ship when he had approached her, sitting in a steamer chair, because she was reading "To The Lighthouse", by Virginia Woolf. Rather more exalted than my parents' first encounter, at a church hop in Burma. I think this was possibly during a trip from Calcutta to England in 1931, which was when Mum had accompanied him for her first taste of overseas travel and her first experience of England.

John and I slotted in between the three children – Ben, Annabel and Rosalind – in age, and we played fairly well together. Eric and Daphne were advocates of free expression, which ideal their offspring adopted with a vengeance. They were all small, blue-eyed and intelligent, with wills of iron. Each one, lucky thing, had the privacy of a bedroom in a thin, narrow Georgian house from whose attic you could see St. Paul's Cathedral and the city centre spread below, fog permitting, in the distance. On a fine day you could read the time on Big Ben with binoculars.

For a while I was scared stiff of Annabel, a small girl who spoke with a deep voice, wore trousers with a snake belt and insisted I call her Dick. She took me up to the Easter Fair on Hampstead Heath, whizzed me down the helter skelter and scared me witless on the Ghost Train, laughing at my timidity. She later became entirely feminine and arty but was always kind. Rosalind resembled a Kate Greenaway illustration, all rosy cheeks and bouncing brown hair but was just as determined as her sister. Ben and John got along well enough, with the odd row. The children were full of confidence, loud ("gun throats" said Gran), were highly intelligent and ran riot. A telling-off from the grown-ups was rare and smacking, of course, not countenanced.

We usually spent Boxing Day with our aunt, uncle and cousins. Our Christmas Day festivities were limited and subdued, as Gran records:

December 23rd 1950
The leghorn started to lay. One egg.

December 24th
Eric, Ben and Annabel came to see us today.

December 25th
Spent Christmas quietly by ourselves. One egg.

December 26th
John came downstairs to sleep. Dulce and Judy went to Eric's. One egg.

On Christmas Eve Dad, disguised as Father Christmas, would creep into our bedrooms dressed in Gran's red dressing gown. Christmas dinner consisted of a rabbit or one of our chickens plus a glass of sherry for the adults. After the King's Speech on the radio the grown-ups would collapse, exhausted, into their chairs, making the most of their two days off work. On this particular Christmas, John moved to his new bedroom, the sunny front room on the ground floor, with his fish tanks and other paraphernalia.

Boxing Day was altogether more interesting and the journey to our relatives' house was an adventure in itself. Firstly, the trolley bus up Child's Hill towards Golders Green, where we changed on to the single decker 210 bus. We then had the choice of two routes – the Underground to Hampstead then a stroll through Flask Walk, or a single decker 210 bus. The latter took us past the famous Bull and Bush pub and Manor House, in Golders Hill Park, once the home of ballerina Anna Pavlova. It had also been a hospital after her death, where my father had worked as a male nurse for a while. The final part of the trip took us uphill through a sunken tunnel of trees before emerging at the top of Hampstead Heath by Jack Straw's Castle, another landmark, near Whitestone Pond, where John would take his model sailing boats.

Hampstead was steeped in history. One walk to my relatives' house took us down East Heath Road, past the Vale of Health and its pond to Well Walk, a tree-lined street where they lived in an elegant Georgian town house. John Keats had once lived around the corner and artist John Constable next door, as a blue plaque indicated. The actual well, a chalybeate spring, was a stone's throw away.

I thought my cousins were so lucky. Their home was stuffed full of fascinating objects: my uncle's lead soldiers on the desk in his study, my aunt's paintings, the latest wallpaper (Daphne was always redecorating), mismatched but elegant porcelain, green Wedgwood leaf plates on the dining room dresser and flowers in a vase on the table. Newspapers and glossy magazines were strewn on coffee tables and the chaise longue, which Dad insisted on calling the Charley Lounge. Bookcases overflowing with books were crammed into the many alcoves. Such bounty.

Dad, acutely conscious of his cockney origins, found Boxing Day a trial. Daphne, referring to of my father's wheeling and dealing tendencies, had once jokingly told Dad that he should have been a barrow boy. Hurt, my father muttered to us "What does she know. All she can do is paint kippers on a plate."

My father had lost contact with his family. One of six children, brought up by a harridan of a mother in the East End, he had kept in touch with Connie, his favourite sister then communication failed after she married an American and emigrated to the States. Dad's air of bonhomie and cheek hid a lacked of self-confidence which surfaced when he was with the Hampstead crowd.

The relatives' Christmas Tree tipped the ceiling and was laden with wondrous baubles. Before lunch on an elegant Heal's dining table our parents would disappear to the pub, the Wells Tavern, a few doors down. Hampstead pubs were far superior to those in Cricklewood but my mother still found drinking in a bar a strange practice. We feasted on novel but delicious food, including paté, devils on horseback and syllabub served in tall sundae glasses. Both Eric and Daphne were excellent cooks. Afterwards we children walked Shandy, the friendliest Alsatian dog who ever lived, on the Heath and sailed our boats on Whitestone Pond, unless it had frozen over. Then home for tea, where the dining table would have been miraculously cleared and the things washed and put away by "the help".

"We're rich and you're poor," said Annabel, always outspoken. As I reeled from the implications of this statement, she added "Mind you, I love your mum. In fact, I think I love her more than my mum," she added.

Surely Annabel couldn't mean that? Daphne was pleasant but undemonstrative as far as her children were concerned. How could my cousin prefer someone else's mother to her own?

In 1953, Sir Edmund Hillary and Sherpa Tensing climbed Everest and the following morning a young queen was crowned. We huddled together in the front room of our neighbours Gert and Jim to watch on their new TV. It was set in an enormous wooden case but the actual screen was tiny – and, of course, the picture was black and white flecked with spots of "snow". Even John sat still for most of the time. After seeing King George VI's funeral on Pathé News, we had re-enacted the funeral march up and down the living room carpet to entertain Gran. She laughed soundlessly, her shoulders heaving, as John performed his celebrated imitation of the Duke of Kent, who we thought looked particularly chinless and drippy. Dad couldn't understand my fascination with the Royal Family.

"Parasites!" he exclaimed, bristling with socialist fervour.

Before the coronation, I had been taken by Dad on a bus tour round the processional route, as his company was responsible for erecting some of the stands. The royal blue and gold banners lining Park Lane were smashing, I thought. The tree outside the Dorchester Hotel twinkled with fairy lights. Imagine owning a flat in Mayfair and being able to watch the procession from your own balcony! I was given a tiny replica of Queen Elizabeth's golden coach, the big attraction being the horses which pulled it. I pored over the wedding pictures of Queen Elizabeth and the Duke of Edinburgh in a well-thumbed edition of the Illustrated London News. I adored her lace veil, embroidered with flowers, trailing down some steps while she posed for the camera.

We didn't own a television set but now we were homeowners. Mum and Dad had managed to buy the whole house with the help of a mortgage when the top flat fell vacant in 1950. John, Gran and I had a bedroom each. What luxury, even though I hated the wallpaper in mine and the brown paint on the stairs – but redecoration was out of the question, far too expensive. John installed himself in the ground floor back room overlooking the garden, complete with his six fish tanks, record player – a Collaro, his pride and joy – and assorted cathode ray tubes, with which he played at being an electrical engineer. He also peppered passing cats in the garden with his air rifle but missed a few times. The standard lamp's shade was full of holes. We played cricket in the garden, with John bowling and me batting. Surprise, surprise, I missed and the French window broke. After this had happened for the third time, the bottom part of the window was boarded up by my father.

Dad filched bits of wood, old radiators and other DIY essentials and got to work. He installed central heating, put up shelves and cupboards and found a second-hand washing machine for Mum. He was always busy, up a ladder, hammer in hand, holding a nail between his teeth, with a pencil tucked behind his ear and a beret on his head. He re-pointed the wall of the house and built another shed in the garden, which made three: one for his tools, another for coal and wood, a third for potting seedlings and a general overflow, which John soon filled with vivariums for his slow worms, grass snakes and newts. They kept escaping under the hen house, where I was sent to retrieve them from the gloom, wriggling on my tummy and coming out filthy.

Stomach-churning family rows seemed to be in decline for the time being. I curled up in bed at night, warm now, thanks to the central heating and a cat in the well behind my knees. She purred contentedly, and we both fell asleep.

Chapter 6
THE SEED IS SOWN –
CRICKLEWOOD COLONIALS

Irene Mendieta, my grandmother, aged 18

By the early 1950s the tension in our house was palpable. Dad was working hard at William Moss but his job prospects and money were not good. My mother had been given more responsibility at work and now had a whole house to clean and maintain. To help with finances, we even had lodgers – a young couple – in the back bedroom. Gran was getting older and more cranky, her eyesight was poor and arthritis worsening. John had reached the tempestuous teenage years. The telephone never stopped ringing in our cold hall. I leapt to my feet and sprinted out of the room to answer it.

"Gladstone 2184!"

Inevitably, it was for John.

There were terrible arguments between my parents. In retrospect, I suppose Dad was in the middle of a mid-life crisis. I remember one awful row on the landing upstairs. I can't remember what it was about but I was stuck between the two of them as they raged at one another above my head, frightened and tearful. My grandmother was bobbing around in the background, like a second at a boxing match. Perhaps they were fighting because of Dad flirting with the lodger's wife, an attractive young woman, or because of Gran's interference in family matters, a constant thorn in his side. I know that my father wanted to change his life and that Mum didn't, to the same extent.

My father, always volatile, felt his authority undermined by the rest of the family. The worst aspect of it all was that he and my mother never had any time to themselves: even when we children were out of the house or in bed, Gran was always there, rooted to her armchair, asking questions. They were always financial problems, of course.

Our suburb was changing its character. Cricklewood was becoming multicultural. Jewish families were moving further out, to leafier suburbs. In the house where I had once played with my friend Simon there now lived an Anglo-Indian family. I made friends with Bibi, one of the daughters. She was bright, friendly and wore earrings and brass bangles; their house smelled of curry and garlic. Next door Jim and Gert moved further out of town and in came a Jamaican family, part of the influx of Caribbean immigrants brought over to help man the transport system and hospitals after the war. Pakistani ladies dressed in the salwar kameez shopped at the barrow boys', where new items appeared – okra, brinjals (aubergines) and chillis. A few cars parked in our road now and the Broadway was choked with more traffic than ever. We became experts at jaywalking.

Emigration became a serious possibility. Australia was mooted and Mum read "The Sunburnt Country", by Elspeth Huxley. Just as we were getting used to the idea of koala bears and kangaroos, Dad applied for a job in Dunedin, New Zealand – we dragged out our school atlases to find out where it was. This was an awfully long way away and Mum decided to do some research. She found out that the climate in South Island was not actually too different from our own, in the south of England, and wet to boot. This did not bode well and the job application was not pursued. My family were addicted to warm weather and who could blame them?

"Please, Mum, please, can we go to the flicks tonight?"

"Have you saved up enough money, Jude?" asked my mother.

"Yes, I didn't spend my sweet ration money this week. And Gran has given John some. We've got enough for the one-and-sixes, anyway."

What I didn't say was that we had enough pennies between us to buy a forbidden bag of chips on the way home, wrap them in newspaper and eat the lot under the light of a street lamp before we got to the house. Mum disapproved of people eating fish and chips in the street. Only badly brought up people did that – she never used the description "common". Somehow they didn't taste the same at home, warmed up in the oven and eaten on the table in the dining room.

"All right, darling. Take your gloves – it's cold." She knew that my feet and hands were always freezing to the point of numbness in the winter.

Hmm, had better remember to remove gloves before eating those chips. Mum could smell vinegar and the whiff of a chip shop at a thousand paces. I must also try not to chew the ends off my gloves in the exciting parts of the film, which drove Mum mad. They were already full of darns.

This was exciting. A trip to the cinema with my big brother! I had better be good. It would be a change from the rowdy conditions at Saturday Morning Pictures, where cheap tickets gave us entry to watch a mixed programme of Tom Mix, Roy Rogers, Rin Tin Tin, Flash Gordon and cartoons. The manager, in his suit and bow tie, gave us all a pep talk about behaviour before the lights dimmed and an organist emerged from the orchestra pit into the floodlights on stage. After a few tunes the curtains would open and we'd cough expectantly, getting ready to sing along to the words on the screen:

We come along on Saturday morning,
Greeting everybody with a smile.
We come along on Saturday morning,
Knowing it's all worthwhile!

We set off into the crepuscular gloom, my brother and I, he at a fast lope with his long legs and I skipping to keep up with him.

The picture we wanted to see was at the Queen's, our local flea pit, just off Cricklewood Broadway. I'd seen the poster near the bus stop: "Where No Vultures Fly", with a rugged Anthony Steel and a primly glamorous Dinah Sheridan looking dramatic. It was about the establishment of the first game reserve in Kenya. Animals, exotic scenery, excitement and not too much sloppy love interest, it promised to fulfil most of my requirements as a picture-goer.

The lights dimmed and we sat through what seemed like interminable advertisements (Pearl and Dean), trailers for All Next Week and the B picture, whose title and contents I cannot remember. A curtain of smoke from the audience's cigarettes writhed and curled in front of the screen. At last! The credits rolled and the audience stopped slurping their Kia Ora drinks or sucking the last bit of choc ice from its wrapper. The story unfolded. Anthony Steel wore a nice line in khaki shirts and shorts but his hair was too corrugated for me to really fancy him. I tried not to demolish my gloves in the frightening parts and hid my eyes when animals were being slaughtered in an attempt to eradicate tsetse fly. As we staggered to our feet for the strains of "God Save the King" I could only see herds of zebra, wildebeeste and gazelle.

I came out of the cinema in another world, my head filled with visions of tawny plains teeming with wild animals, flat-topped fever trees etched against the skyline and Dinah Sheridan elegantly sipping her gin and tonic on a shady verandah. My first, if vicarious, taste of Africa.

I had always wanted to travel – anything to escape the postwar gloom of London. Still a sepia picture: no one had the money to redecorate, clean off the soot, buy brighter clothes. The nearest I got to colour was seeing the fruit and veg on the barrow boys' market stall, sniffing bags of cereal and spices in the grocer's or picking sweet peas in Dad's garden.

I spent some of the time with Gran in her bedroom. It was a refuge from arguing parents and I loved to hear my grandmother reminisce about the old days. On her bedside table sat a photograph in a delicate silver frame of Mum as a young girl, sitting on a pony near Darjeeling with a view of Mount Everest in the background, one which has long since disappeared. As she brushed her hair she told me how it had once been so long that she could sit on it, and how it had hurt when her ayah brushed it too vigorously. She had few possessions but they included a beautiful dressing table mirror with a tiny drawer and a Burmese teak mirror, both with ornately carved frames.

"Your grandfather's prisoners in Burma made those. They were very talented craftspeople," she said.

I fiddled with Gran's hair using her tortoiseshell-backed brush, inspected her collection of kirby grips in another similar box and admired her skill at darning socks with the aid of a wooden mushroom. She was still a good seamstress, making and mending clothes and bed linen ("sides to middle") on a treadle Singer sewing machine – I can still hear the whirr of its wheel, the clatter of the needle up and down like a piston and the pedal's click. Comforting sounds. She taught me how to do cross stitch and make Dorothy bags. I noticed that Gran's knickers were different to mine, interlock bloomers, and found it hard to believe that this was the same person as the young woman in a smart hat and frilled blouse in one of

Mum's photographs. Her room was a place of refuge and peace where I could sit at the window and dream. From this vantage point I could look down over the gardens, across Ivy Road to the leafier horizon of Gladstone Park and imagine I was watching a country sunset – or, better still, a copper-coloured sun sinking down to the horizon in a flaming African sky.

I was happy enough at home. We didn't have much money but our house was warm, safe and full of a loving family. However, I somehow felt there was more to life than Cricklewood.

Gran was always at home – her only excursions were to the shops – and she could talk for hours about the old days. The wonderful fruit she could pick from the trees – bananas, rambutans, lychees. The very names sounded exotic. She had taken my mother into the forest to watch the working elephants lift, pick and roll heavy teak logs down to the river. Saffron-clad monks came to the door with their begging bowls, then walked along the dusty road to make offerings at the pagoda. She told me how beautiful and graceful the Burmese girls were in their silk, fitted shirts and longyis, with frangipani flowers adorning their glossy black hair, how good the first monsoon rains smelled and of her first, unforgettable sight of the Himalayas by moonlight.

Occasionally old friends from Mum's Burmese days came over for supper. Her best friend, Phyllis, was a secretary who lived above John Lewis on Finchley Road: she was John's godmother. There were Ada and Meg, two more ladies that we sometimes saw in their Maida Vale mansion flat, Merlyn and Phyllis's sister Sybil, who later married well and went to South Africa with her new husband. There seemed to be no men in these women's lives.

Mum's colonial childhood wasn't a bed of roses. Her father had died young and she remembered chafing his icy feet with her hands as he lay dying, trying to warm him up. Gone were her journeys to boarding school, by a paddle steamer on the Irrawaddy River. Gran became a matron at another school and lived in. My mother remained a boarder, one of the poorer ones who slept in different beds and ate different food from the fee-paying girls. Her first task at the beginning of term was to clear the bed frame of bed bugs, which she did with a piece of soap.

Gran was in a reflective mood.

"You know, Jude, our servants lived with their families in a compound near the house. They were a hot-blooded lot and one night there was a terrible fight. One young man stabbed another..... I went down there and told him to give me his kukri, dripping with blood. And do you know, dear, he did!"

On Mum's bedroom wall hung a simple, impressionist watercolour she had bought in Rangoon in the 1920s. I loved this landscape. It showed people strolling up a tree-fringed, red-earth road, carrying brightly-patterned parasols to protect them from the bright tropical sun. Looking at it gave me a warm, serene feeling. My poor mother had brought virtually nothing from the Far East back to England, so the painting was all the more precious. She had, however, managed to pack her trio of bronze figurines to take with her: a lady smoking her cheroot, a warrior with his sword and the chinlone player with a rattan football poised on his toe. Other mementoes lay in our dressing-up box: a ruby-red Mandarin jacket, silk shawls and Mum's old evening dresses, now no longer worn.

Strangely enough, Mum did not talk about those days. She was too busy. When I was very small she had worked for the Ministry of Information and, during the war, watched the Battle of Britain from the roof of University College's Senate house.

"Weren't you frightened, Mum?" I asked.

"No, darling. There were so many air raid warnings it was too much of a fag to go downstairs to the shelter all the time. So we just stood up there and watched."

My horizons had expanded, too. I had left the little private school as I was still battling with sums. Miss Hutchinson frightened me so much my mind went blank when she asked me a question in class. I had sat the Scholarship (Eleven Plus) exam for grammar school one year early but had failed the maths section, which it was essential to pass in the Eleven Plus examination: English, Mathematics and General Knowledge. Students had to pass this exam to gain entrance to a free, state grammar school. If they failed the alternative was a secondary modern, unthinkable in my mother's view.

For this reason, I was moved to the local primary, Mora Road, which was much closer, for the purpose of improving my poor maths rating. I was still a little feeble shrimp and had to learn how to toughen up. I had been used to nasty boys flicking ink pellets in my direction or sticking spiders down my collar and girls calling me names at St Helen's. Our teachers had patrolled the aisles, ruler in hand for miscreants – but I was a goody two-shoes. Anything for a quiet life. John had made me impervious to all teasing and I readily answered to moron, cretin, pea-brain, four eyes or any of the other nicknames he gave me.

Mora Road was a large, redbrick Victorian school surrounded by tarmac playground – no lawns or trees here – and we queued in line each morning to file into the entrances marked Girls and Boys. I was lucky enough to have Mr Whitlock, a wonderful Welsh teacher with a dry sense of humour, and take part in some of the musical revues written by the talented music teacher. Mr Whitlock made a fuss of me and helped me settle in, a fact not unnoticed by Rita, the teacher's pet. She was a pretty girl, blue-eyed with a matching blue ribbon in her curly blonde hair and was often made the class monitor.

One day we were walking past the Ilford factory when I saw Rita on the other side of the street. I looked at her and gave her a nervous smile.

"Wotcha staring at, stare cat?" she shouted.

My first encounter with jealousy; and another would soon follow.

We went on a school camp to St. Mary's Bay, travelled round Kentish castles and Romney Marsh and performed our revue, in competition with other schools. The show started with us all sitting on the floor, holding one another's elbows, to simulate a train. We moved forward on our bottoms, chugging along, singing

We're heading for the sand and sea,
Oh won't you join our company?
Now here's the celebration,

86

Meet me at the station,
Put your suitcase on the rack,
Your bucket, spade, umbrella, mac.....

I was the narrator: my years at a private school and my mum's influence had given me good, clear English pronunciation and some acting ability. This didn't go down too well with one particular girl, Jackie, long used to being joint teacher's pet with Rita. She tormented me by calling me names, putting salt in my cocoa, sticking holly in my camp bed and whispering behind my back, which I detested. I maintained an aloof silence and didn't let it show that she upset me but I was dreadfully homesick. Still, it was a formative life experience. I wasn't a physical fighter but was learning to use my wits and tongue to get myself out of trouble.

Besides toughening me up, this primary school also taught me new skills – performing on a proper stage without dying of embarrassment, playing cricket and juggling. In Coronation year, 1953, we all had to practise country dancing for a festival in Gunnersbury Park, even the boys. Mr. Whitlock persuaded them that learning how to dance would improve their football skills. We'd spend hours skipping, doing "bumps", where the rope passed twice under your feet while you jumped higher, to rhymes such as

Julius Caesar, Roman geezer,
Squashed his nose with a lemon squeezer.

There was also the mixed blessing of kiss chase in the playground, where I was usually caught by one of two boys, both called Alan – unsettling but thrilling. The sweetshop near the school gates beckoned and we filled our faces with fruit gums, sherbet fountains and gobstoppers.

I sat the Eleven Plus exam again and passed this time, though my maths was still weak. I expected to get into the grammar nearest to home but, at Mum's insistence, had put Henrietta Barnett in Hampstead Garden Suburb as my first choice. By now I'd assimilated so well that I considered myself a street kid and wanted to go to the same place as my friends.

"That's a snob school!" I protested. "I'd much rather go to Brondesbury and Kilburn, Mum"

Henrietta Barnett was girls only, what was more.

"It's a good school, never mind 'snob,'" she replied. "You'll like it."

"I won't get in, anyway," I sniffed. "So there."

I had already sat the entrance exam for a scholarship to North London Collegiate (alma mater of Esther Rantzen and Eleanor Bron), a famous school in Edgware with beautiful grounds and thought it was wonderful. I was going through an Angela Brazil phase at the time – she was an author who wrote about life at a girls' boarding school – and considered this to be as exciting as Harry Potter's Hogwarts is today. They had awarded me a place but not a scholarship and of course, my parents couldn't afford to pay. I was very disappointed and promptly lost interest in grammar schools.

My results came through. I had passed and gained a place at Henrietta Barnett. Where education was concerned, Mum's word was law. They sent a uniform list and panic set in. This was going to cost my poor parents a fortune. Mum scouted around, bought some poplin and gabardine at cost price from her good old M&S head office and found a local dressmaker who could sew the blouses and tunics. One day we took the trolley bus to Pullen's, at Temple Fortune, where a forbidding, superior shop assistant measured me up for a blazer, games shorts (divided skirts – how ladylike), gym knickers, regulation plimsolls and a box-pleated gym slip that would make even an eleven-year old look pregnant. We couldn't afford a blazer, just a navy purse on a cord on which the school's emblem, an oak tree, was embroidered in red.

Rumbling under blackened girders, Midland, bound for Cricklewood,
Puffed its sulphur to the sunset where that Land of Laundries stood.
Rumble under, thunder over, train and tram alternate go,
Shake the floor and smudge the ledger, Charrington, Sells Dale and Co."

John Betjeman, from the poem Parliament Hill Fields, 1912

In 1953 the trams or rather trolleybuses still ran under the railway bridge up Child's Hill. They were quieter, cleaner and smoother than the diesel buses but occasionally their long antennae connecting them to the overhead power lines became unstuck, with a shower of sparks. The girders were still black and the trains still rumbled.

When I set off for my first day, I was the only schoolgirl from Cricklewood on the bus. I walked up the hill to the school, in Hampstead Garden Suburb, an imposing building facing a green square flanked by two huge churches. Dame Henrietta Barnett had founded the school in 1911 "to educate bright girls regardless of their means" and the buildings had been designed by Sir Edwin Lutyens. As we registered, I recognized a familiar face: my friend Juliet Wittman, from St. Helen's. We fell into one another's arms with relief but had to split up almost immediately as there were two separate assemblies, one for Christians, the other for Jews. Half the school's intake was Jewish.

To my surprise, I enjoyed Henrietta Barnett. Its parquet flooring gleamed, the classrooms were light and airy and the teaching standards high. Our class teacher, Miss Cronin, who also took French, was one of a dedicated band of teachers who all seemed to favour grey suits. We took it in turns to tidy the classroom and provide flowers and I, naturally, managed to overturn the vase and spill water everywhere at my first attempt.

"You stupid girl!" cried Miss Cronin, as I dabbed ineffectually at the mess. "Get a towel, for goodness sake. Have you no brains?"

I finished the job and lay low. At least I could apply lavender polish to wax my own desk properly once a week, that was something, and keep up with the challenging tasks our teachers set us. The murky intricacies of French, Latin, even Maths, became clear but I could not cope with Physics and Chemistry, taught by an elegantly sarcastic teacher in a lab coat. She gave me my first detention because I couldn't spell "paraffin". The art studio was a revelation and my spidery handwriting was transformed by a jowly, patrician spinster, Miss

Henrietta Barnett School, Hampstead Garden Suburb

Sinclair, who insisted on our using pens with inkwells (no fountain pens until the sixth form and definitely no ballpoints) and practising patterns before we were let loose on the alphabet. We weren't allowed exercise books, only scrap paper on which we had to rule two extra lines at the top of the page to save paper, still in short supply. Miss S transformed my handwriting to the extent that I won a prize at the end of the first year. Our Geography teacher, Mrs Skilling, also laid a solid foundation in cartography and lettering. I resumed piano lessons on the mellow tones of a Broadwood, with Miss Bosely, a sweet lady who wore colourful dirndl skirts, knitted shawls and dangly earrings. She, like the majority of the staff, was a superb teacher. My favourite subject was English, taught by the dainty Miss Gawthrop. I coped with it all but was definitely not top of the class. The bar was raised high and the Jewish girls reigned supreme. Their fathers were doctors, writers, teachers, artists, musicians, businessmen and accountants and some of their mothers worked too. Through my Jewish friends I learned much about wartime persecution, the confines and demands of their religion and the comfortable reassurance of their society.

I came into closer contact with the Jewish girls when I gave up on school dinners. The vast quantities and smell of overcooked cabbage in the canteen made me feel ill, delicate little flower that I was, and I couldn't clear my plate, a mandatory requirement. I persuaded Mum to make me packed lunches (another chore for an overworked woman) and ate them in the assembly hall with my new friends, Juliet included, eating their kosher lunches, surrounded by enormous, pre-Raphaelite paintings of depressed women. I developed an aversion to the smell of gherkins, salami and pickles.

The school was strong on music and the arts and Juliet was to feature in leading roles in many productions. I had saved my pocket money for riding lessons at Stanmore a couple of years earlier but was too embarrassed to leave the house in my second-hand jodhpurs, yellow polo-necked jumper and jacket, getting changed in the Tube station lavatory – what would the street kids think? I wasn't posh, after all. Now I had enough confidence to catch the bus in my riding gear and meet a new school friend to go riding on Hampstead Heath. I loved everything about my Saturday at the stables: the glossy coats of the horses, the sweet smell of hay in mangers, the creak of the saddle as I trotted along, the coarse texture of the mane between my fingers, the aroma of polished leather. As I concentrated on the view between the pricked ears of a favourite pony, I revelled in the achievement of perfecting a smooth canter, the wind in my hair.

The new school was not all a bed of roses. I didn't enjoy PT – too many instruments of torture in the gym – or hockey. I was too tall, weedy and skinny. On the hockey pitch hearty girls with mottled legs, muscles and thunder thighs bore down at frightening speed in the freezing cold, while I vainly tried to pass the ball before being tackled. The lumps I still have on my calves bear witness to these clashes. I was such a wimp.

The gloomy way home with a laden satchel down Hoop Lane involved passing Golders Green Crematorium, which spread over many acres and was festooned with enormous memorials and headstones, sepulchral angels and urns. It was spooky walking past there in the autumn

93

twilight, horse chestnut trees dripping overhead. I boarded the bus at the bottom of the hill, steeling myself for comments about my beret (another hated object) from cheeky boys, and envying the girls from Ada Foster's Stage School, attended a few years later by singer Elaine Page, star of Evita and Cats. They climbed on at the same stop and could wear whatever they liked. The walk to Temple Fortune was shorter, prettier (glowing flowering cherries in springtime) but the bus ride cost a few pence more. It took about an hour to get home – and then we had piles of homework, not a novelty but more this time, much more.

During my first winter at grammar school, illness struck. My nose streamed, I came down with 'flu then recurrent tonsillitis. I began to feel I was getting behind with my school work. In fact, I wasn't but it felt like it. John, too, caught 'flu and perfected the art of fainting. One day I was reading in the dining room when I watched John, sick again, walk out into the lean-to and pass out with a crash, just missing the mangle.

PART TWO

AFRICA

Chapter 7
NORTHERN RHODESIA –
A VOYAGE OF DISCOVERY

Table Mountain, seen from Bloubergstrand

Rumblings of discontent continued at home.

"I dunno, Dulce," said Dad, "I'm never going to get promotion. That blighter Stan is blocking my way. It's a case of dead man's shoes. Maybe I should start looking overseas."

There was talk of finding a job in Kenya but these seemed to be few and far between in the building trade. Besides, the Mau Mau disturbances were rife, hundreds of Africans were being forced to take oaths and were being killed, and a few Europeans, too. A State of Emergency had been declared and the British Army was sent out to help.

My mother said nothing as she cleared the table. She liked her job, we now had a whole house to live in and she didn't want the boat rocked. Gran paid no attention: she had heard Dad's complaints before. She remained glued to the wireless, listening to a boxing match. She got agitated on such occasions, clenched her tiny fists and punched along with the boxers.

"Give him hell," she muttered.

John was in his room, playing music at top volume. I said nothing and buried my head in Latin homework. They hadn't asked me for my opinion, anyway.

Then, in 1954, Dad came home with and advertisement for work with a building firm in Northern Rhodesia. Where on earth was that?

The atlas was plonked on our dining table once more in what was to be a defining moment for our little family. We found out that Northern Rhodesia was a landlocked country in Central Africa, about 24 times the size of the United Kingdom but with a small population of three million people. It was drained by the river systems of the Congo and Zambezi rivers, whose headwaters rose within its borders, and contained a huge swamp next to its largest lake, Bangweulu. A British Protectorate, it was bordered by Tanganyika in the north, Nyasaland to the east, Southern Rhodesia, the Caprivi Strip (an outlier of South West Africa) and the Belgian Congo.

I listened to the murmuring of my parents as they thrashed out the pros and cons of emigration late at night in the dining room, which lay directly beneath my bedroom. What I didn't realize was that Dad had given Mum an ultimatum: come with me or it is the end of our marriage. It was agreed that Dad should fly out to Lusaka, the capital city, and try the job, with a building company.

It was time for Jack the lad to reinvent himself.

All too soon my father left. He was collected in a taxi early one morning for a flight from Heathrow Airport and I can't even remember saying goodbye. A lonely Marks and Spencer wooden coat hanger dangled in the hall, inscribed in Biro "Dad – Do Not Take This". Poor Dad, he was bossed around by his family right up to the time of departure.

Airmail post was in its infancy then and we were not to hear for another three weeks about his trip, whether he had arrived safely and if he liked his new job. Eventually short but pithy postcards arrived, sent from his stops en route during the four-day flight. Passengers took off in the morning, came down for lunch and refuelling, took off again, sometimes landed for tea and finally rested at an overnight stop. I followed my father's progress avidly and traced his journey in pencil in the atlas.

Grand Hotel, Sliema, Malta:
Haven't seen the George Cross yet! Nice view of harbour. Bumpy flight.

Wadi Halfa:
On the Nile! No sign of General Gordon.
New Stanley Hotel, Nairobi:
Where's my sjambok (whip made from hippo hide)?
Blokes bring their guns down to dinner and leave them on the table while they're eating. (This was because of the Mau Mau disturbances: people carried their guns around with them.)

We never got a postcard from Lusaka. It wasn't the sort of place you would send a postcard from. Dad was billeted at the Lusaka Hotel on Cairo Road, the broad main street, so called because it formed part of Cecil Rhodes' dream, never realized, of a continuous road from Cape Town to Cairo. It had been established as the principal administrative centre because it was more central than Livingstone, the former capital, being a suitable crossroads for all the provinces. After a few years the powers that be discovered that the place flooded during the rainy season but by then it was too late to change things: a typical case of external rules and plans ignoring local geography. The place looked more like a Wild West town than a capital city. The name Lusaka was supposedly derived from that of the original Lenje chief, Lusakaas, who once lived there but I preferred the other root, Fisakasaka, meaning scrub thorn bush.

The broad main street was a dusty expanse wide enough for a span of six oxen and cart to turn round in, its shops fronted by verandahs to give shade from the harsh African sun. There were even hitching rails for horses fringing the uneven, concrete pavements. The town centre was rough and ready, almost a frontier place and one of my father's first memories is of a drunk being forcibly ejected through the swinging half-doors of the Corner Bar in the Lusaka Hotel.

Life in England went on much as before, except that there was no Dad around. We missed his jokes, the cuddles, his ability to fix anything from a leaking radiator to a flaking wall, flowers in the garden, family outings to the park. Mum, under pressure, argued with Gran. A few months later news came that Dad had changed his job and was now working for the Northern Rhodesia Government, the NRG that was to dominate our lives for the next ten years. His talents and energy were to be devoted to the Public Works Department, which managed all public roads, buildings and transport. His first posting was to Kasama, in the Northern Province – in the bush. Young as I was, I could see that Mum was tempted to go out to join her husband and take me with her.

John had made it clear he didn't want to go. He was in the third year of the Sixth Form at Marylebone Grammar, trying to improve his Maths marks to go to university. In fact, he lazed around and his grades didn't improve, quite the reverse. He was offered a place at Battersea Polytechnic, reading Chemical Engineering. He was informed that he would not be going to the main campus but to the "annexe" in Putney, a converted shop. This was not the academic life John had anticipated and he switched to read Psychology at University College after the first year – talking his way in, no doubt. He had inherited Dad's charm. He was not the least bit concerned about the impending departure of his mother and sister.

Gran was slowing down. She was also half-blind: a few years' previously she had been operated on for a brain haemorrhage and now only had one eye. She'd been given a glass one and couldn't be bothered to wear it half the time as it made her eyes water. This horrified visitors but we were used to it! What's more, her mind was as acute as ever and she could hunt for anything we'd mislaid.

"Eyes and no eyes!" she would cry. "I can find more with my one eye than you can with your two."

Mum was finding the winter months a trial – catching buses and walking to work in all weathers, housekeeping and, worse still, suffering from arthritis in her precious hands. With crippled fingers, how could she carry on typing? And she was lonely. She had to choose between staying put or dividing the family if she joined my father. For me, there was no contest. I wanted to be with both my parents, even if it meant an unknown country and the possibility of boarding school while my parents were in the bush.

Early in 1955, the decision was made. Mum and I were going to Africa. I was incandescent with excitement and, looking back, quite heartless at the prospect of leaving John and Gran, school and friends. I had never been abroad before. Endless forms were completed and we were given the necessary inoculations and X-rays to prove we didn't have pulmonary tuberculosis. Suitcases and tea chests were packed with household goods to set up home in the bush. NRG provided employees and their families with houses and hard furnishings and we were expected to supply the rest. Our sea passage was booked. We were to travel on the Braemar Castle from Tilbury on 24th March 1955, then take the train from Cape Town all the way up through Southern Africa until we disembarked at the railhead, Ndola.

The pain of separation didn't hit me until the morning of our departure. I made my bed for the last time, gave the cats their milk and listened to the news of the radio. We said goodbye to Gran at the house. She stood on the front doorstep, a little old lady in her soft brown skirt and cardigan, still in her shapeless broad bean slippers. Tears streamed down her cheeks, even from her sightless eye.

"Be a good girl, bhatcha, and look after your Mum," she said.

The day was dismal and grey as we took the taxi to the ship. In those days the Port Of London boasted 26 miles of docks. John helped us with our luggage into the cabin, a windowless cell in the bowels of the ship which smelled of diesel. The Braemar Castle was one of the new One-Class ships but we were definitely travelling steerage. Poor Mum's eyes were moist but she stayed in control as she bade goodbye to her beloved son. I tried to picture John back in the house, left behind in England with his grandmother to cope with. He'd be finishing school, going to university and running a home on a shoestring this year with both parents thousands of miles away. It wasn't as though he could pick up a phone to say hello. There were no telephones where we were going.

Immediately after our departure, there was a newspaper strike which last for almost a month, followed by Churchill's resignation on 5th April. I can't imagine now how bereft and isolated Gran must have felt.

We spent two weeks on board ship, sleeping in our little hole below decks. The Braemar didn't have her full complement of cargo because her arrival in the UK had been delayed by storms and shippers had transferred their goods to other vessels. She also had no stabilizers so consequently when we hit rough weather in the Bay of Biscay she bounced around like a cork. I learned the difference between pitching and yawing – our ship did both. The dining room, once full of passengers tucking into bacon and eggs at breakfast, emptied so that soon it was just a few of us. Crockery and cutlery slid around the table, crashing into the low rail round its edge. Some brave souls sat in deckchairs under rugs and were handed out mugs of Bovril for elevenses. I was sick just once, in our hell hole, as the ship groaned and shuddered through heavy seas. Mum wasn't so lucky and continued to feel ill for the duration of the voyage.

Our first port of call was Las Palmas, Gran Tenerife. We docked at night and were taken for a quick taxi ride round the seedy-looking town, where street vendors plied us with lace, shawls and linen tablecloths. Later, a group of flamenco dancers came on board to entertain the passengers. Entranced, I watched their graceful whirling and stamping to the sound of guitars and castanets and forgot about the time. I incurred Mum's wrath by getting back to our cabin after midnight.

"Did you think I'd been whisked off by white slave traders, Mum?" I joked.

She gave me a brisk slap on the face. I put my hand up to my cheek, horrified. It was hardly more than a tap but Mum had never, ever hit me before. She burst into tears. This was a revelation and taught me how much my mother worried about me without betraying her feelings.

The clouds lifted and soon the weather was baking hot. We anchored off Ascension Island, a red volcanic peak studded with radio masts. Flying fish skimmed over the waves. The water was so clear that I caught my first glimpse of a hammerhead shark from the ship's rail and at night the sea glowed with phosphorescence. On the foc'sle the off-duty crew removed their blue shirts and developed tans, looking far more desirable than most of the male passengers.

The ship ploughed on across the Atlantic Ocean. Where we had once found the meals exciting and plentiful we were now suffering from a surfeit of nourishment and not enough exercise. I couldn't believe the amount of food tossed out of the kitchen portholes each day. All sorts of events were organized to amuse the passengers – films, card and casino evenings, race nights, dances and the inevitable fancy dress. The men's winner, dressed in a bowler hat, braces, cardboard box and little else, was The British Taxpayer and the ladies' was a pretty woman in a black evening dress fringed with green crêpe paper. She was a Grass Widow, a term which meant nothing to me. Mum sat wistfully at the dances, missing Dad as her partner – better ballroom dancers than this lot.

When we crossed the Equator the crew dressed up for the Crossing-the-Line ceremony, presided over by Neptune. The ship's captain wielded a cut-throat razor, men fought with pillows on a greasy pole over the tiny swimming pool and generally larked around. I was more interested in the next landfall – St. Helena, where Napoleon had once been exiled. Another volcanic island, this one was lush and green and we were allowed to go ashore. As we climbed down ladders a pair of huge manta rays swam alongside. They were as big as the small boats waiting to collect us, their huge, sail-like fins flapping just below the rowers, who poked at them with their oars. The small town smelled and looked excitingly exotic and we climbed up Jacob's Ladder, steps cut into the steep hillside, up to Longwood House, Napoleon's island prison.

The seas were getting rougher as we hit the Cape rollers. By now we had our sea legs and scarcely noticed the heavy swell. It was as though we were looking at the horizon from a slow-motion roller coaster. Suddenly, one morning, there it was – Table Mountain, rising straight out of the sea mist like a distant, fairytale castle. It didn't look real. We went below to finish our packing and prepare for immigration formalities, which took place on board, so we didn't see the ship pull into harbour. When we climbed back to the deck we were blasted by intense sunlight, despite the fact that it was autumn, with a chilly, stiff breeze. The rugged skyline of Table Mountain and the Cape Range loomed above us. Customs sheds glinted under a blue sky. Hatches were opened, cranes lifted out nets full of cargo from the hold and some cars were hauled off the deck, greased against the salt. Africa!

We lurched ashore, understanding the meaning of the expression "sailor's roll". Coffee-coloured men speaking a guttural language grabbed our bags and we stood under the S in the customs shed to identify our boxes. Adderley Street looked clean and scrubbed after London. People of all colours mingled on the streets but the park benches were segregated, with signs saying "Blankes – Nie Blankes."

The next part of our trek continued on the Blue Train. We were given a small compartment with two green, leather bunks, a table and a washbasin. We were served hot drinks in there, where I admired the skill of the Afrikaner steward as he poured in milk and coffee from chrome pots simultaneously, from a great height, in a steady stream. The bedding boys were Cape Coloureds. More segregation. The journey was a thrilling live geography lesson, crossing through provinces and countries. Some of their names have faded into history. From Cape

Province, we crossed the Orange Free State and Transvaal into Bechuanaland, through Southern and into Northern Rhodesia. We sped through the fertile coastal plain, past lush vineyards and orchards full of peach and apricot trees. White, thatched cottages with tall Dutch gables huddled at the base of the mountains. We drank our tea and watched the sea recede as the train snaked up the Berg in the Hex River Pass. It was well named and easy to imagine witches flying around the surrounding crags, where spiky aloes, proteas and bleached grasses poked between the dramatic rock formations. We ate supper in a spotless dining car then retired to our compartment, where I was too excited to sleep. Lightning flashed over the semi-desert of the Karroo, spotlighting kopjes and the stark outlines of flat-topped trees.

Dawn broke on a dusty plateau, spotted with the occasional herd of sheep, scrubby bush, white farmhouses flanked by windmills and dorps. There were villages full of round mud huts, cattle wandering through the scrubby bush and carts pulled by donkeys. Women with large headdresses carried huge bundles of wood or water pots on their heads. Africans on bicycles and mothers with babies swaddled on their backs stared as we swept past level crossings on the veld. Our journey was punctuated by meals with strange foods – mealies, gem squash, boerwors – and endless cups of strong coffee. We read, dozed and watched. The sun shone and a brilliant moon illuminated the wide open spaces of the savannah at night.

We changed trains at Bulawayo at night, with much shouting from the porters trundling our luggage. We were now on a Rhodesia Railways steam train, a beauty, and climbing down into the low veld towards the mighty Zambezi valley. There we would cross over the gorge dividing Northern and Southern Rhodesia by a bridge constructed in 1906 by Dorman Long, a firm from Stockton in north-east England, home of Stephenson's Rocket and other pioneering steam engines. It was quite a feat of engineering, as old photographs show.

By the time we reached Ndola, four days later, I was suffering from sensory overload. We had traversed scrubby bush, deserts, huge prairies of maize, pastures, forests, escarpments and mighty rivers. We had crossed the Zambezi gorge at Victoria Falls, thundering in full spate at the end of the rainy season with so much spray that we could hardly see the cascading wall of water. We leaned out of the windows, yelled with excitement and got drenched. We'd changed trains in Bulawayo, from South Africa Railways to Rhodesia Railways, seen mine dumps and headgear and glimpsed antelope and monkeys. On one stretch of high veld, clumps of granite kopjes looked as though they had been scattered by a giant. At every stop there were crowds of people, black faces upturned, bare feet smudged with dust, hands outstretched. I was shocked to see how poor they looked. Some were clad in little more than rags. We tossed children coins, sweets and pencils. The third class passengers bought wizened oranges, bananas, peanuts and posho (maize porridge) for they were not allowed (nor could afford) to use the restaurant car. We, the lucky ones, were travelling second class.

At last, we pulled into Ndola station. Our eyes scanned the waiting crowd.

"There's Dad," I shouted.

He looked smart in his bush shirt and shorts and his

highly polished shoes gleamed in the bright sunlight of the high veld. He was thinner, though, and had flecks of grey in his hair. He and Mum embraced each other, choked with emotion. My father's first year in Africa had not been easy and he'd suffered from two bad doses of malaria. We clambered down the steps gingerly into the dust – the station had no platform – and a swarming throng of black faces who buzzed like bees.

Ah, the bliss of a bed which was immobile, with clean, crisp sheets in the government rest house. Dinner was a stilted affair and I was acutely conscious of the row of uniformed waiters standing to attention behind our chairs, backs to the wall, anticipating our every move. Each one wore a fez and uniform of long tunic and trousers but their feet were bare. Their white teeth and taffeta sashes gleamed in the dim light of the dining room as we sipped our Brown Windsor Soup and waded through Bream Meuniere, Beef Casserole and Sponge Pudding, bland in the extreme. Outside, a full moon shone so brightly that we could walk to our rooms without torches. The balmy air was heavy with the scent of wood-smoke and jasmine.

The next morning, 14th April, Mum sent a telegram to Gran saying that we had arrived safely. Poor Gran was preoccupied with saving money, selling my old school blouses to Juliet for 10/- and paying bills – £1.10.0 for 4cwt of coal. Dad had some supplies to collect and he took us along to a diner for ice cream before we set off on the last lap of our long journey – 150 miles into the bush.

We could have been in America, sitting on chrome and plastic chairs and eating off glass-topped tables while the juke box churned out the latest pop music. A lady with a foreign accent served us.

"She's an Afrikaner," whispered Dad.

We sat in the shade of the golden shower and bougainvillaea creepers on the verandah at the rest house while Dad finished his errands, listening to the murmuring of the staff inside and the burbling of weaver birds above. These alien, vivid colours, smells and sounds would form part of our everyday lives and become as common as the London plane trees or the chatter of house sparrows.

Dad arrived in a vanette with his driver, Luka. We squeezed into the front bench seat and set off down the tarmac road to Mufulira, a copper mining town, beyond which we would travel for 45 miles through a part of the Belgian Congo on an atrocious road called the Pedicle.

"Very bad road ahead, sah," said Luka, for the benefit of Mum and myself. Dad had travelled down the day before and knew all too well just how bad it was. We crossed the border at Mokambo. The barrier lifted and revealed the dreaded highway.

This road was to become uncomfortably familiar but I can't forget that first journey on the long, straight, red road going on and on, gradually rising and falling into infinity. "MMBA – Miles and Miles of Bloody Africa", the expats called it. Cicadas shrilled in the dense, low forest which crowded into the roadside and clouds of yellow butterflies settled on puddles, of which there were many, in the deeply potholed surface. Corrugations rattled our teeth, gullies and sudden dips made our bottoms bump and our bodies sway as we alternately grounded when we hit or swerved to avoid them. At least there was only a little dust. The day grew hotter and we stuck uncomfortably to the plastic seats. We took off our shoes and Dad opened the windows and the air vents, which simply blew an equally scorching draught on to our faces, along with dust, scraps of dried grass and the occasional insect.

We passed lorries which had foundered in the drainage ditch or got stuck in the mud, some with punctures, others missing wheels or wings, many with crumpled bodies, tilting at crazy angles. One or two Africans sat by their disabled vehicles, eating, having a smoke or staring into space. They didn't seem worried. There were no views, no expanses of tawny grassland with statuesque trees. No resemblance at all, in fact, to "Where No Vultures Fly." Only endless bush – miombo woodland, the sunburnt road, dusty grass on the verges and broken vehicles. My illusions were shattered.

Hot and sticky, we peeled ourselves off the leatherette seats and on to Chembe ferry, the pontoon which crossed the Luapula River. Luka drove the vanette up the ramp with a clatter. A few locals walked on, a couple carrying chickens. The word chembe means fish eagle but we didn't see any that day. After the rains, the current was strong and the diesel engine chugged us upstream so that we could float downstream to the opposite bank. We turned our faces into the wind, which ruffled our hair and cooled the sweat from our bodies. We gratefully stopped for a cup of tea with the PWD supervisor.

"Do you ladies need the PK?" said Dick.

We looked bemused.

"The PK – the piccanin kaya," Dad laughed. "The little room. The lavatory. Look out for snakes."

Was he joking? Evidently not. Snakes loved to wriggle into comforting thatched roofs. In his previous bachelor pad, Dad had encountered a nest of cobras snoozing behind the toilet door. Mummy cobra had woken up and reared her head, her hood expanded, her tongue flickering enquiringly. He'd leapt on the seat and got out through the tiny window behind.

We walked in turn to Dick's PK, a scary privy at the bottom of the garden. We bent low under the grass fronds hanging unevenly from the roof to get in. Fortified by our rest stop, we were ready for the final 60 miles of our personal great trek. Another stretch of MMBA, more dirt but smoother now.

We passed through the tsetse control barrier, where a languid guard squirted our vehicle with a flit gun. The town was fly-free, unlike the surrounding bush. As the sun dipped below the horizon and shadows lengthened, we descended slowly into a broad valley. A water tower came into view, then a garage; people walked along the road, carrying mattocks and bundles. Fort Rosebery. It didn't look fortified – no walls, stockades or guard posts. It was just a little town in the bush. We had arrived at our new home.

Chapter 8
COMING HOME

Boma herd of cattle with egrets

In those days it was Fort Rosebery, named after a lord, an English Liberal imperialist who had served under Gladstone as Foreign Secretary, later becoming Prime Minister. Lord Rosebery wasn't a brilliant politician but he had three ambitions: to own a Derby winner, marry an heiress and be rich. He'd achieved all three. Now the town is called Mansa, after the small river that runs through it.

Our first house was a small, two-bedroomed bungalow. Hardly visible from the red laterite road, it was screened by flat-topped bush trees and a small grove of cassias, which dripped with panicles of yellow blossom when we first pulled in to the drive. Many tree trunks were covered by branching tunnels of red dust, made by white ants (termites). Agama lizards, blueskops, loved this grove in front of the house and scuttled off as we approached. The Africans were terrified of all reptiles and were especially wary of these large specimens, who could run at tremendous speed. They lay along the bark facing upwards, their grey, mottled bodies virtually invisible, indigo heads bobbing up and down like an Indian dancer to focus on their prey. To one side of the house lay a rickety carport under a frayed thatched roof, next to the Rhodesian boiler and its accompanying woodpile, while at the rear my father's vegetable garden and rough grass sloped downhill towards the servants' kaya and the golf course beyond.

The house was unprepossessing. It was built of local red brick on a base of dingy white stucco, the latter permanently stained by a tide mark of red dust round its base, with steel-framed, ant-proof windows and a corrugated iron roof. The latter seemed to have a life of its own, crackling loudly as it expanded and contracted beneath the sun's rays and rendering all conversation impossible when subjected to a tropical downpour. The bungalow floor was well above ground level – to escape flooding in the rains – and we entered via the front steps and a cement stoep, painted ox blood red and polished to a high sheen by the houseboy. All the servants were called "boys", a term derived from the Portuguese word for bearer. It was applied to all staff, whether eight or eighty, which I found odd.

Dad parked the vanette in the dusk and we were formally introduced to the staff: Simon, the houseboy and Tandeo, the garden boy. They bent one knee and shook our hands, one arm placed on the elbow of the other, then clapped their hands softly. This showed respect for the person they were meeting and indicated that no weapons were being carried. It was the traditional Bemba greeting.

"Mwapoleni mukwai, bwana" said Simon. "Mwapoleni mukwai, dona. You are welcome."

Simon's family were hovering discreetly in the background, waiting to see what the rest of the bwana's family looked like. Our arrival also meant supplies and their monthly ration of tea, soap, washing powder, sugar and mealie (maize) meal. This retinue would silently appear each time the cold lorry arrived from the line of rail, well after dark, with its precious cargo of meat in the steel-lined, ice-packed box.

Simon was smartly dressed in his starched and pressed safari suit uniform and spoke good English. He was tall for a Bemba, handsome with flashing teeth and his trim, woolly hair neatly parted on the side of his head. In contrast, we were travel worn, scruffy and covered in red dust. Skinny Tandeo wore his own ragged shirt and shorts with gazelle-like grace; he gazed shyly at the ground and said nothing, as his command of our language was nil. Luckily, Dad could communicate with a person of any nationality with blind confidence and bonhomie, through a mixture of sign language and a few (usually inaccurate) words of the vernacular, with some inevitable misunderstandings all round. This really embarrassed the family but it must have worked because his employees thought the world of him.

The "boys" carried in our suitcases, collecting their bonsela with cupped hands.

"Don't spend it all at the beer hall," Dad instructed.

We sank wearily into Morris chairs, standard government issue in our sparsely furnished lounge.

Top: *The bridge over the gorge, Victoria Falls*
Bottom: *Chembe Ferry, Luapula River (Photo: Alan Kitching)*

These were made from mukwa, a local hardwood but were amazingly comfortable. Their slatted backs were adjustable, the substantial arms wide and long enough for the safe parking of one's drink, book and ashtray. The seat cushions rested on a base of buck hide (riempie) webbing strips. They were sturdy and utilitarian pieces of furniture but my parents loved them so much that they eventually took a pair back to England when they retired. Some reed mats, a Morris sofa, a rickety coffee table and the radio completed the décor. Dad hadn't got round to curtains yet.

Simon immediately wheedled his way into Mum's good books by bringing in a tray of tea, unasked. He was an excellent cook, baked wonderful bread and perfect Victoria sponge cakes and made soufflé omelettes to die for.

A deep, tropical darkness suddenly descended, lamps were lit and we ate our supper to the hiss of a Tilly lamp. I was given a hurricane lantern to take to my room where I immediately fell asleep, immune to the cacophony outside of tree frogs, crickets, an owl and the odd, alarming shriek of some unidentified small mammal. I had come home.

After a few days' grace, my mother started work at PWD, working as secretary to the chief engineer. I had a few weeks to spend at home before starting school, to settle in and explore. Bush life would seem boringly routine in later years but at first it was all totally exotic and exciting.

Each day a flock of noisy bulbuls woke me up, chattering in the tree by the bedroom window while it was still dark. These brown, crested birds, the African equivalent of the house sparrow, started their burbling before the sun was up. Then Simon would knock gently on the door, heralding early morning tea. My family couldn't function without regular cups of the stuff and, as far as Dad was concerned, the earlier the better. Outside, I could hear the gardener sweeping round the house with his hand-brush of twigs, swish, swish.

After breakfast (pawpaw with lemon, cereal and vile powdered milk, toast, more tea) my parents walked to work along the dusty roads for a seven o'clock start. They had no car, initially but Dad was eventually given the use of a short wheel base Land Rover which we christened Dreamboat. The Boma drums announced the beginning of the office day, echoing round the valley.

The Boma (a Bantu name for a stock-proof enclosure) was the headquarters of the Provincial Administration, the PA, staffed by the DC (District Commissioner). The pecking order was DC, DOs (District Officers), DAs (District Assistants), Cadets and clerical staff, right down to the Boma messengers, who dressed in purple tunics and matching shorts edged in red. There were also other messengers in rural areas, kapasus, who acted as informal policemen.

Periodically PA officers went on tour (ulendo) to oversee their particular patch of Native Authority land. They bumped around in Land Rovers festooned with canvas water bags draped over the bumper wing mirrors, used bicycles when the road ended and walked, pitching tents where there was no rest house. A team of bearers accompanied them on these safaris, cooking, doing the laundry and lighting fires. The PA dealt with agricultural problems and taxes, sorted out domestic and criminal issues and operated in tandem with the local chiefs.

While I lived in Fort Rosebery, Luapula Province (formerly part of the Northern Province) became a separate entity, with its own Provincial Commissioner – PC – as well as a DC. It was all very military, colonial and confusing, involving a language studded with acronyms. You were saluted in offices, at border posts and even walking into a friend's front gate. Everything – furniture, cutlery, stationery, car number plates – was stamped with NRG, Northern Rhodesian Government or sometimes FRN, Federation of Rhodesia and Nyasaland. Land Rovers and school uniforms were government green.

There was an unofficial hierarchy in this little town – very colonial British. The Provincial Administration were at the top of the tree, closely followed by the Northern Rhodesia Police(NRP) and possibly the more professional departments such as Education, Health and Information. Lower down the scale the Public Works Department, Water Affairs, Agriculture and Forestry trundled along together, leaving the more practical category of Trade (shop owners and managers, garages, haulage and transport companies) at the bottom. Offshoots of indeterminate rank included priests, nuns, missionaries and miners. There were no postal workers as letters were not delivered to the house but to a Post Box, number 3 in our case.

Our town must have had a population of no more than 180 Europeans. There were two townships, African and European, separated by a stream. Most of the government offices were clustered around the Boma, where residents paid their rents, water and electricity bills and taxes, registered their vehicles, and obtained driving licences. Africans collected their situpas here, a form of work permit and pass which guaranteed their residence within the town. Even European travellers were supposed to report to the DC. In this way the administration kept tabs on everybody.

The Public Works Department, where my parents worked (Dad as a Stores Officer in Roads and Buildings, Mum as private secretary in the main offices where she worked for the Chief Engineer) was situated on the edge of the small shopping and industrial area, opposite the bus station – Thatcher Hobson, later to become CARS, Central African Road Services. The Club, with its tennis courts and cricket pitch, was a focal point for social activity. It sat above the Boma and what was optimistically called the golf course, crisscrossed by footpaths made by the locals and small animals, studded with some beautiful trees, including one enormous mango, a relic of the Arab slave trade, and a field used for agricultural shows and other gatherings, below the courthouse. The only other building of note, on the other side of the river was the European Hospital, the former DC's house, surrounded by graceful jacaranda trees which were covered in mauve scented blooms before the rains. During my stay the old swimming pool here was revived for everyone's use, although its cleanliness was suspect. One lady who swam there every morning swore she had caught bilharzia from it. The town was surrounded by tsetse fly country

Top: *Dad's first house in Fort Rosebery*
Centre: *Mum in living room of No 23, our first family house*
Bottom: *Rear view of No 23*

but the Boma owned a herd of cattle which grazed on and around the golf course, usually attended by a flock of white egrets foraging for insects. We envied the PA families their supply of fresh milk. An airstrip lay a few miles out of town, above the valley. That was to be my little world outside school for the next few years.

My parents must have felt as though they had time-travelled straight from pre-war Burma, 1936 to Central Africa, 1955 as there were many similarities. They settled in readily.

Mum felt no pain at abandoning her London business suits, confining suspender belts, stockings and high heels for cotton dresses and sandals. She had a nice boss, a Scot whose soft speech and quiet demeanour hid a sharp sense of humour and a sense of the ridiculous. He loved the onomatopoeic quality of the African languages and was fond of pronouncing local place names such as Shikamushile, Sindabele (singe-your-belly) and Sesheke (she-shakey). Dad, ever the dandy, cut a fine figure in his immaculately ironed shirt and shorts, knee length socks and glistening shoes. His shirt, in true NRG fashion, sported two chest pockets with buttoned flaps: one bristled with pens and pencils sharpened at the ready, the second held his packet of 50 Life cigarettes and lighter. A pair of knee-length khaki socks and gleaming brown shoes completed his outfit. Customs officials or doctors wore long white socks and only people who knew no better wore short socks with sandals. Dad was fair-skinned and wore a hat in the hot, midday sun but Mum avoided going out of doors at noon, anyway, if humanly possible. She had shielded her face from the sun's rays since her youth and maintained her soft skin and clear complexion until old age, unlike the leathery, suntanned visages of many European matrons in the tropics.

My parents knew they would be in Fort Rosebery for the remainder of Dad's first three-year tour of duty, when they would be given overseas passages for home leave. After this time they might stay in the same town or Dad might be posted somewhere else. Government servants were not permitted to buy land in the country or indulge in commercial activity but I knew that my parents cherished ideas that they would settle somewhere in Rhodesia when Dad retired. Their days in Fort Rosebery were the happiest of their lives.

After breakfast I took a bath, stubbing my toe on the duck-board alongside, still half awake. Then I made myself scarce while Simon set to, cleaning the house. Once he had finished clearing up in the kitchen, he made a beeline for the bedrooms and bathroom, leaving the lounge until last, shaking out the threadbare reed and duiker mats out on the stoep. He couldn't shake them out of the windows as they were covered with fly screens, which were fixed, the bane of our cats. I lingered when it was floor polishing day, as I loved to watch Simon's performance on the brushes. He would apply a liberal slather of Cobra wax then attach the strapped brushes to his feet. He hummed as he polished, dancing rhythmically. Yes, I learned a few good moves from Simon. Evidence of his diligent application of floor polish could be seen on our furniture, which bore a red tide mark round its base. In an effort to eke out the tin, Mum would thin the polish with methylated spirits, whose strong smell would permeate the entire house until we flung open all windows to the breeze.

Later on in the morning Simon tackled the ironing. A deal table was covered with a blanket and sheet, one iron filled with hot charcoal and a second flatiron placed on the stove to warm. With these primitive implements Simon would produce piles of beautifully crisp laundry. Shirts were gleaming white and impeccably starched, trousers and shorts given razor-sharp creases and dresses and skirts hung from the pantry door.

The first time I left the house on foot I got lost. It was a small town – at that time there were only 22 European families – and Dad had driven us round it only once. I had a good sense of direction and easily identified the way to the Club, the fig tree under which the market was held, the small shopping area, the Boma with its flagpole and semicircle of white painted stones, the road down to the bridge over the River Mansa, the White Fathers' mission and the small loop of residential roads. I completed a circuit round the block and returned to where I thought the house was and..... couldn't find it. I panicked, trudging up and down the steeply cambered road in my sandals, past bungalows partly obscured by heavy swathes of foliage. There was nobody to ask: all the Europeans had gone to work, children were at school and the few Africans I saw looked at me, curiously. I couldn't speak Chibemba and was tongue-tied. Besides, I didn't even know the number of our house or the name of our street. In fact, neither had a name. Our address was a post box, like everyone else's. It had just rained, everything steamed in the heat and sweat was trickling down my neck and into my shirt. It was only half-past nine in the morning and I was already melting. Water gurgled down the storm drains and through the culverts that ran below

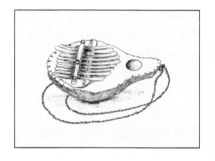

Top left: *African hand-piano*
Top right: *Blueskop lizard*
Bottom: *On the kitchen windowsill*

the road. A bird sang insistently, its harsh, repetitive call sounding like a rusty swing, probably a hoopoe.

At last, I found it. It crouched below its canopy of billowing leaves and yellow blossoms, looking very like its neighbour. It was just a modest little bungalow, hiding in the bundu.

I went into the kitchen for a cold drink – well, as cold as it could be from the larder. We had no electricity and no fridge for our first three years in the bush, nor any piped water initially. A water bowser drawn by two oxen brought a supply up from the river to pour into our tank. All water had to be boiled for at least five minutes at this altitude, to get rid of a bewildering variety of dysentery-inducing bugs.

"Simon, which bottles are for the drinking water?" I asked.

We used old liquor bottles for water and I had already made the mistake of seizing one in a hurry, in my thirst, swigging a mouthful of neat gin by mistake.

Simon had finished his cleaning and was now kneading dough on the kitchen table. The black, cast-iron stove had just been lit and stoked with a huge log which protruded from its open door. Its brand name was Magic ("bloomin' magic if you can cook on it," said Dad). I could never understand why they didn't chop up the log and put in small pieces of wood but then I was ignorant of the density and impenetrable hardness of the local trees. The kitchen was simple: the stove stood along one wall, open shelves bordered a second and the sink and its draining board occupied the third. A deal table and solitary chair stood in the middle of the room. The fourth wall opened into the scullery and its walk-in larder, equipped with an ironing table, shelves for the oil lamps and a wooden meat safe; this was zinc-screened, its legs standing in tin cans filled with paraffin to deter ants. Flour, biscuits, sugar, any dry goods and even some cigarettes were kept in tins – no sealed plastic containers in those days – to deter insects. From the scullery Simon could look out through a large, fly-screened window to the patch between us and the next property. Everything was open, there were no fences to be seen. Steps led from the ever-open door to the outside sink, in which Simon was soaking the day's laundry, to be attacked with a piece of Sunlight washing soap cut from a long, yellow bar. The Africans could only afford the cheaper sort, which resembled blue cheese and smelled like it, too. Detergent powder, in the form of Tide and Daz, had yet to make an appearance. My mother washed our undies and delicate clothes with Lux flakes.

Tandeo was now chopping wood with a hand axe to feed into the boiler fire, for lighting in the afternoon. The timing of this was critical as there had to be hot water for washing up and for baths. Leave it too late to bathe and you would find scalding steam spurting out of the taps. The Rhodesian boiler looked like a larger version of the outdoor pizza ovens seen in Mediterranean countries, the difference being the 44-gallon oil drum inserted above the fire to warm the water. Oil drums were used as scaffolding, water tanks, for traditional beer-brewing and, cut in half, to make a braaivleis. The "toc, toc" of the gardener's chopping mingled with the softer "pock, pock" of Simon's wife pounding corn or cassava with her pestle and mortar near the servants' quarters.

Once my parents were safely at work, the kitchen steps became an epicentre of social life. Simon and Tandeo sat there for tea breaks and a smoke, stubbing out their cigarettes carefully so that they could re-light them later. A stream of callers would appear, chatter endlessly then stroll, loose-limbed, in the direction of the golf course, taking the path back to the African township. Servants would call with chits (notes) for the bwana or the dona in the absence of a telephone system. Small boys and women came round peddling tomatoes, beans, tiny eggs or animal skins and people would just come to pass the time of day. Sometimes I would be summoned to the back door to take a look. After a chorus of "mwapoleni mukwais" the courtesies would have to be gone through before selling and bargaining commenced.

"And how are you today, dona?"

" I am well. And you?"

"I am just all right. I am bringing you some tomatoes and sweet batats (potatoes) from my village."

"Have you come far?"

"Aiee, too far, dona. I have been walking too much. My village is six miles out on the Kawambwa road. You give me one drink water, please. The sun it is very hot today."

And so on and so on. It was impolite to hurry such formalities. In fact, you couldn't hurry anything. African life was slow. Things could always be done mailo – tomorrow or "just now" (in a minute), whereas Europeans demanded that it be done now now, or in other words straight away! They couldn't understand why we whites were always in such a rush.

Simon could also hold a perfectly good conversation with next door's houseboy, even though their respective back door steps were 150 yards apart. A drama school could teach them nothing about the art of voice projection. Still, if I was reading in the living room this babble didn't bother me. Our bungalow was designed like many others, with the kitchen and bedroom wings projecting from each end of the living and dining area, affording privacy for working/chattering/laughing staff at one end and tired bwanas at the other.

At 12.30, to the accompaniment of Boma drums, my parents returned home for lunch, prepared and served by Simon. Conversation would centre on work – what projects Dad had on in the buildings department, how some silly bugger had fallen off the scaffolding and how his workmates had giggled with embarrassment, what appointments had been gazetted (appeared in the Government Gazette, the civil servants' bible) and other such boring topics. My ears pricked up at the occasional exciting snippet of gossip.

"Do you know, Jack, Fred and Mrs W are being so soppy together at work, it's quite distracting. She's not getting through all the typing she should. Her husband must live on another planet – he just can't see what's going on," said Mum.

She was referring to the affair being conducted by an accountant and the pretty wife of an agricultural officer who worked as a clerk at PWD.

"What's more," Mum continued, "they keep passing love letters to one another in the SIV book. I found one there this morning. I passed it back to her, of course, and she had the grace to blush."

"What's an SIV?" I piped up.

Mum gave me a stern look. I think she had forgotten I was there.

"It's a Stores Issue Voucher", she said. "You haven't heard any of this, by the way" she added, looking intently at me.

"SIV!" I giggled. "They should call it Sinful Indulgence in Vice."

"Change the subject, Dulce, " said Dad.

I was surprised. Normally Dad was the one to drop juicy bits of gossip and Mum would keep a secret unto death. On this occasion, she really had forgotten I was around. That happened when they started talking PWD.

More tea, then Dad would switch on our wheezing, crackly radio for the local news and Mum would take a nap in the chair. Dad retreated to the bedroom and plunged himself under the counterpane for a quarter of an hour before they walked back to work for the afternoon. Simon retired to his house but Tandeo continued in the garden, where Dad had showed him how to dig a vegetable patch, with raised beds. Seedlings were sheltered by stick frames covered with elephant grass. Later on, when the sun began to sink in the sky, the gardener would flood the furrows round the beds and tiny, vivid blue waxwings arrived to drink and bathe.

Tandeo rested under a tree, strumming a mournful dirge on his kalimba, a hand piano made from a hollowed-out gourd with metal keys. The sun shone brassily from a pale sky and I sat on the kitchen steps, watching the small lizards who sunbathed there. They were beautifully marked, striped with cream and brown on top, shading to purple, violet then grey on their bellies. Some became tame, if I sat still enough, regarding me with beady eyes. It was too hot to think. I lay on the sofa, book in hand and drifted off.

The drums galvanized me into action. Four o'clock and time for the Club, social mecca of the town. Twice a week a library opened in the end room, stuffed higgledy-piggledy with yellowed paperbacks and dusty, musty volumes whose pages were speckled with mould. The population were great readers, however, and there was a varied selection to choose from. You soon got used to silverfish crawling out or the odd squashed mosquito embedded between pages.

By 4.15 Stan Tully, proprietor of the Mansa Hotel, was already sitting in his chair outside the bar for his daily sundowner but I was intent on bagging one of the two tennis courts. Picking a couple of ball-boys from the ragged gang hanging around the courts, I started knocking up, practising my serve against the grass screens. My parents and other grown-ups arrived and had time to play a couple of sets before it got dark. Calls of Umupila! and Ndeshya! rang around the court as shadows lengthened and the temperature dropped. The courts were made from crushed antheap, a free commodity that was in limitless supply in this area, and they looked attractive at this time of day, glowing pinkly before a backdrop of tawny grass and the glossy, bottle green of the mango trees. Gasping for a drink, Mum and I swallowed some ice-cold Mazoe orange squash and water and headed for home. Dad stayed on for his daily ration of Castle beer and a chin wag.

"Don't be late, Jack," reminded Mum.

She and I walked home. The sunset was quick and dusk was short-lived in the tropics.

Sometimes there would be letters to read, including precious overseas mail which took between two and three weeks to arrive, a precious newspaper or magazine. My parents collected mail from the postbox near PWD.

In January, 1956 Gran recorded in her diary that there was smog all over London and 1st February was the coldest day of the century so far in London, minus 20^0 Fahrenheit. The water cistern in Cedar Road froze and she couldn't make a decent fire. She was cold and miserable.

Dad's job was to light the lamps at home before darkness fell. This was a job that could have been entrusted to the servants but no, this was my mother's way of ensuring my father got home well in time for dinner. There was no question of her lighting the lamps, of course. Like driving a Land Rover, lighting fires, killing snakes and tuning the radio to the correct station, that was man's work. Inevitably, Dad failed his curfew instructions and arrived home late. He loved to talk and would have become embroiled in the latest gossip. Mum would be seething.

"Your father can talk the hind leg off a donkey," she grumbled.

Dad walked in at last and faced the music.

"It's so inconsiderate. We'll eat supper late and Simon is waiting to get home. Honestly, man," she said. What she really meant was that she wanted Dad in the bungalow, safe from the temptations of one beer too many or the attention of ladies perched on bar stools. It was all part of the parental power struggle.

"I only had two beers, dear," was Dad's standard, mild reply.

After supper Simon brought in the tea tray, bade us goodnight and Dad hunched over the temperamental radio to tune it into the BBC World Service. The marching strains of Lillibullero and six pips announced the Six O'Clock News (GMT, 8.00pm Northern Rhodesian time), to which my parents listened with hushed reverence. They lit their cigarettes, drank their tea and read until bedtime. The hurricane lantern was too dim to read by so I would stay up a little later. I was told to watch the Aladdin oil lamp on its niche in the corner of the room and turn down the wick if it flared up, as was its custom. Invariably, I became too engrossed in my book and the lamp's flame would scorch the ceiling. Our house was full of lamp shelves surmounted by burnt patches. In an emergency there were always candles, some stored in my mother's Burmese lacquered box originally designed for betel nuts. Bed, cool sheets and a sound night's sleep beckoned, accompanied by bush stirrings, chirrups and shrieks.

Chapter 9
FRIENDS, FOOD AND FIREFLIES

Betty de Wet and Jude

After a few weeks in our new home, children who boarded in schools on the line of rail came home for their holidays. Fort Rosebery had only one small primary school so I was to become a boarder at Jean Rennie, the secondary school in Lusaka.

The first girl to arrive home was Jean, whose divorced father lived a few doors away in a ramshackle cottage, a real bachelor pad. It was rumoured that Guy, the father, was the disgraced son of an English aristocrat who had been reduced to running a chain of African general stores in the bush.

Guy's house was a mess. The gloomy lounge was full of broken-backed chairs covered in newspapers and dogs but he had a PK of character. There was always plenty to read in there and I smiled at the cartoon on the back of the door. This was a skilful pencil sketch of a raddled-looking woman, knees apart, knickers at half mast, sitting on the throne, entitled "The Relief of Ladysmith."

When Guy was in a good mood he was amusing and very good company. More often, he communed with the gin bottle and Jean, waif-like, wandered down to me. We climbed trees, explored the scrubby golf course and read books, Jean preferring paperback romances with lurid pictures of semi-dressed sirens on their covers. My new friend was no brainbox but, being a true white African, she knew what made things tick. Trotting down to one of her father's shops one day, wearing my tennis shorts and shirt, barefoot Jean put me straight. A group of young Africans hung around the verandah, sniggering. They looked furtively in our direction, whispered behind their hands and pointed – at me.

"That muntu says he would like to marry you," said Jean, giving me a euphemistic version of what he had actually said.

She was the first person to tell me that Africans married girls as young as 10 years' old so that, at 13, I was highly eligible. Wearing shorts, I was flaunting my fertility and availability, in their eyes. Bare legs were taboo, whereas exposed breasts were quite acceptable to African men at that time. The local women always wore lengths of chitenge cloth to ankle level, even if they were wearing European-style dresses or were riding a bicycle. They walked along the roads carrying pots on their heads and babies slung on their backs but would nonchalantly hoist the baby down to breastfeed, regardless of who was present. Mrs. Graham swore that some even pulled out a boob and stuck it in the sugar bowl before sticking the nipple in a baby's mouth! She had seen it in the tea room.

Generally, women stayed firmly in the background. They stayed in their villages to cook, look after their children and work on the land. All domestic servants and government employees were men or boys: they were the educated ones. It was rare to see a woman employed as a maid or a nanny.

Unfortunately, Jean was going home to her mother in South Africa when her school holidays were over. A shy, gawky teenager, I was dreading the prospect of a new school, boarding at that, where I knew no-one. Dad asked around and found out that Guy's neighbours, the Grahams, had a daughter who was a Jean Rennie boarder and arranged for us to meet. I had already walked her dog, Sally, an intelligent but nervous collie.

Betty de Wet was an Afrikaner, confident, sunny and friendly. She was everything that I was not – small, stocky, pretty, with an already burgeoning bosom, aged 13 going on 30. She knew how to cook, sew a dress, play hockey, jive, go on safari in the bush and, most importantly, talk to boys. She initiated me into the arts of teenagerdom – blue jeans, rock records, makeup and fun – and took me under her young but maternal wing.

We would spend hours in her house, a rambling thatched affair, listening to records and eating bananas and mangoes.

"Plus, you must never eat green mangoes, hey – they give you sores round your mouth. Good for making chutney, though," said Betty, looking up from her copy of Fair Lady, a South African magazine never seen in our house.

One day Betty decided we were going to do some serious baking in her kitchen. Like many bush kitchens, this was a separate building connected to the main house by a covered, thatched walkway, a design which ensured the house remained cool. It also prevented any fire from spreading should the wood-burning stove get out of control in the kitchen. I looked nervously at the roof for snakes.

My new friend shooed the cook-boy out and we got to work. As she arranged her arsenal of ingredients on the table she uncovered a large scorpion lurking behind a tin of Royal baking powder. It faced us defiantly, its quivering tail erect and ready to strike. I gasped but, before I could bolt, Betty calmly picked up the insect in a tea towel and deposited it in a jar of methylated spirits.

"Sis, man. Let's watch it vrek," she said, coolly.

We carried on with our measuring and mixing, perspiring gently in the hot afternoon. The scorpion twitched in its death throes in the purple liquid, its movements growing more and more feeble as it gradually but most definitely expired. I watched, fascinated and horrified. Betty appeared not to notice, humming as she sifted flour, rubbed in Holsum cooking fat and whisked eggs vigorously in a bowl. Was I impressed! That was one of many cooking sessions in her kitchen – milk tarts, koeksisters (a plaited sweet doughnut drenched in golden syrup) and cakes appeared with Betty's effortless skill.

Betty's mother and stepfather managed the largest grocery store in town, Zlotnik's for a former Polish refugee, Zloty, who lived in some luxury in Luanshya, on the Copperbelt. They adored their daughter but she was free to do pretty much as she pleased. Betty introduced me to many forbidden pleasures, such as walking

On Betty's kitchen table

barefoot, swimming naked in the Mansa river and trying on her mother's jewellery: Mrs. Graham had a penchant for dangly earrings but my ears, sadly, were unpierced. "Only common girls have their ears pierced" was the received wisdom among government daughters.

One afternoon, bored after a hard game of tennis, Betty persuaded me to play gooseberry and walk down to the river with her and the current boyfriend, Ian. His dog, a Rhodesian ridgeback, was a powerful swimmer and loved to retrieve sticks. We reached a fast flowing, deep section where the piccanins had slung a knotted rope from an overhanging branch to use as a swing. It was nearly dusk and the river bank was empty as we threw the first stick for Simba. He plunged in, grabbed it and appeared to struggle against the current as he swam back to us. He reached the bank and bounded out with a tremendous leap, followed by the gaping jaws of a crocodile. A croc, in our little river! The speed of the reptile was incredible. It scrambled up the bank after the dog, who sprang back, barking. We yelled and the croc swung round, lashing its tail to try to knock him into the water. Ian grabbed his pet's collar and we retreated further up the bank, Simba barking frantically and straining to get back into the water, stupid animal. We flung sticks at the croc and it lay still, almost invisible apart from its prominent, yellow eyes and snout poking above the water. My legs had turned to jelly and I was rooted to the spot. Suddenly, the sinister creature submerged and was gone.

We ran back to the Club and burst into the bar.

"There's a croc in the river! He nearly caught Simba! I'm telling you, man, it was huge, hey" gasped Betty to the assembled drinkers.

"Come on, Betty, you're imagining it," said Betty's stepfather, a mild-mannered Scot. "It was most probably a leguaan."

"Honestly, Dad it was a croc, true as Bob," said Betty.

The men laughed and returned to their beers. A croc in the Mansa river? Never.

A week later the townspeople had to eat their words when Dennis Gaunt, the game warden, had his little dog, a Jack Russell, eaten by a crocodile in the river. A hunt was mounted and the reptile was shot. Or was there just one? We never knew – but I never swam in the river again.

A crocodile was one of the many perils which lay in wait for pet dogs. Practically every white person owned a dog. They were called local names – Simba (lion), Sterek (strong), Iwe (Chibemba for hey, you!) or something fanciful, such as Satan, Sheba or Shah. One friend called her two Mosi (smoke) and Tunya (thunder), after the local name for the Victoria Falls, Mosi oa Tunya, the Smoke That Thunders. One of our dogs and a litter of puppies died of distemper, one was almost blinded by a spitting cobra, another almost died of billary and one cat died giving birth to kittens that were too big for her small frame. There were no vets in the Luapula Province. There were local dogs wandering around, yellow hounds with amber eyes and curly tails and rabies was an ever- present possibility. Our dogs were given annual injections and wore metal tags on their collars to show that this had been done. If there was a rabies scare a "tie-up" would be declared, when a dog was supposed to be confined so that it couldn't come into contact with another; dogs without tags or collars were shot. It was a harsh but effective way of controlling the disease.

I paid the price for walking barefoot. Betty's feet were hardened by years of going without shoes but mine were still tender, with soft, Pommie soles. I got jiggers, eggs which burrowed into your skin and emerged as maggoty larvae. Dr. Preece extracted them at the clinic, gouging my foot without anaesthetic, a painful experience.

"That'll teach you to walk round without shoes," he said.

Betty may have escaped jiggers but she got pootsies. All washing hung outside had to be ironed as pootsie flies could lay eggs in them, especially in the rainy season; the emerging grub would burrow under the skin to feed and grow. Ugh. Betty's houseboy dried their washing on the garden hedge and hadn't been careful enough with his ironing. The poor girl got pootsies all over her back. One night her mother and I spent an hour picking these out, smearing Vaseline on the spot, waiting for the maggot to emerge for air, plucking it out with tweezers then popping it over the heat of a Tilly lamp.

"Ma we!" exclaimed Mrs. Graham as she examined her daughter's back and pulled out a squirming maggot. "There are meningi pootsies, man!"

"Aina! It's sore, hey," Betty squealed.

It was a curiously satisfying experience for us amateur paramedics but agony for the sufferer.

Mum knew I was missing our pets. My longing intensified when we were invited out of town to a braaivleis party at Bahati, a manganese mine in the bush. The Australian manager and his wife lived in a large house with a brood of six children and a menagerie of animals. They occasionally came to the Club for a film or tennis tournament in their sturdy American station wagon, where the kids would come tumbling out of the car like puppies. At night they were simply put to sleep like sardines in the back on a mattress, a common practice. They were a jolly lot, always bursting into song. "Come on, kids, join in!" their father cried as he pulled out of the car park.

Roll along, Land Rover, roll along,
For it's time we were singing you a song.
Mufulira may be fine
But give me Bahati Mine,
Roll along, Land Rover, roll along!

There was a lot of singing – and drinking – at the party. Besides the Land Rover song we had The Wild Colonial Boy, The Foggy, Foggy Dew and Waltzing Matilda. The grown-ups drank and drank and grew maudlin. Mum was giving Dad the look which said "Time we were going, Jack" but, as usual, he was ignoring her. Oh, no! They were singing "I'll Take You Home Again, Kathleen". It was like the Galtymore Dance Club all over again.

I wandered into the garden to take a closer look at the animals. There were dogs, cats, monkeys, birds, two bushbuck who picked their way through the house on dainty hooves and two tame warthogs, Mildred and Stewart, who drank from the waterhole on their knees. One of the cats had produced a litter of kittens. Would I like one? She was a pretty little thing, tortoiseshell and affectionate. We took her home that night.

Only a week or so later Jean asked "Would you like to go to Samfya?"

"Where's that?"

"It's on the big lake, about 45 miles away. It's like the seaside. There's white sand, you can swim. Dad fishes there sometimes. Maybe he could take us one Sunday."

Guy, however, was not to be persuaded. He got only one day a week off – Sunday – and he wasn't going to sacrifice it to spend a few hours driving up and down a bumpy bush road so that his daughter could have a swim. His buddy who owned the boat wouldn't be there, anyway. What did he want to sit on a beach for?

"Ask your dad," Jean wheedled, "Maybe he could take us?"

"It's no good, Jean, he doesn't have a car. He doesn't even have a government Land Rover."

Samfya was a government station of about nine houses and offices on the shore of Lake Bangweulu. It was popular with Fort Rosebery families for a day out or a weekend's camping and, over long holidays like Rhodes' and Founders' (Rogues and Scroungers) weekend, townies would come up from the Copperbelt, 150 miles away.

Dad knew I was longing to go. One morning he sent a chit home from work, saying "Jude, Get your swimsuit and towel out, Mr. A. has to deliver some stores to Samfya. He'll be collecting you and Jean at 9.30. Love, Dad"

I rushed off to the bedroom and got my things, plus a sandwich and a gin bottle of squash. I was ready.

143

Top: *Samfya, 1955*
Bottom: *With Dad's .22 rifle, 1956*

Mr. A, one of the PWD foremen, pulled up in his Bedford vanette with Dad and Jean on the bench seat alongside. Oh no, he'd got his wretched dog, a bull mastiff cross, with him. Mr. A. looked like his dog: he was brisk, burly, with a moustache and red face. The Africans called him Bwana Punda, Mr. Shout. As I stood on the front steps the dog leapt out of the back of the vanette and shot across the drive, where my young cat recoiled, ears back, frantically looking for a tree to climb. She never made it. The dog pounced and seized the cat by the scruff of her neck, shaking her like a rat. We ran towards the dog and Mr. A. grabbed his collar. The cat, dripping with blood, crawled into the undergrowth.

"Don't worry, Jude," said Dad. "She'll be fine. You go. You must go. Jean will be so disappointed if you don't."

I knew my cat would not be fine but I got into the vanette. Mr. A, the pig, was now in the passenger seat and made us two girls sit in the back. He wanted his African driver at the wheel for the Samfya road was treacherous, narrow and sandy, with patches of black cotton soil where it crossed the dambos, swampy areas. Mr. A. wanted to be chauffeured in style. He had a load of bricks, oxygen cylinders and sacks in the back but we would add extra weight, to make the vehicle more stable. Chivalry was a word unknown in Mr. A's vocabulary. Perhaps he felt ashamed about his dog and couldn't face us. I didn't know and I didn't care.

That journey and my first view of the lake passed in a mist of tears. We slithered along the road and were soon choking on fine, white dust. We sat on sacks and put scarves over our noses and mouths, like bandits. Naked children gazed open-mouthed as we drove past villages, the older ones waving, as their mothers pounded millet. Chickens ran in front of the vanette and escaped with their lives. Women were hoeing small plots of land dotted with tree stumps, straight-backed, digging the blade backwards between their toes and others walked along the road, carrying huge bundles of wood on their heads. We passed the Samfya airstrip, climbed a long hill and there it was, Lake Bangweulu, "where the water meets the sky". It was dazzling. Mr. A. dropped us off at the small, deserted beach, below the clutch of bungalows on the hilltop, while he went off to the local PWD stores. We looked as white as a pair of ghosts after the dusty journey but washed most of it off our bodies with a swim, which I was too miserable to appreciate. We only had an hour or two before our home journey, in the short African twilight. The dambo reeds glowed red as we passed and we saw one or two buck coming down to drink. Egrets stalked around like large, white moths on legs.

When we reached town it was dark. The tree frogs were tuning up and bats flew round the garden, catching plenty of mosquitoes, we hoped. As we reached our drive I noticed the fireflies were out, winking away. They were a cheerful sight but they couldn't cure my misery today. I didn't need to ask what had happened to my sweet little tortoiseshell cat. I looked at Dad and he shook his head, silently. It had been a sudden death, the first of many I would see in Africa. It was a sobering experience.

Mum was slowly getting to grips with a new job and feeding us on my parents' modest salaries. She and my Dad sent back every month to Gran and John so in effect they were keeping two households going. The supply of local fruit and vegetables was sporadic: the market under

Fish traps, Luapula River

the giant fig tree near the Mansa Hotel sold tiny tomatoes, groundnuts, bananas and limp local lettuce or spinach. Poor soils meant produce low in vitamins and trace elements. At least, we had guavas, lemons and pawpaws to eat from our garden. As we had no refrigerator, meat had to be casseroled and was often too tough to eat in any other way. Chickens were scrawny and local fish from the Luapula River or the lake were a real treat. If a work colleague had been out shooting in the bush we were sometimes given biltong, dry cured meat. Dad did his best to provide us with fresh fruit and vegetables but the rainy season was a lean period, paradoxically – heavy showers washed seedlings away and leached out nutrients, besides which there were pests and mildew to contend with. By the end of a three-year tour we were all tired and deficient in vital minerals, even though Mum got into the habit of dosing us with supplements.

After the euphoria of arrival, enjoying the wonders of sunshine, space and servants we were beginning to find that life in Africa was not all a bed of roses.

Chapter 10
SCHOOL DAYS
1955

Jean Rennie School, Kabulonga

There was no choice of schooling for me in the bush. I soon learnt that there was an educational hierarchy, the ranking being: firstly, a posh, expensive school overseas (the PA were given financial help with fees and air fares); secondly, not quite as posh a school in Southern Rhodesia, e.g. Chisipite; thirdly, the Dominican Convent in Lusaka for Catholics and irreligious parents with some spare cash; finally, the government boarding school in Lusaka for the rest of us, including me.

After a few weeks in our new home it was time to get ready for Jean Rennie, the lowest school in the above pecking order. It was another girls only establishment, although its twin boys' school, Gilbert Rennie, lay a few playing fields away. I looked with distaste at the new uniform: striped pink and white blouse, grey gym-slip, grey socks and black, lace-up shoes. All those layers in this heat! Were they mad? At least Mum had been able to get one of the local tailors to run up my gym-slips, shapeless garments, on his treadle Singer machine, for we had none ("kneel down girls, the hem should just touch the floor, no more, no less"). A disgusting grey felt pudding basin hat with a brim completed the outfit. School discipline was strict and woe betide any girl who went to town in a uniform without a hat. Why couldn't we have straw boaters in the hot weather, like the boys? The cold season white blouse, grey flannel skirt and maroon cardigan made more sense in this climate. Mum ran out of Cash's name tapes and spent hours labelling clothes with an indelible pen. A packing frenzy ensued, to be followed by a lifetime of packing and unpacking. My clothes and few personal possessions were bundled into Mum's grey Revelation suitcase, the clothes list taped inside the lid and my name stencilled there as well. She handed me the keys.

"DON'T lose these Jude, please," she said. Mum knew I lost everything unless it was pinned to my person. She looked stern but I knew she was trying not to cry. I tried to be brave as well.

The impending departure loomed. My short spells away from home had been limited to a school trip to the seaside with Mora Road school and overnight stays with friends. Now I was to travel hundreds of miles by Morris army lorry, overnight train and bus to get to a strange place where I knew precisely one person, Betty de Wet. Even she wouldn't be in the same boarding house as me. Still, I consoled myself with the fact that if Mum had done it so could I. At least I wouldn't be as badly off as girls and boys who went overseas for their schooling and only returned to Africa once a year.

By now I was used to bumping around in the back of vehicles, sitting on a hard metal seat and getting covered in dust. We were red from head to toe by the time we reached the Ndola Rest House, where Mrs. Perry ordered us to strip off on the spot and take baths before donning uniform.

"Leave your shoes outside and don't sit on the beds," she cried, pointing to the spotless white counterpanes. She considered schoolchildren an unnecessary evil.

We cleaned our shoes with our hankies and prepared to board the train, a steaming monster with a cow catcher on the front, just like those we'd seen in Wild West films. The klaxon had the same, mournful note as it hooted. Hundreds of boys and girls milled around the station and I was surrounded by a babble of voices with strange, colonial accents.

"How's it?"

"Did you have a lekker hols?"

"Hey, Mafuta, my man!"

"Who's got the playing cards?"

"Which dorm are you in?"

Betty was looking forward to going back to school and being reunited with her boyfriend, Johan.

"I love him to bits!" she said.

Before Betty was whisked away by her mates she took me up to a girl wearing a green dress – the old Lusaka Girls' School uniform – and a brown, slouch hat tied cowboy-fashion under her chin, fastened with a holed Rhodesian penny.

"This is Jill. She's in your boarding house, Sherwood."

"Hi," she said, grabbing my hand. "Come. We must grab a compartment before they're all taken."

Top: *Megan*
Bottom: *Joyce (Photo: John Roulet)*

The klaxon tooted as we passed level crossings and stopped at rural halts, taking on passengers, coal and water. As dawn approached we were passing through European farmers' country. Some pupils stood by the line with their families to hail the train. They climbed up the carriage steps and were greeted with cheers and cries of "Hi, Jumbo, Boetie, Georgie Boy" as they jumped aboard with barely a backward glance while their trunks were loaded into the guard's van. Some of these kids had been going off to boarding school since the age of seven. They were cheerful, fit and tough.

None of us slept a wink in our couchettes. The old timers were too busy catching up on holiday news, playing cards, eating tuck or sipping Coke. I gazed out of the window as the grey, pre-dawn light revealed a different landscape, of prairie grassland dotted with flat-topped trees. Farmhouses and villages were sparse and fields of winter wheat and grass rippled in the wind. Cattle grazed on the maize stubble, herded by small boys wielding sticks. I noticed dairy cattle, fat-tailed sheep and rangy-looking horses, too. I wondered if there would be stables at the school? This flat, open country looked perfect for riding.

"There's the cooling tower! Nearly there," said Jill. "Better get your stuff down." We swung our small suitcases, games kit and bags down from the overhead luggage shelf.

We chugged slowly into Lusaka Station, hissing steam. The city centre looked like a building site. In an effort to cope with the rainy season floods on Cairo Road they had built a drainage channel down the middle. New buildings were going up between the railway track and the road and dust blew into our faces as we alighted in the cold morning light under a bleached, dry season sky. The air felt thin and rarefied. We passed some wooded suburbs as the bus climbed uphill, past Government House to Kabulonga. My stomach was tied up in knots.

Jean Rennie was a brand new school, built on a ridge the edge of the city. Its extensive sports fields were still red laterite and, following a scorched earth policy, those responsible had only left a few indigenous trees for shade. The classrooms were built in the Spanish mission style, with a pantiled roof, long polished verandahs ("Don't run, girls!) and a cloister where the grass was a dust-bowl in winter, and a bog in the summer rains. We weren't supposed to walk on it, anyway – it was reserved for open-air school plays and photographs. Our classrooms had full-length, Crittall windows which squeaked and jammed as you tried to open them, concertina fashion. The gym/assembly hall jutted out near one end and a two-storey tower (which we christened Stalag Luft III) housed the library and the headmistress's office. She was a large lady whose bark was worse than her bite. Across a small road lay the two, barrack-like hostels, the boarding houses, lying in a sea of red dust on which runners of Kikuyu grass were eventually planted. Playing fields lay between us and our brother school, Gilbert Rennie, identical in design to our own.

We went straight into the refectory for breakfast, my first introduction to the stodgy boredom of boarding school food. The cook matron, a Mrs. Van something or other, had a pouter pigeon bosom, big hair and up-swept spectacles. She possessed a limited grasp of nutrition, had no imagination and was probably expected to feed us on a meagre budget. This seemed unfair when one compared it to the cost of maintaining the vast sports fields. She didn't actually cook, of course – that was left to the black staff. The pupils, teachers and matrons were white; the cooks, domestic staff, groundsmen and gardeners were black.

The Lusaka Africans spoke Chinyanja so what little Chibemba I knew was of no use at all. At that time, there were 45 different dialects in the country. The lingua franca spoken throughout southern Africa was Chilapalapa, also called Chikabanga, and nicknamed Fanagalo (meaning "like this"). It had originated in Zululand and been adopted on mines in South Africa where the workforce came from different tribes. Many of my school friends spoke the language and it was used extensively on farms.

Breakfast consisted of mealie, oatmeal and Maltabella (malted mealie) porridge in strict rotation, one slice of toast and, if times were good, a piece of fruit. The oatmeal was invariably lumpy and infested with weevils but we soon learned to pick these out. We were permanently starving. On Sundays we were treated to limp cornflakes after Communion and an apology for a cooked breakfast. Dinners were the worst. The meat (rarely fish) was dolloped on to our plates by the waiters. We were given liver which either looked like burnt cardboard or oozed blood, tough chunks of fatty, tough meat and boerewors with a spicy gristle and sawdust filling. Vegetables came overcooked and mushy but we always wanted more roast potatoes, a rare treat. A slow eater, meals were agony for me as everything on your plate had to be finished before you were allowed second helpings. One kindly waiter with the features of a Bushman would scuttle up to our table shouting "One One! One One!," occasionally adding "Take Two!"

Mrs. Van was keen on fritters – pumpkin fritters, brinjal fritters – and sago (frog spawn), tapioca and semolina, again served in rotation. She occasionally turned up trumps with Zambezi Mud, a chocolate pudding made with evaporated milk and, more rarely, fresh fruit. This consisted of bananas, stewed guavas, the occasional apple which had made its way from the Southern Rhodesian highlands and grapes from the Cape. In retrospect, I suppose this was in the days that preceded refrigerated transport. Once a fussy eater, I learned to eat anything and everything and also speeded up my rate of consumption.

We supplemented school meals with tuck, food parcels sent from home and morsels given by charitable day scholars (day bugs). We roamed round the bush that bordered the playing fields, eating bitter, wild oranges, unripe mangoes and marula fruit. Girls who'd been out for the day down to the Kafue, in the low veld, would bring back baobab pods for us to eat the cream of tartar and seeds inside – monkey bread. After "free weekends" away others would bring strips of home-cured biltong, melktert, koeksisters and cake. The Afrikaner women were champion bakers and could even produce cakes from a bush pit oven.

Wild bees decided to build a nest under the sanatorium window. A farmer's son removed the swarm and gave us the warm, tangy acacia honey straight from the comb. Just before the rains started, clouds of flying ants would emerge from their holes in the ground. They filled the sky and were caught by some of the farm girls, who would pick off the wings and eat them whole. Yes, we were always hungry. Our diet was deficient in fresh fruit and vegetables and the Lusaka water was hard, as it came from boreholes in the limestone rock. These two factors led to our systems bunging up and much dosing with Milk of Magnesia from the house matrons.

The food might have been strange but so were the girls. Our accents ranged from Rhodesian to Polish, to German to Afrikaans; from an American drawl and cockney to Glaswegian so dense that none of us could understand her at first. Our parents were government civil servants, doctors, road foremen, farmers, missionaries, teachers, accountants, mechanics and fitters, engineers, architects and artists. We travelled to Kabulonga from all over the country: from Mongu, Barotseland, Livingstone, farms on the line of rail, from the Copperbelt, from the shores of Lake Tanganyika, from the Northern, Luapula and Eastern Provinces, even from Blantyre and Zomba, in Nyasaland.

Our religions were an assortment of Church of England, Church of Scotland, Dutch Reformed Church, Presbyterian, Methodist, Church of Christ, Seventh Day Adventist and Jehovah's Witness, the last two of these worshipping on a Saturday, and Jewish. Only a few were Catholics. Sometimes we went to church three times a day on Sundays: Holy Communion at the Anglican church in Lusaka, a journey on a smelly bus followed by lots of kneeling on a stone floor in the heat, the only time

I have come close to fainting. If I was being taken out for the day by my friend Joyce and her family I would also attend the Presbyterian service and sometimes an Evening Service in the gym with the Gilbert Rennie boys, where our devotion was both religious and secular.

We were uniformly white, or nominally so, a cultural melting pot with mixed abilities and backgrounds. No wonder our teachers found us difficult to cope with.

Even though I had thought myself mentally prepared, boarding school came as a shock. I was horribly homesick but cried soundlessly on a horsehair mattress into my lumpy pillow in the dormitory cubicle, divided only by green NRG curtains, so the other girls couldn't hear. It would have been too humiliating to appear at breakfast as Jeanette did, red-faced and eyes swollen from crying, for the first two weeks of term, with the other girls exclaiming "agh, shame" in pitying tones. I woke at first light to the incongruous sounds of the black caretaker stoking the boiler with coal, hawking and blowing his nose on to the ground. Occasionally we heard the distinctive "nkoya, nkoya" call of a fish eagle. There was a dam not far away so perhaps he hunted there, but it was a reminder of home.

Most of the girls were friendly and helpful. Some of the Afrikaners tended to be cliquey and spoke in their own language when others were present, which was against the rules. The girls tended to dress in an old fashioned, matronly way, liked country and western music and played Jim Reeves on their wind-up gramophones, a person who sounded soporific and boring to me. The more xenophobic girls called us "die Engels" and "souties" (salties), though never to our faces.

It wasn't until I became an adult that I realized what an insulting term this was, the word being an abbreviation of "soutiepiel", salt penis. The analogy described a person: a man with one leg in Europe, the other in Africa, with his willy dangling in the sea between. Rude though this was, there was more than a grain of truth in the saying. The Afrikaners had been the first European pioneers in southern Africa and, if they were kicked out, had nowhere else to go, unlike we Pommies. These girls' parents were mostly farmers, for some of whom the Great Trek and Boer War might have happened yesterday. We retaliated by calling them hairybacks, plaasies and japies behind their backs. However, a lovely Afrikaner girl from Nkana, Joey, became my first friend. She reinforced the fact that stereotyping a nation or a race was bad. We both cringed when we heard rude kids call the Africans kaffirs, jungle bunnies, makakas (monkeys) and houties (hout – wood, because the locals supposedly had thick skulls). However, we lived in such a cocoon it didn't occur to us that one day Africans would share our classrooms.

My first memory of Megan is of her strapping on a pair of roller skates and belting off down the road, her gym-slip flying. She and Jill were good friends and tennis partners and she became my best buddy. She was seemed diffident at first but I found this concealed a warm, sympathetic personality. She took me under her wing and we became firm friends. Her father was Welsh and had been a miner, but he now worked for Water Affairs; her mother was Australian, a nurse. They lived in Monze, one of the little towns on the line of rail. On first acquaintance my new friend seemed quiet but she proved to be great fun, always pulling my leg. Megan was pretty, clever, with short, dark hair and dancing blue eyes and she created a stir among the boys. She walked with a spring in her step and loved sport. We shared common interests – tennis and dancing, art, books and animals.

I slowly settled into boarding school life or, should I say, accepted my lot. We rose and went to bed early but I perfected the art of reading under the bed covers with a torch. I collected more scrapes from incidents in the gym, bruises from hockey sticks and added grass burns to my lacerations from the dry sports pitches. Our first gym teacher, a sadistic little Brit with short, mannish hair and tree trunk calves, was replaced by a charming woman, a former international hockey player, who did her best to encourage us. She did give me some confidence which nevertheless evaporated when I saw her flying towards me on the hockey pitch, shouting "Tackle me, Judy, tackle me!"

However, I could hold my head up on the tennis court, in the pool and in the classroom, where we were taught by teachers of varied ability. I am told that Gilbert Rennie was modelled on an English public school – perhaps Jean Rennie was too, but I think the boys probably had the pick of teachers. Being mere girls, perhaps we didn't? Many of the staff were government wives, accompanying their husbands on a tour of duty, and didn't stay long. Some were excellent, some not so good and others hopeless. There were no school counsellors, remedial help was absent and there were few excursions. Our French teacher was a former barrister, a Hungarian divorcée, a brilliant woman who taught erratically. She was especially grouchy when she went on a diet – red meat and wine, which we knew from the number of empty Chianti bottles lined up outside her back door. The history and geography teachers were both spinsters, accompanied by their little dogs, a pug and a brindle terrier of indeterminate parentage, Maxie.

Maxie farted unremittingly during lessons. We got our own back by placing a piece of fake dog poo in front of the teacher's desk. Poor Miss Wilson fell for it and held her nose while one of us removed the "poo" from the classroom in a piece of paper. His owner, who taught us geography, was a nice woman, an excellent teacher. She looked permanently harassed, with worry lines between her eyebrows. We fervently wished she could find a nice boyfriend to remove that frown.

Our history teacher clacked around in clumpy high heels, talking non-stop while we struggled to stay awake. We tried and failed to read her closely-typed, purple handouts with blotches run on a banda machine and, when boredom frequently threatened, sidetracked her into talking about her previous life in Livingstone. As she went into raptures over the Bon Accord hotel and the sight of Vic Falls by moonlight, we decided she had a "past". Although she came over as being strict she had a soft centre, did Miss Keir.

One redeeming feature was our music teacher, Mrs. Davies. She was tiny, with a considerable bosom and long, curly hair and always wore incredibly high heels. She put us through our paces and we managed to produce some good sounds. As a treat, she would sing Schubert's "The Earl King", adapted from the Goethe poem. She accompanied herself on the piano, a virtuoso performance. Just listening to the fast, staccato opening makes my wrists ache as it must have been hellish to play. The song concludes with the words "and the child – lay – dead." and a solemn chord. You could have heard a pin drop in the hall. Unfortunately, the other teacher who gave piano lessons was hopeless and because of that and my academic workload I gave it up, something I now regret.

Mrs. Anderson, our maths teacher and also my house mistress, plunged me into a state of abject terror in class. A formidable woman, she was an advocate of the "pose a question, pause and pounce" teaching method. When her eyes swivelled in my direction then asked a question in her dry voice, my mind went blank. My maths was weak, anyway and continued to be so. However, she showed a compassionate side when she took me into her office and gently broke the news to me that my beloved little black cat had died giving birth to kittens. Yes, she had a good heart and I respected Mrs. A.

From being the statutory goody goody I metamorphosed into the class chatterbox and clown, sitting giggling with my mates at the back of the classroom, exasperating my teachers. I was also the unofficial spokesperson for the class where negotiations were concerned.

Things came to a head with our English teacher in School Certificate year. It was one of my best subjects but, because of constant nattering with my mates, I had been moved to the front row in class. I sat next to June Finley-Bissett, a comical Rhodesian character whose father ran the fisheries at Mpulungu, on Lake Tanganyika. He was something of an adventurer, a trader and, it was said, even a smuggler. Mr F-B later made the headlines when he punched a visiting British Labour MP, John Stonehouse, at Lusaka Airport during a "fact-finding" tour to Northern Rhodesia. This same Mr. Stonehouse later faked his own death by leaving a pile of clothes on an Australian beach and disappearing, so June's dad must have realized he was a slime ball.

June had a lot of native wit but struggled with English Lit, particularly when it came to reading out loud. She was stumbling through a passage from The Mayor of Casterbridge when Miss Barnes, a glamorous but sarcastic lady, put up her hand.

"Stop, June, stop. It's not pronounced "wol", it's "will". Say "will.""

"Wol," said June, faintly.

"Will. It's "will," Miss Barnes emphasized. "You are crucifying the English language, girl."

"Wol," June repeated.

Miss Barnes picked up the board rubber, a lump of wood with a felt backing, and hurled it at June. She ducked and it hit Candy, the class swot, sitting immediately behind, almost breaking her pebble glasses. Tears welled up in Candy's eyes and June sat there, stunned. Miss Barnes, enraged, launched into a tirade.

"You stupid girl. You're so thick I don't think you have the right to stay in this class. In fact, I don't even think you know how to speak English."

June, who had red hair and a complexion to match, blushed scarlet.

I sprang to my feet. Hurling blunt instruments and now taunting poor June! I answered back.

"Don't you realize that it'll take ages for June to alter her elocution? It won't do any good shouting at her. And you shouldn't have thrown that board rubber. You could blind someone like that! That's not fair."

"You insolent girl," Miss Barnes yelled. "I won't have it. Go and stand outside....."

"The Headmistress's office" I finished the sentence. "Don't worry, I'm going." I stalked out of the classroom in high dudgeon, aware that the class were silent for once, sitting there with their mouths open. Miss Barnes didn't say anything, either.

The Headmistress told me off in no uncertain terms for defying a teacher's authority. After this verbal tussle the English teacher walked round me like a cat on hot coals and left June alone.

The worst thing about boarding school was its total lack of privacy. Nowhere quiet to read, to dream or even read a letter from home. Even in the bath you had somebody hammering on the door after your ten minutes was up. If we overslept the diddy matron, Miss Tomlinson, also known as Tiny Tank, hauled us unceremoniously out of bed, screeching "Get up, get up, you lazybones!" at the top of her voice. I tried to be neat and tidy but I couldn't even tie up my mosquito net correctly. My fellow boarders swung their nets round and knotted them in one fluid movement. I experienced the same difficulty I have today with duvet covers. I made some good friends, some of them for life, which was some consolation. School days weren't the happiest days of my life, though, far from it.

Chapter 11
HOLIDAYS

Judy with Blondie, Simon and Tandeo

Snow is unknown but light frosts at night are not uncommon between May and September. Intending visitors and residents should therefore provide themselves with such clothing as they would ordinarily wear in England (except, of course, for heavy underclothing). At different times a use will be found for all types of clothes, even a heavy overcoat or fur being occasionally essential. Pullovers and cardigans are necessary in the early mornings and after sunset except during the hottest months.

"A Brief Guide to Northern Rhodesia", chapter on Living
Conditions

With a huge sense of relief, I went home for the holidays, beginning my four years of hybrid existence. I tossed the dreaded uniform into the laundry basket and plunged into a hot bath, expunging smells of school, sweat and dusty roads.

At the end of my first term, the truck deposited me in an alien drive. I saw a plain, blotchy, once whitewashed house with a skirt of red-brown dust, exposed now that the dry season had truly arrived. The acacia trees had lost most of their leaves and the lawn, lush and vivid green when I had left, was now a patch of wiry grass, thin and yellowing, with patches of red earth showing through. Only the blueskop lizards looked the same. Dry leaves crackled underfoot as I jumped down from the tailgate of the truck and sniffed the familiar aroma of wood smoke from the boiler. I bet there would be a fire in the sitting room tonight – lovely.

Mum appeared at the foot of the steps but Dad was further down the drive, dressed in long, khaki trousers, a long-sleeved shirt and a sleeveless jumper against the chill of early evening. His back was turned towards me and he suddenly swung round, beaming. He had a golden cocker spaniel pup in his arms.

"We've called her Blondie," he explained, passing her to me. I held her close, feeling her long, floppy ears like silk against my cheek. I inspected her tender, pink paw pads and thought it wouldn't be long before they hardened up, like my feet. Inhaling that warm, puppy aroma, I noticed she smelled faintly musty.

"I think she needs worming, Dad."

She was adorable. At last I had a holiday companion.

The macho types at the Club called her "bush dog" claiming their Alsatians, terriers and ridgebacks to be far superior but Blondie had her own special qualities. She could tell the difference between our hens, which she tolerated, and anyone else's, which were chased off the premises. She was a wonderful swimmer and retriever and had the nose of a bloodhound. Totally faithful, her small size allowed her to squeeze under tables, unseen and obedient, and gave the impression that she was a pushover. However, she was an effective guard dog. Blondie's worst fault was that she became totally heedless when she was on a particularly interesting scent (game) or within smelling distance of water, including swimming pools. She hated being on her own, for which there was a time limit. After three hours she'd wreak vengeance by chewing whatever object carried our smells – a prayer book, shoes, the newspaper, duiker skin mats on the floor. It was no accident that she'd arrived at our house full of worms as she would eat anything. She had a taste for fine leather with my smell on it. We learned to leave her the biggest bone available, which would occupy her for hours. Blondie's other naughty habit was to roll in animal dung or, better still, the pungent dried fish which was offloaded at the Thatcher Hobson bus station opposite Mum's office. The stink was indescribable and the dog would be put firmly under the standpipe in the PWD yard. Blondie shadowed Mum but was my special pal during the holidays.

Blondie wasn't our first pet in Africa. There had been a dachshund called, confusingly, Judy, who had piddled everywhere. She then killed a pet loerie bird (a green crested parakeet) given to me by the Bahati mine family. She was given to a road foreman who lived in a caravan on the Chembe Road, where Judy had plenty of bush to pee on, and they lived together happily ever after.

Top left: *Titus and the black mamba*
Top right: *Anthill (Photo: Melanie Bousfield)*
Centre: *Chongololo (millipede)*
Bottom: *Village*

The Australians also gave me Blackie, a small cat with a glossy coat who looked more like a miniature puma than a domestic animal. She was terrified of the staff (with good cause – the locals were known to eat cats) but affectionate. One night Mum came into the lounge.

"Blackie hissed and spat at me in the bathroom. Most unlike her."

"Blackie's here," said Dad.

"So what's that in the bathroom?"

Dad took the hurricane lantern and walked gingerly into the bathroom. Sure enough, there was a cobra, rearing up with its hood extended, spitting furiously. It could blind you with its spittle. It was hastily dispatched with a stick.

Snakes were plentiful and particularly liked the cool of our front stoep. Our second house servant, Titus, killed a black mamba in the garden with his panga, one weapon most of the locals carried with them. We learned to be careful of where we put our feet on our bush walks and also remembered to look up as well as down in the forest, where boomslangs could lurk in the trees. Most snakes would glide away if they heard footsteps, apart from puff adders, who coiled up sluggishly on the sand paths, perfectly camouflaged in the barred sunlight slanting through the grass. Once I ran over a green mamba on my bike and pedalled on frantically, straight to the PWD office. I'd heard stories of snakes wrapping themselves round wheels, of bikes and cars, or even getting into engine compartments. One friend ran over a huge python on the Chembe road. He drove on and stopped, thinking he would collect the skin. He checked – yes, it was dead. He picked it up by the tail, whereupon the front end came to life and looked into his eyes, giving him the fright of his young life.

Grizzled Titus came from the Luapula Valley. He was a gentle person with a wall eye because he had caught river blindness as a boy, onchocerciosis, an infection spread by blackflies which was quite common in the country's Northern Provinces. Simon the Gourmet Chef had become too big for his boots. Dad made monthly inspections of his kaya, to spray for mosquitoes, ensure the plumbing worked and check there was no vermin. Once I accompanied him and was astonished to see that Simon owned five suits (more than my father) and that his wife had embroidered "Sleep Well, My Love" in blue silk on his frilly pillow. The standard appropriation of small amounts of tea, coffee, sugar and flour, which was expected, reached dangerous proportions. Simon, a magpie, had then moved on to underwear and jewellery, which was noticeable, not expected or acceptable, especially as Mum had very little of either.

With Blondie and whichever of my friends was around we explored the bush within walking distance of our house. The lush greens of the rainy season had faded to yellows and browns. We passed a gang of prisoners dressed in white shirts and shorts, lazily slashing the grass with their curved jungle knives under the eye of their capitao. The golf course was as dry as a bone, with stubbly grass underfoot, dotted here and there with mango trees, still dark green and heavy with foliage. The trees exposed bare branches to a cloudless sky, hazy with smoke, and dry leaves whipped round our ankles as we walked, looking out for snakes. We paused under the big mango near the river, grateful for the cool shade of its drooping branches.

We tried to hone our bush tracking skills on the golf course, where the sandy "greens" (browns) were covered in spoor. Clumps of holes, inverted, sandy cones, had been made by ant lions, insects which lurked below with pincers to trap unwary ants which fell into these pits. We might see the curving ribbon imprint of a snake, the dainty footprints of guinea fowl and the spoor of some small buck. Once we had even seen the larger pug marks of one of the big cats, which had sent shivers down my spine. We always hoped that the "brown" hadn't been wiped clean with the piece of sacking lying near each hole.

Despite the lack of rain, there was always something in flower, with aromatic everlasting flowers, wild gladioli and lilies, even white ground orchids to take home. One of these was the called the copper flower as it was an indicator of the mineral. Bungalows were covered in arching sprays of magenta and bright pink bougainvillaea, golden shower, coral creeper and winter jasmine. Next door, a crock of gold creeper exploded over a tree, full of bugle-shaped flowers as big a soup bowls. Granite kopjes above the African township flamed with scarlet as the spiky aloes bloomed. My friend Joyce told me the legend of the Kaffirboom (Erythrina, coral tree), a tree covered with brilliant red flowers on its ebony, bare branches at this time of year: a black boy was murdered by villains; his soul rose to heaven but fragments of his red shirt, the flowers, remained on the tree. Seed pods burst open with a loud "crack" and Blondie came home covered in blackjacks and burrs. Her dense fur coat and long, silky ears also attracted ticks, which Mum removed each evening sitting on the stoep. When she appeared with a bowl of water and the dreaded tweezers, Blondie ran for cover. We were told to check our bodies and hair for ticks, too, as they caused billary in animals and tick fever in humans. We took off our tackies, emptying them of bleached grass, small stones, seeds and red dust.

When the grass dried and flattened in the six-month drought, from May to November, it was easier and safer to walk in the bush and get down to the river, where Blondie chased pied wagtails. They jumped between boulders, their tails wagging in a thoroughly tantalizing fashion. Just as the panting dog swam frantically to catch them they hopped on to the next rock, always just out of reach. I dabbled my feet in the water, admiring the water lilies, until one of the local nurses told me that water snails lived under the flowers and were host to the liver fluke that caused bilharzia ("Billy Harris"). It is interesting to note that only a few years ago John discovered that tilapia, a species of chiclid in lakes like Bangweulu ate the water snails and so eradicated the bilharzia amoeba.

Below the Mansa River bridge the river widened, with beaches of white sand, which is where Betty and I took our illicit swims – until the crocodile incident. Sometimes we'd see the Boma herd grazing on the golf course, chestnut cattle with extravagantly curved, Biblical-looking horns followed by cattle egrets scavenging for insects. The PA families were so lucky to have fresh milk. We made do with Nespray and KLIM ("milk" spelled backwards) dried milk, sold in large tins which Dad saved for his plant seedlings. No tin was ever wasted in Africa – these were the days before plastic bags and containers – and paper bags were carefully folded and put away. KLIM tins were especially in demand for plants. My parents were inveterate hoarders of paper, rubber bands, string, pencils, you name it. I couldn't blame them – the war had taught them not to throw things away. They didn't have to be told about recycling and conservation.

I found that Africa was full of insects and creepy crawlies. Neon-bright beetles, whirring grasshoppers in flight, large hunting spiders which jumped around the floor in a scary fashion and small, beautifully patterned ones which could give you a nasty bite. There were the constant flies, mosquitoes which emerged in the evening so that you had to keep your legs well covered, beautiful moths with a wing span as large as that of a small bird, butterflies which fluttered round pools of water or heaps of dung, stag's horn beetles, vicious hornets and some big squashy looking bombers which bashed themselves against the lamps at night. Millipedes (chongololos) marched across the road and curled into tight balls when threatened.

Huge anthills, constructed by industrious termites from the red earth, were liberally sprinkled through the bush. They were even more visible through the trees in the dry season and a neighbour had built a rondavel on his. There were little grey termite mounds on some dambos which resembled headstones in a cemetery. There were ants on every square inch of Africa – white ants (termites), red ones which bit you, brown ones, little back sugar ants, Matabele ants which marched in pairs through the forest and loved to hang around the wood pile. They buzzed angrily if you trod on them and attacked with their fierce pincers. It was said they could cover a bird or an animal and, by some secret signal, all bite at once, the shock fatally wounding their prey and a story was doing the rounds that an army of ants had swarmed over a baby in a pram and killed it. I thought that ants were destined to take over the world – they were well organized and relentless. If an army of ants decided to walk through your house you just opened the doors and let them through. Blondie's flapping ears usually alerted us to an overnight invasion of red ants, sometimes called fire ants or siafu and no wonder. Sometimes we poured paraffin on them to exterminate the ravening horde and would sweep them out the next day, like tea leaves. For hours afterwards we'd itch and scratch, imagining the ants were still with us. Mum said that ants were a sign that you were about to leave a house and this turned out to be the case where our family was concerned.

We walked home from the Club one night after a film, the moonlight as bright as day. A solitary chicken was cheeping from the carport. Suddenly, red hot needles pierced my ankles. We had been invaded.

"Ants!" I yelled, kicking off my flip-flops. I found one shoe down the bottom of the garden the next day. "Bring a torch."

Dad rushed out and flashed the light over the carport. The hens looked down blearily from their perches on the beams.

"Aubreys! Bloody things," he said. Dad called any insect "aubrey" after an eponymous former army pal who was tall, thin and gangly. "What's making the noise?"

The carport floor was a black mass of soldier Matabele ants. We picked our way gingerly inside and picked up the bird who had given the alarm, a chick too small to fly. The poor little thing was covered in large, biting insects.

They wouldn't release their grip and we had to douse the bird in paraffin before the predators relaxed their pincers. We gave the chick a bath with soapy water and took her into the kitchen, where cockroaches scuttled out of the way as we approached with the hurricane lantern.

"Blasted things" said Mum. "How the devil do you get rid of them, for God's sake?"

The brown, armour-plated insects waved their long feelers and brazenly established eye contact, then clacked as they bolted into the many cracks and holes in the wall. Even though we sprayed and cleaned regularly, cockroaches were a part of life. Periodically we had a cockroach cull but knew that Big Daddy and his mate would be lurking somewhere in the recesses of the building, waiting to go forth and multiply. Everything had to be stored in tins or bottles to keep insects at bay. Betty called them "gogos" and I, tall and skinny, was given this nickname at school, like Dad's mate Aubrey.

We settled the chick on the crosspiece of the kitchen chair to roost and dry out, by the oven. She was fine the following morning.

"Those chickens aren't giving us many eggs," said Dad at lunchtime the next day.

It was one of those chilly, windy days that sometimes occurred in the dry season, when a high, cloudy haze and smoke from bush fires hid the sun. Dad was in a bad mood. He hated the cold.

"The ants gave them a shock, perhaps. Maybe there's a mongoose in the garden," said Mum. "They love eggs."

"If there is one, it's black," replied Dad. "They'll pinch anything. I've been having trouble at the stores. My pickaxes are disappearing. And tools! Those guys will break anything. 'Give us the job and I will finish the tools, bwana.' That's their motto."

Dad was on a roll now.

"And this cold weather. My back hurts much better. It's that damned Land Rover, bouncing on these dirt roads."

Whether Dad's backache was imaginary or not, he soon had something to complain about. Taking my suitcase out to the car, he slipped on the reed mat placed by the front door. It shot from under his feet on the highly-polished floor. Dad had really done his back in this time.

"Bloody mats! They're lethal," he shouted to Mum who, in her innocence, was trying to make the house look more cosy. "For crying out loud, Dulce, it's crazy to have mats on such a slippery floor."

Mats were henceforth banned from the hallway and stoep. Dad tried to banish them from the living room but Mum insisted the big one remained until they bought their first carpet, a square of Axminster, chosen with care and the purchase faithfully recorded in Mum's diary. She was busy making curtains, painstakingly hand-sewing them from material kindly donated by the Cloth Buying Department at Marks and Spencer's Head Office.

One day we had a windfall: a leopard had been killing chickens in a nearby village and the children feared for their lives. A hunting party set out: you needed a special permit to hunt leopard as it was Royal Game. They killed it and Dad was given the cured skin. It took pride of place in our living room, where Blondie would give its extremities a stealthy chew until it finally fell apart.

The dusty garden was taking shape. Dad's vegetable patch was in full production now and small birds, LBJs (little brown jobs) loved to bathe in the watered furrows. The flower beds next to the house were full of zinnias and petunias, larkspur and lobelia grown from packets of Kirchoff's seeds. Tiny pawpaw seedlings were growing fast and would produce fruit by the end of the year and the garden was already producing bananas, guavas and granadillas (passion fruit). As it was customary for civil servants to be transferred every three years, after home leave, little attention was paid to creating permanent gardens. Dad was the exception to this rule and planted trees and shrubs wherever he went, scrounging stuff from Forestry or Agriculture Department contacts and growing plants from cuttings or seeds which he had collected. Our gardens usually contained frangipani bushes, jacaranda and flamboyant trees, bougainvillaea, coral creeper, morning glory and moonflowers.

Tandeo wanted to leave.

"Are you unhappy?" asked Dad. "Do you want more pay?"

No, Tandeo explained in his own language. He was homesick. He had no power. He wanted to go back to his village.

"Where is your village?"

Kawambwa, he replied. Kawambwa! That was over 100 miles away. Not to worry, said Tandeo, he would walk. He could not afford the Thatcher Hobson bus. It was not very far. There were members of his clan in many villages along the way where he could get food and where he could stop for the night.

We were sorry to see him go but it was a good time of year for Tandeo to leave. The roads and paths would be dry and there would be fewer flies or mosquitoes. Nobody walked back to their villages in the rains, unless they had been bewitched. The rainy season made the locals miserable. They were used to living, cooking and eating out of doors and only used their huts at night. This seemed to be the season when spells were cast and people bewitched. Had another one today, Dad would say. Been bewitched, silly bugger. He's gone off to the swamps to die.

Tandeo's family might have wanted him back in the village to work: this was a busy time of year for the men in their bush gardens. Many of them had gone to work on the Copperbelt mines, leaving villages full of predominantly mothers, grannies and children. The Bemba had been nomadic hunter-gatherers when they had arrived in this area 200 years ago but had adopted the least line of resistance on these poor soils, the slash-and-burn method of cultivation, chitimene.

In the dry season the men would select a patch of bush, hack branches off the hardwood trees with pangas and pile brushwood in an area of an acre or two, not bothering to remove the hardwood stumps. In this process they would have accidents – fall out of trees, chop off limbs, break legs – though not as many as you'd expect. They set fire to the brushwood, an exercise which often got out of hand, burning large swathes of bush. Bush fires were also started to encourage fresh grass to grow, providing food for buck which would then be hunted. Piccanins would play around with matches and light fires for the sheer hell of it.

Once the fire had died down in a "garden", the ash and soil would be piled into beds, mounds which I thought looked like graves. The women and children planted crops – cassava, beans, pumpkin, millet, cabbage – in time for the first rains to encourage the seeds to germinate. After a year or two the soil on this plot would be exhausted, the garden abandoned and more forest would be cut down and burnt. It was not surprising that so much of the bush consisted of secondary forest, with fire-climax vegetation. This system had worked well while the population was relatively sparse and the cultivated land given 30 years or more to recover but things had now reached the stage where the population was exploding and fallow periods were diminishing, to the detriment of soil fertility and tree cover. No livestock could be kept because of tsetse fly, apart from long-legged, rangy chickens and the odd duck, so that the locals always craved meat – nyama. I had seen ten of them chase after one rabbit in a storm drain.

The men might help erect pole-and-dagga huts near the new field and thatch them but most of their work on the land would be over for the year. The women would cultivate the land, weed it and harvest the crops. Their menfolk carried on drinking beer, hunting small game, fishing in the dambos or rivers, chewing the fat and relaxing under a tree. Many Bemba men provided the labour force for mines on the Copperbelt, to the south of the Congo Pedicle road. The women never stopped – collecting water and firewood, which were two major tasks, pounding millet and cassava, making pots, weaving, cooking, cleaning and looking after the children.

As there were no draught animals and little mechanization, it was evident that the bulk of hard physical work was done by these Bemba women. They walked down dirt roads and bush paths carrying everything on their heads – bundles of firewood, pots of water, enamel bowls full of fruit and vegetables, even a sewing machine on one occasion. Their deportment was impeccable. With a straight neck and back, broad shoulders and pert breasts, a young girl carried things effortlessly and gracefully, sometimes with the extra load of a baby strapped to her back with a cloth. They were happy and smiling and even the old women, with wizened faces and shrunken bosoms, were uncomplaining with the heavy workload.

After the daily fetching and carrying, cassava roots had to be soaked to remove poisonous acid before they could be peeled and dried. Finally, these were pounded into flour in a large mortar and pestle, sometimes by two women, a thumping sound which will be familiar to anyone who has lived in or near an African village. The end result would be a starchy porridge which tastes a little like boiled potatoes, full of carbohydrate but with minimum nutrition, to be mixed with "relish", sweet potato leaves, wild spinach, beans, groundnuts and any other available vegetable. Their other tasks would include cooking, and keeping their huts and the village area well swept to deter snakes. Chickens were kept in little huts on stilts to avoid predators, as was grain to keep out rats. Childcare was often left to grandmothers. The women were clever at crafts such as pottery, weaving and basket-making, knitting and crochet, often conducted outside, sociably in the shade of a tree while small children ran around. I have some beautiful baskets which must be over 50 years old. There were often separate huts for men and women and birth control took place by the simple process of keeping a woman apart from her husband while she was nursing a baby for the first two years of its life. There was little cash around and it was a self-sufficient economy, with much bartering of goods and services.

The other thing that struck me about the Africans was that they were never in a hurry. The only time you saw them run was if they were playing a game of football or hunting something. The pace of life was slow and I think this was partly a function of heat, endemic diseases like malaria or bilharzia and malnutrition. Perhaps they were good at conserving energy and it was we Europeans who were lacking. They were also patient and stoical in the face of illness or pain and would form long, uncomplaining queues at the hospital. Africans could be indifferent to cruelty. My father's staff at PWD would laugh if somebody was injured on a building site and they could be heartless where animals were concerned. Their mission was survival and everything else was of secondary importance.

By September it was getting hot. While the grasses were still bleached pale by the sun and everything seemed exhausted, the miombo forest surrounding the town burst into leaf. It was like a New England autumn as the graceful, mushroom crowns of the msasa trees were suffused in a colour spectrum of gold, bronze, pink, red and lime green, letting dappled shade fall on the forest floor. By the end of the month buds appeared on the graceful jacaranda trees round the hospital where, by October, their grey trunks and feathery-leaved branches would sit above a lilac carpet of fallen blossom. Finally, the golf course would be peppered with wild gladioli and the orange puffballs of fire lilies pushing through baked earth.

It was a great time of year for excursions – a visit to one of Dad's bush "jobs", going to the lake or a rare shopping trip to the Copperbelt. Mufulira was the closest town to the Congo border but we would sometimes travel to the railhead at Ndola. After a quick slurp of tea we would pile into the Land Rover or the car and set off in the grey light just before dawn, while it was still cool. As the sun rose over the glistening, fresh tree foliage I felt that the bush was playing a symphony. The strings soared, flutes trilled and the trees sang. The sight of an endless sparkling, vivid forest against a background of intensely blue African sky was like champagne to the senses. As it grew hotter, I wound down the window to feel the wind in my hair. Often, I stuck my bare feet out, for added cooling up a billowing skirt, to Mum's disgust. No air conditioned cars in those days. The perfumes of newly opened forest flowers wafted on the air and mingled with the familiar base notes of wood smoke and dust as the cicadas struck up their shrilling chorus. Christmas beetles, my classmates called them.

October was always spent at school, sweltering under a brassy sky. Suicide month. The gym windows were painted white to reflect and diminish the sun's rays but it was still unbearably, suffocatingly hot. The gym was reserved for public examinations, which we sweltered through accompanied by the noisome whiff of rope, dusty wood, chalk and sweaty tackies. Why the powers-that-be planned a school year in which the exams fell during the hottest, most humid month and the long holidays were slap-bang in the middle of the rains, when bush travel was difficult if not well nigh impossible, was beyond us students. We cursed the government as sweat dripped off our noses and on to our exam papers.

The flamboyant trees along Cairo Road sent out exuberant sprays of flaming orange flowers, always a sign that the rains were not far away. There would be rumblings of thunder, lightning displays and towering cumulus for days, sometimes weeks before the rains finally arrived. With the first real downpour we celebrated, like pagans heralding the arrival of the rain god.

With the rain came the insects, mosquitoes and the pungent whiff of formic acid (from Matabele ants) and stink bugs on the wind. Clouds of flying ants surged from holes in the ground. Grass grew to elephant height and the golf course became as green as any in England. Water surged down the concrete storm drains in Lusaka and killed a piccanin. Spears of corn pushed through the red soil and cucumber and melon vines romped away over the mounds in bush clearings.

In our part of the world, dirt roads became muddy morasses, with sections deeply rutted or washed away. Instead of bucketing down a road, riding the vehicle like a bucking horse, we slithered and squelched along, spinning the steering wheel into and out of skids, avoiding huge potholes which had appeared overnight, big enough to swallow a Land Rover, plunging through fords which had become raging torrents. One year, the Congo Pedicle had 50 lorries stuck in a 45-mile stretch. Dambos were often impassable and the Luapula River sometimes swelled to a mile in width. It would rain most afternoons, battering on our tin roof so that all conversation became impossible. Our house had no gutters so water poured off the roof in a sheet, a miniature Victoria Falls. We didn't care. We were home for the holidays.

And summer came in December, when the flame lilies bloomed.

Chapter 12
CLUB LIFE

Dad and friend with man-eating lion

My parents were not barflies but there was no denying that the Club was the hub of social life in our small bush town. For the first couple of years I was allowed in on a limited basis, for tennis, to play ping-pong in the back room, take out library books or attend the traveling cinema.

"Are you going to bioscope tonight?" asked Jean.

This was another word for the cinema, films, flicks, movies. In Lusaka it was a real social occasion and patrons would dress up to the nines, the men in suits, the ladies in proper dresses and high heels. It wasn't like that in the bundu.

The Information Service brought round films, many of indifferent quality, "in blurred sepia and Latvian", as one wag remarked, and ground to a halt between reels as there was only one projector. We kids didn't mind as there was chance to enter the generally forbidden zone of the bar to get a Fanta or Coke, if you were lucky, and some Willards chips (crisps) during the interval. If there were potatoes you could even buy proper chips, also called chips. Very confusing. Squash was a vegetable, not a drink – here you asked for a "cool drink".

Anxious to fit in with my classmates at school, I was getting good at speaking Rhodesian and teased Mum with my authentic "Kabulonga accent". She was not impressed. I was a chameleon, struggling to fit in.

In those pre-television days we soaked up the Pathé newsreels that preceded the feature film and the stilted documentaries on travel, wildlife and educational topics. One such film showed goods being offloaded at Mombasa docks, including huge rolls of paper.

"I wonder what they're for?" I asked.

"Elephants' toilet rolls," said Pat Byrne, the agent from the transport company who was also a fabulous dancer.

Audience participation at the cinema was vigorous – oohs and aahs in the love scenes, jeers for the baddies and clapping when events took a satisfactory turn. An added bonus was the bar boys being asked to do a tribal dance during the interval, like a pair of performing seals. However, Bwalya and Mutapuka seemed to enjoy it and certainly appreciated the whip-round for cash that followed.

The Club was a cosy place but this soon changed. White ants had decimated the timbers and buckets had to be placed under the thatch every rainy season. Off came the roof and we enjoyed some cinema shows in the black, velvet African night with a star-studded sky above.

Those stars! You almost felt you could touch the Milky Way, see Orion striding round in his winking belt and be guided by the Southern Cross. The new tin roof was watertight but no one could hear themselves speak, or the music, for that matter, in the rainy season. Progress.

The Club's main function was to provide copious amounts of beer for the local population. Drinking took place on a heroic scale and the bar only closed when the last drinker chose to lurch home or the beer ran out. Our first neighbours, the Boltons, were avid Club patrons. Noelene was Australian and gave me my first haircut, slicing off my long plaits before I started school. Tiny was a South African of enormous girth who, when pickled, would swing from the beams under the Club's thatched roof, singing lustily. On one occasion he lost his trousers but continued singing. The bar was where tired workers quenched their thirst after a hot, dusty day, exchanged gossip and read the newspaper. A few ladies perched on bar stools but Mum preferred a table beside the wall, with the dog safely stashed underneath, or the verandah overlooking the tennis court.

Nina was never seen on the verandah. She was a true bar fly who specialized in revealing dresses ("backless, topless, frontless", Dad said) and very high heels. She had once been an air hostess but her charms had faded a little, probably because of her love affair with the gin bottle. She fluttered her eyelashes at the men, peering seductively at them through a curtain of dark hair, sadly now greying at the roots. Still, she was fun, even if she overstepped the mark. After a long session at the bar one night Nina climbed down from her bar stool and stepped into her high heels, unfortunately putting her right foot into the left shoe and vice versa. She tottered out of the door, regardless. It was rumoured that her less than ample bosom had popped out of a strapless number while dancing with the Provincial Commissioner at one of the Club hops.

"It was all right, Dulce. He'd got a warm spoon with him in his top pocket," chortled Dad, later.

"Don't be coarse, Jack," Mum replied, frilly-lipped.

Nina was the second wife of Luapula Joe, the local transport manager. He was a diminutive, dapper man with smoothed-back, grey hair and an immaculately trimmed moustache. His eyebrows and eyelashes were startlingly black in comparison and Dad swore he had seen Nina apply mascara to his long lashes with a brush in the bar. I wasn't so sure: Dad was famous for embellishing his stories. Joe had a flamboyant taste in clothes and cars and could be seen driving round in his latest American behemoth. This was huge, with fins and a radiator grill that looked like a set of shark's teeth. Joe was so tiny you could only just make out his head above the steering wheel.

He went to the Boma to register his new car, a 1959 Chevrolet with white-walled tyres, wraparound bumpers, fins, the lot. My brother thought his car was fabulous. Joe closed the door with a satisfying clunk, strutted up the steps and presented his documents at the counter to register the vehicle at the Management Board offices.

"What colour is it, Joe?" asked Bill Jackman, the accountant.

"Champagne Mist," replied Joe, proudly.

"Pink," wrote Bill.

When I was a little older I was allowed to go to quizzes, whist drives, bingo and the dances. Mum kept a wary eye on me, especially when the miners from Bahati were in town. They were reputed to be a wild bunch. Little did Mum realize that the ex-public school PA types had impeccable manners but were the randiest of the lot. You never went out on to the verandah to cool down with those chaps. My parents were excellent ballroom dancers and covered the floor easily and gracefully. Mum could stay on the dance floor and could outlast Dad. Two beers were his limit, after which his wide smile expanded even further and he got sleepy.

"Your mother's on great form tonight, Judy!" said one of the young district officers, whirling past with Mum in his arms. "What's she on?" he asked?

"Water!" I shouted above the din of the record player.

Looking on, I observed the antics of the grown-ups at play. There were the Smiths, always first on the dance floor, their small, chunky figures swooping and twirling in utter seriousness to "Bye, Bye Blackbird". Bob Dickson, a Scot, looked like a lounge lizard but boy, could he move. The young District Officers bounced energetically to the music and danced as though they were on the parade ground but they were good to jive with, being strong and supple. You just had to watch that they didn't fling you out of the door or slam you into the wall with their exuberance. At least they had been taught the Gay Gordons, The Dashing White Sergeant and the Eightsome Reel at an early age, being good sons of Empire. If the miners came into town we had a few Volkspiele numbers, which consisted of folk dances accompanied by an accordion, involving linked arms, Afrikaners singing in unison and much energy. Dad used to call these dances Bokkie Trots.

One of the young Scottish girls was in great demand. She was tiny, extremely pretty and the lads buzzed round her like bees round a honeypot. My friend Anne, the PC's daughter and I had never seen such quantities of mascara on a pair of eyelashes. The boys called her Panda but Anne christened her Blackout or, alternatively, MacLulu. Secretly we were both green with envy at her pulling power. She swayed her hips extravagantly as she jived, balancing on high stiletto heels; she waved her arms in the air and wound her long fingers, their nails ablaze with colour, round her partner's neck as they came together.

"Hmm," said Mum. "She looks like a prawn on heat."

I privately thought this was sour grapes. It must feel good to be like MacLulu – small, dainty, soignée, always shorter than your partner. She had dropped out of her expensive private school, to her father's chagrin, and was killing time at home until she went to secretarial college.

I was always at school for one of the big Club occasions, Burns Night. The Scottish Mafia, as Dad called them, turned out in force: they formed a large section of every ex-pat community, their accents veering from broadest Glaswegian to refined Edinburgh, and Fort Rosebery was no exception. They were teachers, clergymen, missionaries, mechanics, doctors and dentists, miners and farmers and 99% were drinkers. The Scots reminisced about the beauty of their homeland, the lochs, glens and mountains but we noticed that few went back home there when they retired, preferring the sunshine and golf courses of Natal. They played golf rather than tennis, baked scones, saved money and moaned about the indolence of the Africans.

From my mother's letters, I note that the main room at the Club was decorated with swathes of tartan and mock white heather, haggis had been flown in from wherever and the bar well stocked. The whisky ration was one bottle for two people at the dinner table. Beforehand, men were seen muttering scraps of Robbie Burns to themselves over their desks and digging their kilts out of mothballs. The ladies wore long white dresses, with tartan sashes, and a search was mounted for a piper. In later years, one of my boyfriends would oblige and I was amazed at the noise of bagpipes at close quarters – I thought my ears would burst. On one memorable occasion Mum's boss got well and truly plastered, danced and kissed all the women in the room and incurred the displeasure of his wife. Thoroughly inebriated, he sank to his knees and rolled up his trouser legs, pretending to be Toulouse-Lautrec. She turned her back on him but he followed, still on his knees! On Burns Night the Club would be drunk dry. There would be many thick heads in town the next day.

New Year's Eve was the big night out of the year for Europeans in colonial Rhodesia. Ex-pats keenly missed their families back in the old country and Christmases in Africa were not the same. 31st December was a time for people to let their hair down with their friends and sleep it off the following day. The South Africans called it Old Year's Night. There was always a do in the Club, with dancing of all persuasions and a supper, edible or otherwise. One year a wife experimented and made a risotto which no Italian would have recognized. The bulk of it was tipped unceremoniously by disgusted diners on to the tennis court, under cover of darkness. The arrival of the new year was celebrated twice, once at midnight and then at 2.00am, African time, when a wheezy radio was tuned in to the BBC World Service to catch the chimes of Big Ben in London. Everybody linked arms for Auld Lang Syne and more kissing ensued, at which point I dived for cover. By this stage the party-goers were definitely the worse for wear. The men were bursting into song and the women were getting maudlin and tearful from a surfeit of drink, homesickness and cigarette smoke. The young bloods had grabbed a couple of spears from behind the bar and were stalking round each other, chanting "Hold him down, you Zulu warrior, hold him down, you Zulu chief, chief chief....."

"It's time we went home," said Mum, raising an eyebrow at my father.

"I'll just have one more beer, Dulce."

Mum and I walked home by torchlight as Dad was in no fit state to drive. Somebody had already tipped a Land Rover into a storm drain. Luckily, the rain had stopped, the trees dripped and tree frogs and crickets were in full voice.

Dad rolled home in the wee small hours. Mum walked with him to collect Dreamboat from the Club the next day.

"What's that bottle of champagne doing in the back seat, Jack?" she asked.

"Bob got a load in. He was handing them out," said Dad.

"That's very generous. Are you sure?"

"Yes, dear."

A couple of days later Dad was caught out.

191

"Do you know," said Bob Dickson in the bar, "When I got back to my table I was sure there were three bottles left and blow me, some bugger had lifted one. Would you believe it," he muttered, shaking his head.

Mum overheard this and gave Dad a roasting.

"For God's sake, Jack! You must have been totally puddled. How could you think Bob had given you a bottle of champagne? You must take it back at once."

"Yes, dear."

Just before we went on leave, in 1957, Gordon came into our lives. Mum and Dad brought him home from the Club for supper and we were instantly entertained. He told the most wonderful stories of his old life as a shop assistant in Harrods and had a wicked sense of humour How he had arrived in Africa as a manager for the African Lakes Corporation, who ran a chain of general goods stores (Mandala) in the bush, was a mystery.

Gordon had belonged to the Highgate Harriers as a competitive walker and demonstrated the method to us, with rolling hips and elbows akimbo. He was a natural comic and looked so funny in ultra short shorts and short socks, mincing around with his pert little bottom sticking out. Mum and I were speechless with laughter. Betty christened Gordon "Superb" – his favourite adjective. There was no doubt that he was camp, unconventional and arty. He stuck out like a sore thumb among the hearty men at the Club. It was rumoured he was gay but he had a girlfriend, currently working for a radio station in Australia, called Psitch.

Gordon was a natural actor and much in demand for shows put on at the Club. His piece de resistance was playing the part of Amanda in "Private Lives", wearing a turban, Mum's Spanish shawl, a flapper dress, someone's nylons dyed white and an agonizing pair of high heels with pointed toes.

"Christ, how do you girls get into these things," he expostulated, as he struggled with the stockings and shoes.

Gordon's house mate, Tony, was playing opposite him as Eliot. They performed their balcony scene, followed by "Some Day I'll Find You" (piano accompaniment by Mum) to rapturous applause. They were very nervous beforehand as the Governor of Northern Rhodesia, Sir Arthur Benson, was to be the guest of honour. They needn't have worried because he was as convulsed as everybody else, helpless with laughter in the front row with tears streaming down his face.

Gordon was a great correspondent and I loved getting his letters at school.

Buckingham Palace
6th February, 1957

Your mum and dad are both in excellent health and your mother is most pleased as she had her tennis racquet back yesterday and we intend to play. Your dad is dancing around on hot bricks this morning; they have had another letter from John and he and his "Yiddisher Momma" (John's latest girlfriend, who was Jewish) seem to be hitting it off very well. John had evidently been to meet the aged parents and all

Left: *Carving pestle and mortar*
Bottom: *Judy and Joyce by Mansa River, 1956*

(except Papa!) had accepted him with open arms. At present her mother and father are on a cruise in the Caribbean! Whacko!!! You won't need to go to Wembley for the ice-skating – John will probably give you a private rink as a present! He describes her as "very exotic" with long hair and long fingernails. Ugh. I can't stand them like that myself..... Still, it might be worth it in the long run.

I went on a pay trip down to Samfya last Thursday. Unfortunately, I had left my bathing costume at home but it was such a beautiful day that I decided to swim and risk the consequences. Now, however, I have regretted it as I was burnt by the sun in a rather awkward spot. Naturally enough, I have a generous tan over the most part of my body so there were no ill effects generally but there is naturally one particular area which is generally covered from the light of the sun and which was glaringly white. It soon turned a deep beetroot colour and for several days was most painful to sit on. The skin is all peeling off but is almost OK now. Shall not become a nudist again without taking proper precautions.

Sunday, 10th February.

I am now writing this letter sitting in bed and as I am unable to find a pen in the shambles that is my bedroom (there are about six around somewhere) I finish this in NRG copying indelible pencil – you are honoured.
Nothing is happening at the minute (as per usual) though Mother M – la vieille mère grise – has been

*away for two days and a deathly 'ush reigned over
the accounts department – thank heaven.* (Gordon
is referring to a colleague who was a bit of a
gossip)..... *Went to play tennis this afternoon, tho' I
only managed to get one set in before it really poured
with rain. So annoying. We played table tennis
afterwards and then (of all things) Happy Families!
We were all in hysterics by the time we finished.
Au revoir then,*

Love, Gordon.

Gordon was a non-stop talker and entertainer. He
would get so carried away that Mum and Dad would
take themselves off to bed. Thus, he frequently stayed
the night, sleeping on our Morris sofa covered in a
government-issue grey blanket.

At breakfast one morning he said excitedly "It was
bright moonlight last night and, blow me, there was a
leopard walking down your drive, bold as brass!"

"How many beers had you drunk then, Gordon?"
asked Dad.

"You lucky thing!" I exclaimed. "I wish I'd been awake."

"You wouldn't have seen it," said Dad, crushingly.
"Your bedroom's at the back."

Leopards occasionally came into town at night. They
were particularly partial to well-fed dogs belonging
to Europeans. The provincial commissioner's dog, a
brindled boxer called Guti, had been attacked by either a
leopard or hyena, we didn't know which. The animal had
crashed through the fly-screen in the back kitchen while
a rip-roaring party was in progress and almost killed

Guti. The dog was left with a huge hole on the back of his neck; luckily, he was a big, strong creature and survived.

Soon after Gordon's leopard sighting, our chickens started disappearing. Dad found a few bloodstained feathers, spoor and signs of a struggle in the carport, where they lived. A leopard could climb up to the hens' roosting beams, no trouble. He decided to get the gardener to build a hide in a tree on the edge of the golf course, set some bait and wait up there one night, .22 rifle at the ready. He stuck it out until two o'clock in the morning then retreated to a warm bed.

"Typical," said Mum.

The leopard struck again that night – he must have waited for Dad to leave his post – and more chickens disappeared.

We found out what had happened to the leopard because it made headlines, even in the British newspapers. Early one morning, when it was barely light, our pregnant neighbour was walking from the main house along the covered walkway to her kitchen when a leopard sprang out of the bush. Terrified, she flew into the kitchen and bolted the door, where the cook found her shivering with fear an hour later. Poor girl, her husband (a district officer) was on tour and the fright caused her to lose the baby.

The leopard, thwarted, walked on to the verandah of the bungalow next door, where Ian Mackinson threw a bicycle at it. The animal ran off, a hunt was mounted and Dennis Gaunt, from the Game Department, finally shot it. I was furious that all this excitement had happened while we were away on long leave. High drama in Fort Rosebery, Town of Tedium – and I'd missed it! I still hadn't seen a real live leopard, worse luck.

197

Chapter 13
WILD THING

Makishi Mask

Seventeen, seventeen,
Cool and solid seventeen,
Young enough to dance and sing,
Old enough to get that swing.

Seventeen, just been kissed,
Graduated and got that twist,
Kind of love I can't resist
At seventeen.

"You're going to wear that record out," said Betty.

Those saxophone riffs in the middle of the record are engraved on my memory. This was supposedly the first rock and roll record specifically written for girls. It was fast paced and easy to dance to and one reviewer said "it was the best fun you could have with your clothes on". I totally agreed. I bopped around on our red, polished floor practising steps, my paisley circular skirt and frothy petticoat whipping round in a satisfactory swish. When I finally turned seventeen, Betty wrote asking for "Seventeen" played for my birthday on the Radio Rhodesia pop requests programme. Too late. By that time, I had discovered proper rock 'n' roll, not the rookie version.

Carol introduced me to the record that changed my life. I was rather scared of her mum, a tiny but vociferous Lancashire lady – but her dad was a sweetie. Mr. Sugden had been an undertaker in his former life, which perhaps accounted for his lugubrious manner. He now worked in PWD, with my father. Carol was considered a wild child but she was good fun. Back to "Seventeen" –

Now, sloppy shirt, old blue jeans,
Dirty shoes by all means,
Patch of blonde, peroxide hair,
Juke box baby, ain't no square.
Seventeen, hot rod queen,
Cutest girl you've ever seen.
Tell the world I'm really keen
On my hep cat doll of seventeen.

Yes, that was Carol.

An equally uncontrollable Rhodesian Ridgeback dog called Shah completed the family. He leapt up at me when I called, placed his paws on my shoulders and did his best to lick me to death.

"Coom 'ere, Shah," Mrs. Sugden yelled, to no avail.

Carole walked calmly to the door.

"Leave off, you stupid dog. Gerroff Jude," she said, calmly. "Voetsek. He's as daft as a brush." Shah dropped down and wagged his tail vigorously, doing his best to kneecap me. "Come in. I've got this new record. It's helluva good."

Carol didn't say "coom". She was being educated, at great expense, at Lusaka Convent but Mrs. Sugden despaired that it wasn't teaching her daughter much in the way of decorum.

We went into Carol's bedroom, an enviably seductive boudoir with a red-shaded bedside light, scented with an indefinably exotic perfume. She took a 78 disc out of its sleeve and placed it reverently on the turntable.

I had never heard anything like it. Elvis had burst into our teenage lives. His first record, "That's All Right, Mama," had exploded on the scene on 5th July 1954, his music a unique blend of blues, country and western and gospel music. I thought his greasy hair and slobbery lips looked soppy but wow, could he sing, smile – and move, we realized, when we saw his films later. The ripples had finally spread to Fort Rosebery in 1956.

My parents wrote to me at school and told me how the "first rock 'n' roll record", Bill Haley's "Rock Around the Clock" had been played at the Club to a stunned audience. No, Carol and I considered Bill positively tame compared to Elvis Presley.

Does rock 'n' roll have an effect on a girl's hormones? Mine kicked in later than those of my school friends.

Most of them were farmers' daughters and had witnessed the causes and effects of sex from an early age. They had been surrounded by copulating bulls, rampant stallions and fierce cockerels marking their claim on the female of the species on the land. Besides, their mothers often gave birth at home, with little outside medical help. Virginia's father, a white hunter, had told her how careful you had to be of elephant bulls when they were in musth: sweat oozed from the glands near their eyes, they sought mates and became dangerous. I knew how wilful our bitches became when they were on heat. The overall message was that animals and people became slightly dotty, if not totally crazy, when they were in love.

I had started my periods early – on board ship, on our way to Africa in fact – but hadn't really made the important connection between these, sex, pregnancy and childbirth. My mum had not enlightened me fully about the facts of life. Joke-telling sessions behind the curtains of our dormitory cubicles filled in the large gaps in my knowledge of the subject. Midge Ramsden, a farmer's daughter, had a particularly large fund of stories about a naughty girl called Little Eva.

Puberty meant the start of years of long, heavy, painful periods. My cycle was two weeks on, six weeks off.

"Have you 'come on' yet?" girls asked.

I was anaemic and dosed daily by matron with foul iron medicine which tasted of blood and rust. At school, I trained myself to wake early to wash my sheets in the ablutions room, a Spartan affair equipped with pinky-red carbolic soap and scratchy toilet paper stamped "NRG". Mum had given me Cuticura soap to use, which was medicated, dark cobalt blue and smelled much nicer.

I crept quietly into the end toilet cubicle to dispose of the hateful sanitary towel in the incinerator, whose brand name was Jackson. Once everyone woke up and the wash-room was full, everyone would know. There would be cries of "She's in Jackson! She's 'on'! She's got The Curse!" Other girls, bolder than me, wouldn't care that their condition was being broadcast.

Dawn managed to get a packet of Tampax from her friend Dionne, who worked part-time at the Woodlands chemist up the hill. We thought she was being daring. Surely a virgin couldn't wear a tampon? She applied it with care in Jackson on Saturday, hair wash day, encouraged and guided by her noisy friends on the other side of the toilet door.

"Have you got it in yet? Put one leg up on the toilet. Relax!"

"Ow, no it's just..... ooh, that's better."

Dawn emerged gingerly from the toilet to cries of "Yea". She staggered around, bandy legged, all day before she realized she had left in the cardboard applicator as well as the tampon. After a while I took the plunge and oh, what bliss. No more chafing, no more disgusting paraphernalia of belts and safety pins. No more large packets of pads handed to you in a brown paper bag, supposedly for modesty's sake but in fact shouting out loud to all and sundry that yes, you'd got your period. Boys didn't know how lucky they were.

We talked about sex behind the closed curtains of our cubicles. Did we know anyone who had gone "all the way" yet? (Some of the bolder, more mature girls admitted they had been tempted.) If so, did it hurt? It was crazy if you did. Boys wouldn't respect you and besides, you might get pregnant and be an unmarried mother. Boys didn't always use French letters and no one would dish out contraceptives for single girls. It would be too shameful.

I started to develop a bosom. It grew and grew. I don't think my mother knew what to do with it, as she had small breasts and had never worn a bra. I was getting lascivious looks from the Africans when I walked past the shops to the PWD offices, bursting forth in my T shirt. Eventually my mate June, 13 going on 30, took me in hand, provided women's magazines with the necessary adverts and accompanied me to Kee's in Lusaka on a rare shopping trip to buy the right one. Lacy, feminine lingerie was frowned on at school so it had to be cotton circular-stitched bras, with conical cups and complicated straps. Suddenly one's naturally rounded, soft breasts were hard, pert and thrusting almost up to shoulder level. Bras added another layer to our already bulky school uniforms – ugh.

(As a prefect in the sixth form we rebelled against these uniforms and designed dresses which were much cooler and more comfortable. The school later changed the uniform and used my design.)

"I dreamt I raced with the winds in my Maidenform bra....."

Fat chance. I had never been much of a runner and now, in addition, I had these two growing blobs to contend with. Hair started to grow in unexpected places and June, once again, introduced me to the mysteries of Mum roll-on deodorant and mini razors.

However, my long legs and bosom were beginning to attract attention from the right quarter, had I but noticed it. I was ill-equipped for close encounters with boys, still being painfully shy, gauche and clumsy. I couldn't run fast but I could swim, play tennis and dance.

School dances had been torture. Each Saturday night saw us in the gym with our brother school, Gilbert Rennie, the girls ranged in chairs in front of the wall bars, the boys on the prowl in the centre of the floor. The anxiety of it all, waiting to be asked to dance. I could foxtrot, quickstep, waltz and even tango with the best of them, having been primed by Mum and Dad, expert dancers since their youth. I loomed above the heads of my partners, earnest sons of the soil with spiky crew cuts or Brylcreemed short back and sides. Even the taller chaps, some of whom were very good looking, tended to dance as if they were on the parade ground, their feet marching stolidly in time to the music, if one was lucky; lurching and swooping at random if they had no sense of rhythm, treading on their partners' toes, one sweaty hand pressed in the small of the girl's back, the other pumping her right arm frantically up and down. Luckily, cringing in my seat by the wall, I was rescued by a good dancer called George, early on. We were not romantically attached but we danced regularly together for years, two shy souls.

The arrival of rock 'n' roll was a release for both sexes. It didn't matter too much if the girl was taller than the boy, she could still gyrate, twirl and step around her partner without being in a clinch. If he was useless, the girl didn't get her feet stamped on. I must have learned something, watching Simon shuffle around on his floor brushes, because I found I could jive. I could do the steps, respond to my partner's moves or help him out if he didn't know how and move my body in a loose-limbed, sinuous way like the Africans. This gave me enormous confidence. I was in demand. Disreputable, edgy characters with duck's-arse hairdos, drainpipe trousers and brothel creeper shoes asked me to jive. My girlfriends gasped. Did I know what a reputation Barry had, or that Richard was a two timer? Never mind, they were great dancers. I didn't have to kiss them! I was an innocent abroad.

Going out with boys was a formal ritual at school. Our contact with them was limited to the period between prep and supper time on weekdays, the Saturday hop in the gym and Sunday afternoons. We were allowed to walk, talk and picnic on the grass between the school and the boarding houses or on the playing fields. There were few trees to shelter under or hide behind with your boyfriend and a teacher marched up and down periodically to ensure there was no foul play. Once you had seen the boy a few times he asked you to get "hitched", after which seeing another boy or girl was forbidden until you "chucked" your chosen one, or were chucked. Some sports were mixed – athletics, some tennis tournaments – and we had played badminton in the school gym in Saturdays until the headmistress decided it was "unladylike". We had joint church services in town or in one another's gyms, offering a chance for the exchange of flirtatious glances. A couple of racy girls broke out of the dorm after their School Certificate exams to see their boyfriends. As all our windows had immoveable gauze fly screens, they must have bribed the nightwatchman to let them out. They had hoped to stroll back into breakfast, where no one would be any the wiser for their disappearance but someone snitched, they were caught and promptly expelled.

I watched these activities from the sidelines, initially surprised and uninterested. At the tender age of 13, some of these girls were on their third and fourth boyfriends and seemed like old, married women. They had no urge to continue their education after school, to travel or have proper careers. When they left school they wanted to settle down, marry, have a nice house and children. They would probably marry one of the local farmers or a mining engineer on the Copperbelt. They paid good wages up there and the copper bonus was riding high. My friends Megan, Jill and I discussed this at length.

"Never marry a farmer, Jude." Megan shook her head emphatically. "Your life's not your own and it's such hard work."

I can't remember when I started to fancy the opposite sex but, when I did, it was bewildering, for me and my family. I changed overnight from being a contented, bookish, submissive daughter into a moody rebel. I became explosive, uncommunicative and disconnected. They must have thought they were living with a stranger.

I couldn't get out of bed in the morning but stayed up till all hours in the holidays. I could dance all night but wasn't allowed to. I played loud music, at top volume, which drove Dad mad. It was so loud that piccanins walking along the road would halt in their tracks and dance as they heard Little Richard shriek the opening bar of "Lucille". My parents bought me a tiny transistor radio which I took to school and crouched over on Sunday evenings, listening to the Hit Parade broadcast from Lourenco Marques, the commercial station. I experimented with lipstick, started to use shampoo instead of Lux flakes and vinegar and slathered on Nulon hand cream. In Lusaka, where the water was hard, I even added hair conditioner. Dad grumbled and couldn't see why I needed such cosmetic aids.

Frantic periods of activity – tennis, swimming, partying, dressmaking if there was a big dance coming up, writing sketches for a revue – were interspersed with periods of intense inertia, boredom and sleep. My bedroom was a mess and the second matron, a cockney widow wreathed in a haze of cigarette smoke, told me my cubicle was "like a pigsty". I smarted at this and resolved to do better.

The following extract is taken from "A Brief Guide to Northern Rhodesia," the section on Climate and Clothing:

Women
Washable cotton and lightweight frocks are most frequently worn by women during the day. The smarter type of afternoon dress is handy for cocktail or sundowner parties. Warm suits are necessary during the coldest months and even woollen or "jeep" coats have their uses. At dinners, dances or other formal functions, long evening frocks are generally worn. A smart hat is naturally indispensable on special occasions..... Dress patterns are obtainable in the larger cities.

I don't think these guidelines applied to us in the bush. No mention is made of slacks or jeans, of course, and I don't think my mother owned a single smart hat. I remember going to one wedding and making a fascinator out of pipe cleaners. Dress patterns had to be bought in Lusaka on trips to Kees, or scrounged from friends.

There would be short, sharp surges of creativity. The house would be covered with drawing paper, if I was sketching caricatures to put on the Club walls for a dance. With my pocket money I'd walk to the Mandala store for some cheap fabric and run up a dress – once we'd got a little hand sewing machine. It was a time for Horrocks glazed print cotton salvaged by Mum, gingham, rick-rack braid, bias binding and buttons, ribbons, and organza for frilly petticoats. I practised making linings for jackets and sewing French seams, sexy straight skirts with slits down the back, roll collars, Peter Pan collars, drainpipe trousers that measured four inches round the bottom..... Titus would have to wait until I had cleared the dining table of paper patterns and fabric before he could lay the table for lunch. He would be running late, on top of which the lounge would look as though a bomb had hit it, with pins, cotton and scraps of fraying material everywhere. Scraps of Butterick tissue paper pattern floated to the floor.

"For crying out loud!" Dad exclaimed. "House is full of bloody loud music and rubbish. And those pins! If I sit on one of your pins again, Jude, you'll be for it."

Mum made soothing noises. Dad had been a male nurse in the army before the war and was pathological about pins or tin tacks causing tetanus, or at least some ghastly infection. He'd tried to train me how to bandage a wound neatly but I had failed. Despite Dad's moans, my parents clubbed together and bought me a cheap hand-operated Singer sewing machine.

Formerly open and talkative, I became defensive and evasive when questioned about what my day or evening had been like. I had become a teenager, even though the breed hadn't been invented. At a department store you went to the Junior Miss department, where they put you in clothes identical to your mother's, just in a smaller size.

In retrospect, I have to pity my poor parents. After the initial euphoria of sunshine, having help in the house and a social life, my mother missed her son and had a nubile daughter to contend with. Her lovely Scottish boss had been transferred and been replaced by a man whom my father called The Bald-Headed Old Bastard. He gave my mother plenty of extra work, with no extra pay, and the accounts to deal with. His wife drove a Mercedes and was intent on giving candlelit suppers for the elite. She would come round to Dad and cadge some choice free vegetables (succulent carrots, leeks, fresh lettuces) to serve with the meal. My parents were not invited to any of these fancy dinners, being definitely below the salt. The couple lived in one of the new, large houses on the edge of town and she was intent on creating an impressive garden to go with it. PWD lorries were seen dumping quantities of black dambo soil on to her drive and my father decided Mrs B-H O B should have a title, MBE – More Black Earth.

Colonial wives were often paid low salaries and were given few rights. Even in post-colonial times financial parity with men was uncommon, even though a man and a woman might perform identical jobs. A single woman's reputation was all important, as was remaining a virgin and birth control was not available unless one was married. My intelligent mother found all this hard

209

to take as she'd held down a good job in London and was clued up about birth control, having attended the Marie Stopes clinic when she had first arrived in England from Burma. The colonial round of coffee mornings, bridge parties and gossip was not her scene. However, she loved her tennis, walking the dog and the relaxed attitude of people. Friends popped in and out of one another's houses unannounced (there were no telephones, anyway). There would always be a cup of tea or a beer in readiness, food, time for a chat or even a bed at short notice. My father would often bring home somebody from the Club for the night, often a fellow civil servant on tour or indeed anyone passing through. It was not uncommon to walk into the living room and find a body on the sofa, someone who had passed out after one beer or whisky too many.

I began to find objects of attraction closer to home. Some of the Gilbert Rennie guys looked like Adonis, there was no denying it. Taller than their English counterparts, their hair streaked by the hot sun, their muscles rippled under their short-sleeved shirts and iron thighs emerged from their short, tailored shorts. Even the sixth formers didn't wear slacks. If you went out with a member of the rugby team, it was considered that you had really made it. However, their conversation was limited, mainly to sport and cars. Being naïve, I didn't realize this was a worldwide phenomenon. Secretly, I was envious because they picked the prettiest girls and wouldn't have given me a second look, anyway. I was also painfully shy.

My parents' friends seemed ancient to me, though they must have been in their thirties or forties. Most men wore the unofficial colonial uniform to work: white or khaki short-sleeved shirt, knee-length, heavily starched khaki shorts, long socks turned over at the top and highly-polished, lace-up shoes. Watching Dad shaving in his underwear in the bathroom, I saw that he was deeply tanned from his face to the V of his collar line, from his elbows to his fingertips and for a four-inch patch in the knee area. Everywhere else was a milky white.

My mother, ever dexterous, cut my father's hair and soon other men started coming round after work for their haircuts.

"Pass Fred (Bert, Bill, whoever) some tea, would you, Jude?" asked my mother. I would oblige.

"Sit down and tell me how you're getting on at school," the customer would say.

I sat down in the only available chair, opposite him. Oh God, he was wearing Desert Rat shorts, wasn't he, with loose cotton Y fronts underneath, sitting with his legs wide apart. You could see everything above those gnarled thighs. It was enough to put you off sex for life. I averted my eyes and soon learned to avoid Mum's barbering sessions.

A new intake of PA staff arrived. Unlike the previous lot, who were mainly married and had seen service in other bush postings or other colonies, the fresh crop of District Officers, District Assistants and cadets were mainly in their twenties and single. They arrived looking weedy, pale and wet behind the ears, with floppy, public school haircuts and accents. I conferred with my friends and we all agreed that they looked like babies but might turn out to be promising.

In our School Certificate year we received some boys and girls from L'Athénée school, Elizabethville (now Lubumbashi), for a fortnight. They were the essence of sophistication and we regarded them with awe. The girls wore provocative white gamine blouses with the top button undone and skin-tight straight skirts, with a revealing slit at the back. The boys were equally dashing, in their drainpipe trousers and loafer shoes. They accompanied us to lessons, dances and to the swimming pool, where one girl dazzled everybody by turning up in a white swimsuit which turned totally transparent when wet.

In our next school holidays we were given the opportunity to spend a fortnight in Elisabethville. Even though our French mistress exhorted us to go, for the sake of our language skills, I declined. My holidays were too precious to spend away from home. Besides, I was beginning to gain a little confidence and have some fun.

Chapter 14
WHERE THE WATER MEETS THE SKY

Porcupine

Despite that awful first excursion to the shores of Lake Bangweulu, Samfya was to become a special place for me. Our hearts never failed to lift when we crested the final hill and saw the blue expanse of water, fading indefinably to the cloudless sky above. We'd pass the cliff-top bungalows, drive past the harbour and its government buildings (PWD, Fisheries, Forestry, Water Development and Irrigation, Bangweulu Water Transport) to the beach below the little town. Tangy scents of eucalyptus and pine trees filled the breeze and we loved the sensation of hot, white sand squeaking beneath our toes. Wavelets lapped gently on the shore and halyards chinked on the few small dinghies lying there. It was our African version of the seaside.

Beyond the horizon lay the Bangweulu swamps, a huge expanse of dark green papyrus (sudd) and buff-coloured reeds and bulrushes, criss-crossed by a network of narrow channels and broader, man-made canals. In

213

the rainy season chunks of papyrus floated off into the lake and at one time a sudd island completely blocked the small beach where we used to swim. The swamps were the haunt of large Nile crocodiles and a wealth of bird life: heron, ibis and egret, jacana trotting inquisitively among the lily beds, the elusive shoebill stork and other water birds. The fishermen were equally at home, punting with long paddles in their dugout canoes, casting their nets, laying wicker fish traps or line-fishing. Just visible above the reeds, standing in their canoes, they glided slowly, languidly, their feet and boats hidden from view. It was as though they were propelled magically through the reeds, walking on water. Beyond the swamps and fringing the lake lay lagoons, dambos, grasslands and patches of forest on the many anthills studding the plains. Red lechwe, the shy, splay-footed sitatunga which could walk on floating reed-mats, oribi and other buck roamed over the grasslands.

People had inhabited the swamps for hundreds of years. The first settlers were called the Ba'twa (wild men), who lived by fishing and hunting from temporary shelters. Some of the locals maintained they had webbed feet. By the early 1950s, they had become assimilated into the surrounding tribes and more had settled in permanent villages. However, in the dry season they still used temporary fishing camps, reed shelters close to the shoals and only retreated to their main settlements in the rains, when the flooded area would expand by as much as 28 miles round the edges. The Ushi, who lived in the swamps now, walked like buck on the narrow paths, leaving behind a straight line of footprints rather than the staggered left foot, right foot pattern.

The lake and its swamps had been formed as part of the great Rift Valley upheaval, aeons ago in geological time. The faulting produced the valley itself, which stretches from above the Red Sea, plunging south through East and Central Africa, with deep lakes in its base, from Lake Rudolph (Turkana) in the north to Lake Nyasa in the south. Mountains were formed, including the Mountains of the Moon in the Ruwenzori massif and volcanoes, such as Mount Kenya and Kilimanjaro, were active. Bangweulu lies in a shallow depression produced when the land surface tilted, altering the drainage pattern. The headwaters of the Congo river system now flow into the north end of the lake, the principal river being the Chambishi, and the Luapula drains the lake to the south before curving up in a hook to flow into Lake Mweru. The Lualaba (Luvua) flows out of Mweru and is one of the sources of the great Congo River, nearly 3,000 miles long. As the river straddles the equator the rains fall on one part or another, ensuring a steady, murky flow.

The lake and its vast swamps attracted all sorts of people. Its shores were densely populated by tribes who depended on lake tilapia (bream) for their diet and trade. Mwamfuli, a couple of miles from Samfya, was a large fishing village whose drums throbbed through the night every weekend after pay day. Even at night, you knew you were passing the village because of the pungent smell of dried fish. Fishermen would spread their nets on to the wide beach to dry. On dark nights they would take their canoes into the bay and fish for the small, sardine-like shoals which were attracted to plankton on the surface. Lights winking in the bows, they would cast their nets or catch the fish with what looked like oversized butterfly nets, a magical sight when the moon shone.

Hunters, white and black, shot the crocodiles, valued for their meat and skin. Both hunter and hunted were nocturnal. The men went out at night in motor boats with bulala lamps to look for their prey, killing the engine when they spotted it. The croc's eyes would glint redly in the light and reveal the best place for the bullet, between the eyes. One of my friend's fathers was a white hunter – crocs in the wet season, buck and big game in the dry. Sport fishermen headed out in boats to catch the striped tiger-fish, which sported shark-like teeth and were a distant relative of the piranha. They also caught yellowbelly and catfish, along with the tasty bream. The locals and a few hardy sportsmen whose vehicles were rugged enough to cross the grassland tracks tracked the buck, bushpig, buffalo, lion, leopard and occasional elephant. If you didn't have a Land Rover it was a case of a long walk through the bush and camping. In those days, Bangweulu's remoteness and its many diseases lent its wildlife protection.

We Pommies were amateurs when it came to the lake. Huddled on our travel rugs and towels, we'd munch our sandwiches ("bloody sand in the sandwiches", Dad remarked once more), drink warm beers and cool drinks which were no longer cool and struggle up the sandy hill to the tennis court after our swim. The Rhodesians and Afrikaners, white Africans, knew better. They rolled up in their pick-up trucks or fat American cars from the Copperbelt over long weekends like Rhodes and Founders and unpacked everything necessary for creature comfort. Trailers were unhitched, speedboats launched, water skis offloaded and camp set up: tables and folding chairs, barbecues, crates of Castle beer and Coca-Cola kept cold on the long journey in cool boxes packed with dry ice, succulent steaks and boerewors to cook, awnings to sit under, tents to sleep in, rods to fish with and rifles for hunting. Sometimes there were even fridges plugged into the car ignition. Yes, they were organized. The girls wore the latest fashion in swimsuits and some even had bikinis! Speedboats buzzed around in the bay and teenagers water skied. As dusk fell fires would be lit and partying would carry on well into the night. Considering the amount of alcohol consumed it's a wonder nobody drowned. The Copperbelt types only made it for long holiday weekends – the rest of the time it was left for us to monopolise the beach and peace reigned.

The lake gave me my first taste of sailing, water skiing, skinny-dipping and even hunting, as an unwilling gun-bearer. Hot sun, cool water, the mingling scents of pine and wild jasmine, soft silvery-white sand. There was a backdrop of trees draped with flame creeper to give us some shade and a little rondavel on the headland. It was an irresistible setting for a young girl intent on romance.

Poor Dad, he got nagged to death by me, and Mum to a lesser extent, to travel to Samfya on Sundays, my parents' one day off during the week. They had to work on Saturday mornings. He so wanted to have a lie-in, get on in the garden, have a quiet beer in the Club before lunch then an afternoon snooze. We had other ideas. Thoughts of the beach, a picnic, a swim, even a game of tennis later, appealed to us, plus the prospect of some new company.

"Plee-ase, Dad, please can we go?"

"It's all right for you two, you don't have to drive on that bloody road. It's no good for the car, either. I've had the suspension fixed once already and it cost me a packet."

It was true that the Samfya road's corrugations and potholes would shorten the life of any vehicle, especially the Ford Consul we'd bought on our first home leave, a car not destined for bush roads. It went through springs, shock absorbers and fan belts like a dose of salts and punctures, too, on the stony bits of road. Dad couldn't afford new tyres so we had retreads. One of his favourite expressions to describe an ugly woman, was "a face like four miles of bad road".

Samfya was a breath of fresh air, a chance to see an uninterrupted view – the lake was 45 miles wide at that point – and meet new people. The handful of families who lived there all got on well together, in contrast to Fort Rosebery, large enough for class warfare and cliques. No wonder we nicknamed it Fort Rowsbery. Perhaps because of its isolation or its attractive setting, romance must have been in the air in the lakeside town because many of the wives fell pregnant.

"Stagnant, again!" Dad would announce after one of his business runs to the lake. "Is it something in the water?"

There would always be one or two roly-poly ladies on the beach. One day I saw Mrs. S, a large lady but a ferocious tennis player, sitting on the beach in her black swimsuit. I didn't think she could be pregnant – she was too old.

"Why is Mrs. S sitting in a rubber ring, John?" I whispered to my brother.

Top: *Makoro, Lake Bangweulu*
Bottom: *Samfya Boma (Photo: Alan Kitching)*

"That's not a rubber ring. That's ALL Mrs. S," replied John. "Perhaps she's got pneumatic fever."

John had come to Fort Rosebery in 1957. He loved to swim but rarely sunbathed. Hiding his skinny frame under many towels, he would lie in the shade, reading a book. He would be joined by some of the local white African matrons whose husbands fiddled around with speedboats, fished and water-skied. They didn't like swimming. Their job was to keep the food and beers coming and watch the children. Their husbands were often PWD men, road foremen and mechanics who spent long periods in the bush and loved it. The Poms built and sailed their dinghies, GP14s, and even built a small yacht club at the top of the beach. The DC's wife painted some tiles to decorate the bar and the new club was christened with a beery roof-wetting ceremony. As I grew older I was asked to help rig the boats and to crew but, being a girl, was rarely given a chance to man the tiller. Sailing along in a gentle breeze, with the waves lapping gently beneath the bows, trailing my hand in the water, was totally peaceful. If a stiff wind blew up I would be leaping round the boat, hauling sheets in as we tacked to and fro. My stomach muscles ached. I was getting fitter.

The early hours of the afternoon were siesta time, punctuated by the odd plop! as an overheated body hit the water. Walking to it was agony as the white sand was red hot. The dogs, exhausted after retrieving sticks or digging holes, lay panting in the shade. One of the Fisheries boys had a pet otter who didn't know the meaning of the word 'nap'. He would flop around our dozing bodies, nip our toes with needle-sharp teeth and cover us with sand with a whisk of his long, flat tail. Blondie, likewise, would take herself off for a swim and shake herself all over us. She'd had her midday snooze and didn't see why we should continue with ours.

As the shadows lengthened we brewed up for tea and took our last dip, trying to prolong our day off. Dad was on one leg to be off.

"Come on, you lot, get out and get dressed," he said, packing up the car and ignoring our pleas to stay longer and longer. "If we leave too late I'll catch everyone else's dust. It's all right for you, Jude, you don't have work in the morning."

"Don't moan, Jack," said Mum, "For goodness' sake, it's her holiday. Freda's invited us up for a sundowner before we leave."

Poor Dad. We strong-willed women usually got our way and Dad would be the last one on the road, following the dust of the other cars and squinting as he drove towards the setting sun. We tried to avoid driving at night – too much chance of hitting an unlit cyclist, walker or wild animal or, in later years, of being hijacked and robbed. If we broke down or had a puncture there would be no help until the following morning. Dad was not a good driver at the best of times and even worse in the dark. Some of his African drivers came to grief on the Samfya road, which was narrow, winding with dambos which flooded in the rainy season. One driver wrote off a precious Bedford vanette.

"How did you do this, Mumba?" said Dad, surveying the wreckage.

"A tree stood up in the middle of the road, bwana, and I hit it," Mumba replied.

Selfishly, I didn't mind driving home in the dark. We could open the windows as we wouldn't be sucking in dust from any cars in front, allowing cool night air to flow over our sunburnt arms. The car headlights picked out all sorts of nocturnal creatures: a buck crossing the road, a civet cat on the prowl, the odd reclusive porcupine shuffling along. The weirdest were the spring hares, mice-like rodents with huge ears and long legs.

As the years went by I was invited to stay with Bill and Freda, my parents' friends in Samfya. Freda was witty, elegant and a superb cook. She specialized in puddings, one of which was a strawberry mousse affair.

"We have something like this at school, Freda," I said, "Only it's chocolate. We call it Zambezi Mud."

"Do you?! Well we'd better give this a name. How about Bangweulu Blood?"

On one of my visits there was another guest, Dr. Hugh Cott, a renowned biologist. He was conducting a survey on the lake's ecosystem, in which he concluded that if too many crocodiles were killed the game fish would multiply at the expense of the edible tilapia and other species. He was also a keen birdwatcher and observer of local customs.

One night he decided to take his tape recorder to a local village, where there was a celebration planned, as he was interested in African music. The ANC (African National Congress) flag fluttered above the proceedings, its orange, gold and black swirling in the firelight. It was the first time I became aware of tribal identity and the groundswell of feeling that would develop into the African nationalist movement. The drums were deafening and the women chanted along in a wailing, repetitive dirge. They shuffled around in a circle, wringing their hands, rhythmically stamping on the dusty earth, bottoms and bosoms thrust out, hips gyrating, working themselves into a trance-like state. I felt almost hypnotized myself. Then the men took the floor, leaping around, whirling like dervishes, making imaginary swoops at their prey with spears as the women sang louder and ululated to their energetic display. It was thrilling and a bit scary.

One of the young DOs was amazed when I told him about it.

"You're mad. That boffin obviously doesn't understand the dangers of going into a village at night. The locals were probably drunk to the eyeballs with native beer and doped with dagga. They could have got carried away and attacked you, for goodness' sake."

Still, I felt honoured that we had been invited. Perhaps I should have felt threatened but I didn't. I decided not to tell Mum and Dad or they might put a stop to my enlightening visits to Bill and Freda.

As I grew older, some of the boys who had cars or Land Rovers would take us to Samfya for the day. We used to pile into Bill Jackman's Vauxhall Cresta, squeezed in like sardines, some of us with our legs sticking out of the rear windows. Our favourite, noisiest number was "Personality", a pop song of the time:

Over and Over, I'll be a fool for you,
Over and over, what else can I do?
'Cos you've got...
PERSONALITY!
WALK (with personality),

TALK (with personality),
SMILE (with personality),
CHARM (with personality),
LOVE (with personality)
But you've gotta great big heart!

We sang, we talked, we waved to Africans in the villages who shouted "Kwacha!" in return.

If we were lucky, we'd be offered a ride in Roy Williams' little red MG sports car. Roy was in charge of Bangweulu Water Transport, a familiar figure in the area, a real character. "Bwana Fulwe" the piccanins shouted as he tore through the villages. They loved him because he was the crocodile hunter, the saviour of Mwamfuli. One memorable Boxing Day he had shot a huge beast, a fifteen footer, which had killed a child in the village. He idled up to it in a small speedboat, killing the engine as he approached. Taking careful aim, he shot it perfectly, between the eyes. A crowd of people hauled the croc up on to the beach, ululating and singing. We were persuaded to stand by the dead animal, one foot on its head. The stench was unbearable, both from the croc and the sweaty bodies surrounding it.

Chapter 15
TAKING FLIGHT

36 Cedar Road, 1957

In 1957 it was time for my father's first home leave. The whole house had to be packed up to be put into storage and tempers frayed as we stuffed its contents into tea chests, wooden boxes and trunks. Dad was a meticulous packer and neat printer, and we still have evidence of his stencilled handiwork on sundry pieces of wood now recycled as furniture. By the end of this procedure we were exhausted, emotional and ready to go – leave-happy. We decided to celebrate by going to the Easter braaivleis at the Club, where a whole lamb was roasted on a spit and washed down with copious amounts of Castle beer.

The usual bumpy journey down to Ndola made us feel more queasy than usual and by the time we arrived at the airport Mum and I abandoned my father to the mercies of the check-in and dashed to the Ladies. The sacrificial lamb was exacting its revenge. It later transpired that the whole of Fort Rosebery had been stricken with the trots. We put our luggage and ourselves on the scales and I felt aggrieved that I was only allowed the same amount of baggage as the enormous matron who preceded me. I couldn't wait to board our tiny BOAC Viking aircraft, which more resembled a flying beetle than a sleek dragonfly. My first flight!

It was the end of the rainy season but the thunderclouds were massing as we took off at midday. We quickly lost sight of the ground and plunged into the murk, cruising at a paltry 10,000 feet in an unpressurised cabin. Our ears popped and oohs and ahs echoed round the cabin as we bucketed around the sky, hit by side winds and bumped by thermals, plunging one minute and soaring as though we were in a high-speed lift the next. The plane shuddered and groaned, its engines roaring. I got the giggles.

"Look at those pieces of string, Jude," shouted Dad, pointing to the lightning conductors streaming from the wingtips. "They're holding the plane together."

They were necessary, that was obvious, as flashes backlit the clouds, thunder rumbled and rain spattered the portholes, streaming horizontally along the steamy glass. The pilot's laconic voice came over the intercom and told us to expect "a little turbulence".

Night had fallen by the time we landed in Leopoldville, capital of the Belgian Congo, in a warm, soupy atmosphere that smelled of wood smoke, palm oil, drains and something indefinably continental, Gauloises cigarettes, perhaps? By the time we reached our hotel, a cavernous pile on the banks of the Congo River, Mum and I were beyond expressing interest in its ambience. We dashed straight to the bathroom, where I spent most of the night with stomach cramps and worse. Oblivious to cool jazz playing at the bar, the charms of the candlelit restaurant or the prospect of fillet steak and pommes frites, Mum and I stayed confined to the bedroom. Dad, desperate for some cheery company and a drink, sought the bar and found us some bottled water.

"Parlez-vous anglais, mate?" he asked the barman, undaunted by his total lack of French. "Gimme a beer."

By the time daylight broke I was on intimate terms with the bathroom, every crack on its high ceiling, the curious geckos on the wall, one noisy cricket who had somehow got indoors and the operation of the bidet, an appliance hitherto unknown to me. I heard the dawn chorus of a thousand birds and, through the palm trees, watched the sun rise over the vast, pearly expanse of the Congo River, so wide that its far bank was invisible. Fishing trawlers and pirogues sailed past our upstairs window, blackly silhouetted against the shimmer of the water, heavy with chunks of silt and papyrus reed islands floating downstream on the current. Soon a cacophony of African voices joined the raucous bird calls and the chug of vessels. We sat at a table laid with crisp white linen and twinkling cutlery; Mum and I managed to nibble a croissant.

The second stage of our journey took us to Douala, French Cameroun, for lunch. We had been flying through thick cloud which now threw wisps over the impenetrable rainforest fringing the airport. In high humidity, we dripped sweat into out chicken chasseur while ceiling fans tried, unsuccessfully, to cool the air.

Our night stop was Kano, northern Nigeria, on the southern edge of the Sahara, where we stepped off the plane into a blast of hot, dusty air, like an enormous hair dryer. There were camels by the runway, a signpost with multiple fingers showing distances and directions to the world's major cities, mud houses and hawk-nosed men swathed in djellabahs, wearing turbans. When the sun set the temperature dropped dramatically and we were cold.

By now we had developed into a jolly, friendly band of travellers on the plane. We talked to the cockpit crew when they stretched their legs, taking turns to walk round the cabin, and I privately decided that the captain was having an affair with the blonde air hostess whose mind was definitely not on her job. The couple sitting opposite us were preparing to meet the wife's parents for the first time in England and the husband kept rehearsing his opening speech.

"Hello, mother-in-law, or do I call you Mummy? How nice to meet you. Enchanté. Sorry if I'm not what you expected....." He broke off. "What do you think, darling?" he asked his wife.

We were fed meals served on china plates, with proper cutlery and a cruet set, bombarded with drinks and informed of our flight's progress with blue printed sheets – map, land speed, air speed, headwinds, position, expected landmarks to be seen through the haze, for we were now crossing the Sahara desert. We peered out of the window at a lunar landscape as we landed at El Golea, an oasis, to refuel. The airstrip was a patch of sand marked by oil drums. You expected Beau Geste or Humphrey Bogart to arrive at any moment. After lunch a sweepstake was run to estimate our arrival time in Algiers. Despite the clear skies, it was very bumpy in the air pockets and passengers were too busy filling their sick bags to calculate the variables to work out our ETA. Having an empty stomach and nothing better to do, I had a go. To my surprise, I won – a mathematical first and last – probably because most of the plane was otherwise engaged.

In Algiers we were bundled on to a bus and escorted by armed guards to our hotel. The country was in the grip of its independence struggle and the pieds noirs, the French colonials, were leaving. We drove from the airport along the coast with the jagged peaks of the High Atlas mountains our backdrop, past vineyards in which the vines were interplanted with roses. The Hotel St. George was situated in a commanding position overlooking the city and the Mediterranean below. A plaque by the entrance proclaimed it to be the site of General Eisenhower's signing of the North African peace treaty in World War II. Moorish in character and design, the place was a treasure house of massive carved doors, elegantly arched rooms, vivid mosaics and tiles, gardens and courtyards. What a pity we were cooped up – we had passed the entrance to the Kasbah and it looked dangerously fascinating.

Next day, the excitement on board was electric. Passengers had put on their best bib and tucker for the return to the mother country and, after lunch in Marseilles (the Mistral was blowing strongly) hearts and stomachs were fluttering. The pretty wife opposite was dressed in a suit, with matching gloves and handbag. Her hat kept falling off the luggage rack overhead.

"Hello, Mummy, hello, Daddy" rehearsed the husband.

My mother was particularly quiet, a sign that she was very nervous. She must have been wondering how much her son would have changed in her two years' absence, and her mother, too. True to form, Dad couldn't stop talking, even though he had to shout above the noise of the engines.

The captain's voice crackled into life on the speakers.

"If you would like to look to your right, ladies and gentlemen, you will see the white cliffs of Dover."

With one accord, everyone surged to the starboard side of the plane to catch the first glimpse of England. The plane lurched alarmingly and the captain's voice said, tersely, "Ladies and gentlemen, would you kindly return to your seats as your movements are disturbing the stability of the aircraft."

Our neighbour retrieved her hat for the umpteenth time and plonked it firmly on her head. Not long to wait now.

After four days' travel, we landed on a grey, spring afternoon at Heathrow Airport. Our little Viking taxied to a halt between sleek, turbo prop airlines. We walked down the steps and across the windy tarmac to the terminal buildings, a scruffy clump of converted Nissen huts.

There was John, looking taller and thinner than ever, his long hair flopping over his forehead, looking suave in a suede jacket. Mum hugged him fiercely and Dad, for once, was speechless with emotion. I was overcome with shyness. How grown up my brother looked. He grinned and kissed me. This was new: he used to screw up his face and proffer a cheek for his little sister. I glanced sideways and noticed that the young husband seemed to be going down well with his new in-laws.

We arrived in style at 36, Cedar Road, in a taxi. The house looked smaller and the hedge definitely needed a good trim. There was Gran, tiny and frail, standing at the front door to welcome us. She had suffered two strokes in our absence, in the winter of 1956 and her one good eye was almost completely sightless. Tears streamed down her cheeks.

For the last two years our house had become a student hostel. To help pay the mortgage and other expenses, three of John's friends had moved in during April the previous year. Their rent was 30/- (£1.50) each a week. The house bore the scars of its occupation by five people, one old, four young, for whom housekeeping was not a priority.

The first explosion came from Dad when he went to the bathroom, newspaper in hand, after breakfast the following day. He settled himself on the lav, looking forward to some peace, when a nerve-shattering shriek of alto sax burst from the wall overhead.

"Bloody hell, John! What's going on?" he yelled.

My brother, addicted to jazz, had connected the hi-fi in his bedroom to speakers all over the house, including one in the bathroom.

"It's too much, Dulce. That boy....."

My mother said nothing. She had her head down, cleaning and tidying after the mess made by her tenants. John was told to disconnect the speakers and help clear up the house. Bonfires were lit in the garden and rubbish bags filled. The phone never stopped ringing, always for John – another source of irritation for Dad.

When it rang in the hall I'd race to get there first.

"Gladstone 2184," I'd say, and wait breathlessly to ferry a message to John from one of his friends or some adoring female.

"Is she the latest?" I'd ask, handing over the phone to John as he gave me a withering look. I was such a nosey little sister, a clinging limpet. Dad grew increasingly irritated with a constantly shrilling doorbell and telephone, something he didn't have to put up with in Africa – yet. Gran relished the company and, along with the budgie, never stopped talking, eager for all the news she had missed. Sometimes she ran out of steam and sat, bemused, amidst the chaos.

I was excused house clearance and decontamination duties because I was in my Overseas School Certificate year. To make sure I kept up with academic work I was sent back to my old school, Henrietta Barnett, for a term.

My old pals greeted me with enthusiasm.

"Gosh, you look brown."

"You've got a funny accent!"

"Did you see any lions?"

"Why aren't you black?"

After the initial flurry of questions, they lost interest and resumed their discussion of more pressing topics, such as the merit of Johnnie Ray's latest record.

My old teachers were less welcoming. My Latin mistress, her jowls quivering, told me that my handwriting (also her subject) had deteriorated and, what's more, my Latin was pathetic.

"I don't know what they teach you out in the colonies," she sniffed.

There were some compensations. I could speak authoritatively about Africa in geography and beat a few people at tennis. The academic competition was as intense as ever but I knew that I was only there for a term and did not feel pressurised. One girl, a good chum, had been wearing braces on her teeth when I left and was now tall, elegant, with perfect teeth and contact lenses. Contact lenses! Juliet had blossomed and wore her hair down to her shoulders instead of confining it to plaits. She was very clued up on politics and the arts now. Yes, my London contemporaries were stylish and sophisticated and I felt like a country cousin.

John's end of year university results came out. They weren't up to scratch and, once again, Dad erupted. John decided discretion was the better part of valour and got out of the house as much as possible during the summer holidays. He had already frightened my parents to death on his Vespa scooter, named The Toy, by skidding on black ice, soon after our arrival, in the depths of rural Surrey. The phone rang at one o'clock in the morning.

My mother sat bolt upright in bed.

"It's John," she said. "Something's happened."

Dad answered the phone. Yes, Mum was right. He got in the car and drove down to Horsham to collect John from hospital. He'd come off The Toy and slid ungracefully on the icy road, knocking out a tooth and collecting gravel and tarmac down one side of his face. John said his passenger had "twitched, the moron," something he'd admonished me never to do.

One side of John's face looked normal but the other was a mangled, bloody mess. I was horrified. Seeing my shocked expression, he covered the injured side with one hand and gave me a lopsided smile.

"It's OK, Jude, I'm still handsome on this side," he said.

Dad, Tony Page and John, Cricklewood 1957

John healed quickly and, sure enough, resumed his normal appearance minus one tooth, later to be capped. Mum persuaded him that The Toy wasn't safe and he sold it. Immediately, he realized he urgently needed wheels: he still rode his bike but that was no good for ferrying round his girlfriends. Unlike the Africans, he couldn't exactly put them on his crossbar or handlebars, could he? He gave Dad the hard sell, his version of Chinese water torture, using all his charm and his considerable powers of argument. Dad was no match for this onslaught and finally surrendered. He also had not forgotten that one of his brothers had been killed in a motorbike accident. Yes, John was allowed to use Dad's precious car.

This was an act of true generosity and selflessness on my father's part. Before our arrival, Dad had ordered his first car, an ivory Consul, the first in a long line of the Ford Motor Company's cars used by our family. Dad cherished this car like a third child, polishing it to gleaming perfection and anxiously listening to every tremor of its engine.

I was half relieved, half sad at the departure of The Toy, which John had ridden with careless nonchalance. He must have held the land speed record for the stretch of the Edgware Road between Cricklewood Broadway and Marble Arch. He would weave between London buses and cars, shave past pedestrians, thread though through traffic jams and jump sets of lights, of which there are many on the Edgware Road. At one point, his mate Tony swore that John had squeezed between a bus and a bollard with no room to spare because Tony's shoulders (broader than John's) had brushed both.

My brother now sat behind the wheel of his father's car, weaving through traffic as though he were still on his old Vespa, holding forth on a range of subjects, cracking jokes and gesticulating passionately with his free hand. I wondered if there wasn't Italian blood somewhere in our ancestry.

Inevitably, he pranged the car in small, tangible ways – a dented door here, a bent bumper there. The final straw occurred when we went up to Hampstead one evening to a coffee bar. London was emerging from its postwar grimness with a rash of coffee bars, skiffle groups and hamburger joints, which we considered groovy. John had even painted a mural in the Two I's coffee bar in Soho, haunt of Tommy Steele, one of my teenage pop idols. Parking on Hampstead High Street was always a battle, if not impossible. John reversed up a side street and eased the car uphill into a vacant spot, edged by Victorian, cast-iron bollards.

"See me in, Jude," he instructed.

I stood in the road and waved him in, running hither and yon as he turned the wheel. Crunch. He'd hit a bollard. Oh, blast.

"You cretin! What the hell were you doing?"

I hadn't seen the bollard, probably because, being a vain teenager, I wasn't wearing my specs.

"You can tell Dad this time," said John. "It's all your fault."

John was banned from driving the Consul, a temporary measure thanks to Mum.

Spring turned into summer and our road looked leafy once more. Thank goodness. In winter the pollarded plane trees, their bark dappled and peeling, always looked as if they had a nasty disease. The house was beginning to look more like its old, pre-student self. John's friends began to creep back to see him, now they were more sure of a favourable reception from the parents.

One day I answered the doorbell to find a tramp, his back turned towards me, leaning over our front gate. His long, black, curly hair coiled over the collar of a filthy paint-spattered raincoat. Panicking, I was about to call Dad when the figure turned round, beamed and asked, in cultured tones "Is John in?" This was Brian, undergraduate of the Slade School of Art, artist, entrepreneur and eccentric, erstwhile student tenant of number 36. The second friend to appear was Tony, a northern jack-the-lad, raven-haired, broad-shouldered and a fabulous dancer who improved my jiving skills. Tony scandalised my mother by appearing shirtless for meals in the hot weather. Brian was a non-student friend, a wide boy with a spotty face and a manic laugh. He had astounded John's friends at parties by throwing flick knives at the garden fence and later married a girl the boys called The Haddock (because of her fish face), moved to Jersey and ran a pub.

Then there were the girls. Patsy, the Jewish heiress from Porchester Gate who drove a baby blue Ford Anglia, holidayed in Venice and had worked on a kibbutz. Her father owned a string of woollen mills which supplied Marks and Spencer with textiles and he adored his daughter. Dad called her Patsy Rock (short for Rockefeller). At Passover, it was a tradition that a matzo wafer should be hidden somewhere in the house and the person who found it be given a prize. One year Patsy was told that if she found it the prize would be a Greek island.

237

My brother was tolerated by the family, after charming his way in, particularly as they were under the impression that he was an unorthodox Jew.

Patsy had half-supplanted Renee, my brother's faithful girlfriend of some years' standing who was now safely rusticated near Reading. There was also busty Jill, an Eng. Lit. student who smoked Balkan Sobranie cigarettes and acted in student productions with Tom Courtenay – and others. I was sometimes taken to the Student Union by John where, expecting stimulating intellectual conversation, I was disappointed to find his cronies smoking and playing cards.

Summer wore on and there was a heat wave which happened, as they do, before school broke up for the holidays. I had forgotten how sticky and smelly London could be in hot weather. My parents had rented a television set to watch Wimbledon and sat glued to it each afternoon, impervious to the heat, the telephone, the doorbell, an atom bomb. I would arrive home, dragging my satchel, puce in the face and have to climb in through the front window, disgusted. I squeezed past John's bike, the bag of tennis racquets and some boxes in the narrow hall to announce my arrival – not that they noticed. John was entrusted with a key but I was not, a decision which was sexist, ageist and every other -ist but one I never questioned.

Chapter 16
THE RETURN OF THE PRODIGAL SON

Second house, Fort Rosebery

All too soon, my summer in London drew to a close. It was time for the long flight back to school. Mum and Dad were following by sea, bringing John with them. He had decided to take time off from his university course and had been allowed to do so by the Psychology Department. My brother must have used his full battery of charm and persuasive powers to secure his release. Perhaps the fact that our house was to be sold helped to decide the matter. Dad simply couldn't keep it going from such a long distance, besides which he still had his children's education to complete and pay for. John's long-term girlfriend, the ever faithful Renee, was snapping at his heels and threatening to follow him to Africa. Gran was to go and live with the Hampstead relatives – more persuasion on Mum's part. Big changes were afoot. My parents preferred life in Africa to life in postwar England and hoped to settle there one day, after their government contracts had expired – or so they told me later. Family plans were not discussed with John and me. I said goodbye to my school friends, knowing that I would see them again one day when I secured a place at an English university, one thing I was determined to do. There were no opportunities for further education in Northern Rhodesia. My good pal Joyce and family were to meet me at Lusaka Airport for the remainder of the holidays before incarceration prior to big exams in November.

My parents and John followed me in the autumn, by sea. A Union Castle boat again, then a long drive of several days up from Cape Town to home on their personal Great Trek.

The Ford Consul now sported a few Dad touches – a sun visor and Venetian blinds in the rear window. John and Dad shared the driving, through the Berg then the Karoo, with its long, straight roads. They didn't like the skyscrapers and urban canyons of central Johannesburg, or its hustling, menacing atmosphere. In Potchefstroom, a dorp in the Transvaal, they asked where the nearest café was and were given blank looks by xenophobic Afrikaners. Finally, they made it to Lusaka and looked in on me at school. They got lost in the dark and stopped to ask for directions from a white man, another Afrikaner.

"You just go up the hill," he pointed, "until you see a flaming sword, ja." He pronounced the "w" in "sword" He was describing the illuminated sword which lit up the Cenotaph, in front of the Secretariat, the Legislative Council offices also know irreverently as The Biscuit Box. "After that you turn left, hey, and you come to the Kabulonga Road. The school's at the top – you can't miss it."

*The Cenotaph with its "flaming sword" and Secretariat,
aka The Biscuit Box, Lusaka*

I was so excited when they arrived – it was the first time my parents had visited me at school. John and Dad emerged wearily from the car and I gave them each a big hug. The car was packed to bursting point with bags and cases and the roof rack was piled high. It was a wonder the springs hadn't given way.

"Where's Mum?" I asked.

A little voice squeaked from the direction of the back seat – my mother, almost submerged by a mountain of luggage.

The family looked round the school for the first time.

"Why, the boarding house looks quite comfortable," said Mum.

"What! You must be joking. It's a cell block. We freeze in winter and roast in summer."

I could have added that the ceiling fans in our prep room wobbled alarmingly and nearly flew off the ceiling when they were turned up high. The prefect always put them on the lowest setting, which hardly shifted the air at all.

The party continued on the final leg of the trip, going the long way round via Kasama. On the road who should they see but Gordon, hitch-hiking up to the coast. He had been expelled from the country, PI'd – declared a prohibited immigrant – so he was off to Australia to find Psitch. He must have upset some bigwig with a plummy voice. Poor Gordon, he never could keep his trap shut. He had no money and goodness knows how he was going to pay for his sea passage.

My parents had been forced to travel through the Northern Province because the Luapula River had flooded spectacularly and the ferry couldn't operate.

Top: *Great North Road*
Centre: *Gordon, hitch-hiking*

Worse still, this meant that Fort Rosebery ran out of beer. This was a crisis of mammoth proportions and there were rumblings of discontent. We already had to pay Congo Basin duty because of our location north of the Pedicle road plus extra for groceries because we lived far from the points of supply. People were fed up. It was this bloody Federation, they affirmed. We lived in a country where copper produced 95% of Northern Rhodesia's wealth and where did it go? To Salisbury, that's where, to be spent on health, education, transport and communications. Our province, all Native Authority land, was low on the Federal Government's list of priorities. We had one doctor to cover an area the size of Wales, crummy roads, no telecommunications apart from the Police radio telephone and transmitter, a primary school in a converted house, no church and no proper hospital. If the Luapula flooded we were sunk.

This episode prompted the powers-that-be to introduce an air service to our province. The old airstrip out of town was resurfaced, regraded, and we were given a little air service once a week in the shape of the DC3, a Dakota. At last we children could fly to Lusaka to school, which we loved despite the noise, heat, discomfort and the fact that the luggage looked as though it could fall on you at any minute, being held in a net in the corner of the cabin. As we didn't fly very high it was fascinating to look at Africa's sunburnt surface from the air.

We moved across the road, into a larger, U-shaped bungalow which had been occupied by the former DC,

Governor flies over N.R. flood area

FORT ROSEBERY, Wednesday.

THREE "VIP" aircraft touched down at the tiny dirt airstrip here this morning within two hours of each other. On board were the Governor of Northern Rhodesia, Sir Evelyn Hone, a planeload of homecoming schoolchildren and two tons of badly needed supplies.

More schoolchildren were shipped across the two-mile wide Chembe Ferry in Government tugs today, to make it the best day the water weary European community has had for several watterlogged weeks.

But the only reliable way to get into Fort Rosebery is to fly in — a motor mechanic from Kitwe took more than a day to get to the Northern Province town by road earlier this week and spent five miserable hours stuck on a sandbank in the middle of Chembe Ferry.

He had to wait for an African canoe to take him off.

Europeans in the district now fear that one road still open to Fort Rosebery — the dirt track from Samfya at the south end of Lake Bangweulu will be washed out if there is more heavy rain. And the road to Kasama is now cut in three places.

A Government official here told of a nightmare three hours through mud and water on the 50-mile trip from Samfya to Fort Rosebery.

With food supplies running out, today's supply plan came just in time to boost stocks. Powdered milk, flour and paraffin are the number one priorities for the white population.

It was the third supply plane to land here within three weeks.

Mr. Peter Hedges, managing director of CBC, the firm organising the "airlifts," said today that it was "almost certain" that another plane would be going up to Fort Rosebery next Wednesday.

"But we are well short of our monthly output," he said, "normally we send about 40 tons up—now we are airlifting only eight tons in a month."

Sir Evelyn Hone's trim little four seater monoplane flew over the flood area today. The Governor was accompanied by the Provincial Commissioner, Mr. G. F. Tredwell, the Acting Minister of Native Affairs, Mr. L. Bean and the Governor's senior Press officer, Mr. B. Clare.

Later he had talks with Mr. Tredwell on the flood situation before returning to Lusaka.

Residents in Fort Rosebery, Samfya and Kawambwa are "putting up" with the rigours of isolation.

Another two months

But it has been six weeks since they were cut off from the south, and most people feel they have at least another two months in "exile."

"These floods are the worst we have ever known," said one man. "The European houses are not threatened, but hundreds and hundreds of Africans have lost their homes or drowned in the floodwaters."

The Africans are still threatened with famine. Stocks of mealie meal are running low and the main diet is now the root crop casava. But the bulk of this season's crop has been completely ruined by floodwaters.

Final comment on the whole situation came from an irate film fan. "We get a cinema show tonight—it is only a once weekly show—and what do they give us?

"Yul Brynner in "The Buccaneers" — nothing but water all over the b—— place. . . ."

Flood report in newspaper, November 1957

with three bedrooms to accommodate all of us. This was old by African standards – 20 or 30 years – and concocted from a mish-mash of architectural styles. Its small, wooden casement windows with eyebrows resembled those of an English country cottage and, no doubt, the built-in dresser in a spacious dining room harked back to some District Commissioner's former life. There were roses in the garden, frangipani bushes, bougainvillaea covering the thatched carport, a rondavel on top of an anthill and an incipient screen of pine trees. Dad revved up into full gardening mode and the house was soon fringed by more flowerbeds and some fantastic moonflowers, also called evening glory, which opened on cue at sunset to let forth their sensuous perfume. Roses twined round the windows beside the bonnet-shaped, blotched blooms of Dutchman's pipe. Despite the fact that we would not be there to see them fully grown, Dad planted many shrubs and trees – jacarandas, poinsettias and flamboyants to add to the existing msasas.

However, the screened corridor that ran round the back of the house, the large but bare kitchen and the tin roof were definitely African. While all the wood looked attractive it was riddled with white ants and the ceiling was made of a cloth of some sort, probably canvas. We were sitting reading after supper one evening, Mum with her customary books, cigarettes and fly swat, when the lounge door fell in, imploded – destroyed from within by termites. The roof space was a haven for thumping, scrabbling, squeaking wildlife – bush babies, mice, the odd snake and a colony of bats. Periodically a stray bat would lose its way and flap into the living room, where John and I would try to stun the creature – not easy – with tennis racquets before removing it outside. The first time, John picked it up for closer inspection and was bitten.

"Oh God, you'll get rabies!"

"Don't be silly, Mum," said John, wrapping a hankie round his finger. "The little buggers have got sharp teeth, though."

We acquired more animals. The community had woken up to the fact that the family were a soft touch when it came to pets and we were constantly looking after people's dogs and cats, sometimes permanently. We often had Sammy, the Norths' young spaniel, who got temporarily blinded by a spitting cobra in the garden. Kay, the departing nursing sister, gave us Maxie to rehouse. He was a large, piebald cat of with a sweet disposition and Dad found him a home at a PWD road camp, 45 miles away.

Some months later an emaciated cat came yowling to the kitchen door.

"He's got the same markings as Maxie," Mum remarked.

The skeletal cat rubbed itself against her legs, purring.

"My God, it is Maxie! He's walked all the way home, through the bush."

"Can you believe it," said Dad, shaking his head. "Well I never."

We couldn't turn him away again but by this time we had Figaro, another tom cat. The two did not get on. Maxie was found a home with some bachelors, a few doors away and soon regained his former girth and contentedness.

Figaro had belonged to our neighbours, who were leaving Northern Rhodesia for good. (There were two destinations for emigrants: Down South and Overseas. The Merrys were going Down South.) He was a beautiful, fluffy marmalade cat of imperious mien and settled in so well it was as if he had always belonged. He sorted Blondie's attempts to chase him with a well-aimed swipe of the paw. Figaro didn't curl up to sleep, he sprawled, in a regal manner – on the top shelf of the larder, on the mantelpiece or a bookshelf, knocking ornaments, tins and glasses flying. On all such occasions he lay like a miniature tiger, swishing his plumy tail gently, looking down at the shattered article with a twitch of his white nose and a waggle of his long, magnificent whiskers, quite unperturbed, as if to say "oh dear, did I do that?" before putting his head between his paws to go to sleep. His other favourite kipping spot was inside the lid of Mum's African sewing basket. When he emerged from his afternoon nap he changed from being a peaceful cashmere ball into a killing machine. Slitty-eyed, he would stalk out of the screen door, tail up, on the hunt for birds, lizards and chameleons. At night, the pupils in his yellow eyes grew huge and black as he waged war on sundry rodents in house and garden. A merciless hunter, Figgy was fond of bringing in the mutilated spoils of the chase – a tail here, an ear and entrails there – for Mum's approval.

This cat had the unnerving habit of flinging himself at the zinc gauze of the dining room fly screen, like a flying squirrel, to attract our attention. He then released his claws gradually, paw by paw, with a loud, metallic crunch which put our teeth on edge.

"Figgy wants some lunch" said John.

"Bloody cat," replied Dad, who nevertheless always got up to let Figgie in. "Still, he's smart. How does he know

Top: *Figaro in Mum's sewing basket lid*
Bottom: *The lordly Figaro on Mum's bed*

that these screens are the only sliding ones in the house? Come on, then, Fig. Come ON!" as the cat teetered on the lowered fly screen, taking a good look from this height at the food on the table.

Dad secretly loved Figaro, even though he swore that the moggie's long hair made him sneeze. Dad was allergic to cat hair, among other things, and had the most spectacular, long-lived head colds seen in Central Africa.

It was beneath Figgy's dignity to mew, though he could sit outside a window and give you a pitiful silent miaow. When my parents were eventually transferred to Lusaka, the cat travelled down after their home leave by plane, in Mum's sewing basket.

"He was the best behaved passenger on the aircraft," said the air hostess when we collected him.

John's arrival broadened my horizons no end. He brought music in the shape of his records and hi-fi and an bottomless pit of jokes. I was his constant companion, a situation he bore with fortitude, and he came with me to the Club to play tennis, even if he did whack me under the lip, above my chin, by mistake one afternoon. I dripped blood on to the sand.

"Look! You've gone right through the skin!" I exclaimed, waggling my lower lip to demonstrate. I still have the scar.

"Don't be so dramatic, Jude," he replied. "I haven't, have I? Oh well, you shouldn't have been standing so close, you clot."

My lower lip swelled.

"Don't worry," said Pete, one of the young District Assistants. "It actually makes you look quite sexy, like Brigitte Bardot."

"Who's she?" I looked blank.

John drove us willingly into the bush or to the lake and was fascinated by the birds, insects and small animals that surrounded us. He always carried his camera and would frequently screech to halt, jettisoning me on to the dashboard.

"Quick, Jude. You see it, there on the bushes? Go and get it and I'll take a photo."

Off I would trot to collect the brightly coloured bug, locust, butterfly, praying mantis, whatever. I drew the line at caterpillars (the hairy ones out here could give you a nasty rash) and spiders.

My brother had to be the one who discovered the nest of a bird-eating spider on our front lawn. He was delighted and got his camera ready. I wasn't too happy about this.

"Jude, get a stick, will you? Look, you can just see his legs poking out."

I could indeed. The spider was under its little trap door of homemade cement, with two hairy legs protruding.

"Give it a poke."

I gingerly prodded the spider. A couple more legs came out, then retreated.

"Again," urged John.

The same thing happened.

"Come on Jude, don't be a sissy. Try again."

I prodded once more. The spider emerged and rushed in a flurry of hairy legs up the bamboo pole. Terrified, I shrieked, dropped the stick and ran.

"What did you do that for? You twit."

"What was I supposed to do, wait until he ran up my arm? Fat chance."

I was unrepentant. I still remembered that scene from "King Solomon's Mines" where Deborah Kerr goes into the bush to change her clothes, coming out with a humongous spider on her dress, upon which Stewart Granger says "Excuse me, madam, I think you have something on your skirt" and she looks down and faints. No, I wasn't taking any chances.

We took Blondie for walks. John couldn't move more than two paces without his cigarettes and lighter: halfway down the golf course he'd pat his shirt pocket and send me back home for them.

"You fetch and carry far too much for John," said Mum. It was true. We all did. He really was the Prodigal Son.

I was in my Overseas School Certificate year. I'd missed a term with going to England but was relying on my good memory and swatting technique to get me through. By "spotting" questions and the revision lessons covering sections of the syllabus I had missed I was arrogant enough to think I would get through and pass with good enough marks to qualify me for entrance into the Sixth Form. Even so, by the end of September I was worried. There were huge gaps in my knowledge, particularly in Biology and French Grammar.

"You weel never pass your School Certificate. You 'ave not put in zee work – pouf," said the Hungarian French mistress.

This made me determined to prove the old bat wrong. Still, there was no doubt I would have to work really hard to catch up.

Hysteria swept through the dorm. The cell block inmates felt that supernatural forces were at work. Sessions were held with an ouija board in the anteroom to the bath cubicles, which had no windows, and some girls claimed that the glass had moved of its own accord, spelling names and predicting marriage, children and other disasters. I was not convinced.

Mary, a sensitive soul, was convinced we had a ghost in our dorm.

"I can hear it moving around," she said, "but I'm too scared to get out of bed. It sort of squeaks."

"We'll sit up and catch it," said Midge, always the bravest. We duly pushed our beds together in a couple of cubicles and pulled open the green curtains (NRG). We waited in the dim, blue light of the ceiling night bulb. I felt my eyelids droop.

Next morning I woke with a start. Oh dear, I hadn't stayed awake. Wonder if the others had?

Midge sniffed. "Trust you to nod off."

"So did you see the ghost?" I asked.

"No, but we heard it, didn't we? Did you know that you grind your teeth when you're asleep? What a racket. It's you, Jude, you're the ghost!"

How embarrassing.

Rosalie and Michelle weren't expecting to do well in their exams. They knew they hadn't worked hard enough and they weren't the least bit bothered. They just wanted to scrape through and do a secretarial course in Salisbury when they left school. As long as they passed Maths and

Eng. Lang., that would be enough, so why sit all the other boring subjects?

Faking illness was one way out. A couple of girls tried the hot water bottle wheeze to give themselves high temperatures but the wily matrons soon sussed that one out.

"How about fainting?" said Rosalie. "I know how to do it. You hold your breath really hard, stick two fingers in your mouth and shut your eyes. Then hold your breath! If you concentrate, you'll pass out. I'll show you. Just stand behind me, somebody, to hold me tightly round the stomach."

Sure enough, Rosalie fainted. When we were sure she'd got her technique just right, we dragged Matron in.

"Matron, Matron! You must come, hey! Rosalie's sick – she's as white as a sheet and she's passed out in the dorm."

Rosalie, an ash blonde with a pale skin, now looked clammy and had turned a convincing shade of green. Matron whisked her off to sick bay and she missed the History exam.

"Yea! I did it!" Rosalie was as pleased as punch.

The rest of us struggled on, without reprieve. Then one morning Jill, the girl who had befriended me on my first train journey to school, woke up and couldn't speak. She had been struck dumb.

At first we thought she was putting it on. But no, she honestly could not speak. Jill was a clever girl but also very sporty, with a trail of boyfriends. She had been practising hard for the tennis singles and had neglected her studies. The teachers had high hopes for her which Jill was beginning to realize she couldn't fulfil: the pressure had pushed her over the edge. She, too was put in to the sick bay; the school doctor called and, it was rumoured, a psychiatrist. After a couple of weeks she came back into the dorm and gradually regained her speech, speaking with a stutter. She passed her exams but not well enough to qualify for the Sixth Form which would have lead her to university.

October came. The heat was appalling and the rains were late. We sweltered in the airless prep room and kept a wary eye on the wobbly ceiling fan above out heads. Our lessons were mainly revision and we were given study days off. Some of our day bug friends took pity on us boarders and took us off to farms for a swim in water tank swimming pools. Cattle grazed listlessly in parched fields of scratchy stubble. The air smelled of dust, generator diesel fumes and silage. Veronica invited me into the gloom of her farmhouse, which was full of massive, dark furniture in the typical Afrikaner style. There were stinkwood coffee tables with ball and claw legs, cane-seated rocking chairs and high, double beds as big as barns. Battered animal skins lay on the floor and we were plied with scones and koeksisters. Packs of rangy farm dogs barked and covered us with drool, panting in the heat. Ouma sat on the stoep, knitting. Knitting, in this heat! I was shown a creamy-white Brahmin bull, the farmer's prize animal. It had broken its leg but Veronica's dad had successfully splinted the break. I was encouraged to run my hand down the silky foreleg and feel the bump of knitted bone. We drove down to the Kafue for picnics in the mopane forest. Twenty miles south of Lusaka, the plateau dropped between cliffs and forested hills to the flood plain of the Kafue River, a tributary of the Zambezi. We might be lucky enough to get a boat trip on the river and feel a gentle breeze fan our hot cheeks.

My good friend, Joyce, was a lifesaver. She had arrived at Jean Rennie a couple of terms after me and was a day pupil, a "day bug". Her parents taught at Munali, the elite high school for African boys. They had been attached to Lubwa, the same Church of Scotland mission which Kenneth Kaunda, later to be the first president of an independent Zambia, had attended. Joyce's mum was a busy lady as she taught all day and half the night at evening classes in Kabwata township. Our school secretary lived at Munali and would take me over to Joyce's sometimes in her Morris Minor. We would go the back way, skirting round the eastern side of Lusaka Airport on a dirt road. Mrs. Martin drove slowly over the corrugations – bump, bump, bump, lurch, lurch, lurch – as we tried to suppress our giggles.

At last the rains came – oh, what blessed relief. The rain gods thoughtfully timed their arrival to coincide with the end of the exams.

We were elated as the holidays approached but sad, too. Some of my good friends would be leaving, to go on to secretarial college or to work, some to complete their education overseas. Just a few of us would be left to board and carry on into the Sixth Form. I hated the prospect of another two years as a boarder but, in my heart of hearts, I knew I had to continue if I wanted to go to a good university. I had passed my school cert well enough to get Matric Exemption, enabling me to go to a South African university. I had even been accepted at Cape Town and I knew that Mum wanted me to go there. Cape Town was a dream city for her. But I was uneasy with the thought of continuing my education in South Africa. I was a fun-loving teenager, not a political animal

256

in the slightest but I was unwittingly developing a social conscience. I was not happy with apartheid. No, it had to be England.

Chapter 17
SUNBURNT, MOONSTRUCK

Ladies' Garden Party, Governor General's visit, 1958

Joyce and I sat in the courtyard round the back of our house, trying to dry our hair away from prying eyes. Wisps of boring, brown thatch had escaped from my set of bristly rollers, designed to capture and control unmanageable hair. They had failed miserably with mine. Joyce's hair was that wonderful Celtic glossy blue-black and her eyes were sapphire blue. A bobby pin dropped on the grass, followed by a roller.

"Damn," I muttered.

As I bent to pick it up John walked round the corner. He looked at us, grinning.

"It Came From Outer Space," he boomed in a hollow voice.

"Oh, shut up," we said in unison.

We were going through the usual pre-dance ritual. Hair-drying would be followed by combing out, teasing and lacquering. Only then, with rock-hard coiffures, would we bathe, apply make-up and dress to kill. The one tiny bathroom in our house would be occupied for some time, to Dad's disgust.

"For God's sake, it's only a hop at the Club!"

Joyce had come up for the holidays and we were on red alert for fresh talent.

John played the role of chaperon, hiding himself away in the record player room and acting as DJ. Although I thought him slim and elegant, as did my girlfriends, he was acutely self-conscious about his skinny legs and never wore shorts. In his charcoal-grey slacks, shirts with sleeves rolled up to the elbows and sunglasses he stuck out like a sore thumb among the Hooray Henrys. His wit far exceeded theirs, though Will gave him a run for his money.

Will was one of the latest intake of District Assistants. They were older than their predecessors, some were graduates and others had seen National Service. Will had been in the Royal Navy and we met in a round-robin tennis tournament, Rooineks versus Hairybacks. He nodded hello in a taciturn fashion as we squared up to our opponents. It was nearly noon and the sun beat down relentlessly as we dived round the sandy court. My partner virtually ignored me but I noticed that he was tall, fair-haired and very fit, with well-muscled, sinewy legs. He played hard, if erratically, and served several aces but his unhappy blue eyes flashed when we lost a point. We walked round the court in virtual silence. To my surprise, we won the game and ran to the net to shake hands with our opponents and each other. Will brushed his floppy hair back from a sweaty forehead, his face softened and he smiled. I noticed that his face was sunburnt and his nose was peeling.

"Well done, partner," he said.

He'd been in town a few months by the time Joyce came up. He was a big hit with the girls and had broken a couple of hearts already.

Will loped up to us at the dance, flashing his most charming smile.

"Aren't you going to introduce us?" he asked.

He shook hands with Joyce, who was wearing a kingfisher blue dress which complemented her eyes. She dimpled, and looked up at Will, fluttered her long black eyelashes and blushed. The two of them got on like a house on fire and I could hear Joyce's silvery laugh at the far end of the room. Will was delighted to find out that Joyce was Scottish, as he played the bagpipes and could dance the Eightsome Reel. We all went on to the bachelors' quarters to continue dancing when they finished at the Club. For the rest of the holidays, Joyce and Will were inseparable. A gang of us spent happy hours playing tennis, dancing, walking or playing very bad golf. Once John had got his record player rigged up at work, where a generator supplied electricity, we were really in business.

John had found a job as Field Secretary at the new Health and Nutrition scheme set up in the town by the World Health Organisation. It needed electricity for its lab machines and John took his hi-fi equipment up there so that we could dance in the porticoed corridors at night. The record player brought the music to life and was so much better than the tinny sound of the old wind-up gramophone. He also had a darkroom and I would spend hours as his lab assistant, bathed in a red light, enduring the stuffiness and stink of chemicals while John developed and enlarged the photos he took for work. He wrote a letter to Gran which is legible as it was typewritten:

Box 55
Fort Rosebery.

29th July, 1958

I am afraid that I have been very remiss in not writing to you but I hope that you will forgive me as I suffer very badly from chronic idleness – due, of course, to vitamin deficiency and congenital indisposition.....

There have only been two highlights in the otherwise monotonous routine of life here. I expect, in the interest that you have always had in the subject in England (boxing!) that you would have enjoyed highlight no 1, the impromptu Luapula title fight between "Killer" K and Battersea Boy P – enfant terrible of the Fort Rosebery Boma. No decision was reached but expert observers have it that it was a win on points for Killer.

John was referring to a punch-up in the Club between one of the young District Assistants who had been romancing an accountant's wife. The DA was transferred soon afterwards.

Highlight number 2 is the arrival for a long stay of a YOUNG FEMALE (John's old girlfriend, now living in Salisbury). So long have I been in rustic seclusion that it took me some time to recognize the creature.....

Unfortunately, Judy will soon be returning for yet another of these inordinately long holidays and my peace will be shattered. She seems to be enjoying life rather more these days and her letters don't sound quite so much like Russian tragedies. Mother has stuck up on the living room wall some of the child's adolescent daubs and the result is, of course, appalling.

My job continues as usual with not too much work at the moment though. All this will soon change, however, when the new £900 instrument (for blood analysis) arrives in a few days; from then on I shall have to work like a slave as it will require very much manipulation to yield very little.

Patricia is now in Israel and I have had a letter from there, I but I don't know as yet how this Iraq business will affect her.....

All my love
John

John's expertise with the camera proved useful at agricultural shows, parties and the remarkable occasion of the visit of Earl Dalhousie, Governor General of the Federation. He looked like someone out of a Gilbert and Sullivan operetta, in full dress uniform, sparkling brass buttons, narrow black trousers with a red strip running down the outside seam, helmet topped by white ostrich plumes. John took a cine film of his arrival in the DC3 at our little airstrip, kicking up clouds of dust as it landed, and the reception that followed. The great and good ladies of the town in smart hats, New Look dresses, high heels and white gloves queued up to be presented.

*The Governor General's
Visit, 1958
(Photos: John Staddon)*

In all the urban areas the climate is healthy. It can, in fact, be described as healthy throughout the whole Territory if reasonable precautions are observed."

"A Brief Guide to Northern Rhodesia", 1960, chapter on Living
Conditions

The Health and Nutrition Scheme monitored the health of the local population, in whom malaria, TB, venereal disease, river blindness and other chronic diseases were prevalent. They paid particular attention to the children, who were weighed, examined and tested for various conditions. John walked around me in the living room at home, conducting a mock examination in the manner of his Danish boss. He stroked his chin thoughtfully.

"Yes. 'ere we 'ave ze prize specimen of European teenager. No sway back, no spleen, no hernia. I zeenk we vill put 'er on ze skin fold machine to show ze Africans vat a fat European looks like," he said, pinching the flesh on my upper arms.

"Ow, that hurt." I aimed for a punch in John's ribs.

"Children, children," said Mum mildly, not looking up from the newspaper. Now we had an air service she was avidly reading the Northern News, pencil at the ready, to finish the crossword.

Two research doctors, one Danish, one Scottish, ran the "Health and Nuts" outfit and, being bachelors, were seized upon by the local matrons for drinks, tennis games and social stimulation. The PA matrons were particularly fond of the Scot, Fergus McCullough, a handsome man with strawberry blond curls and a beard but were incensed when he chose the Mauritian wife of the general store manager as his tennis partner. They were quite a sight on the court: he an energetic, bearded redhead, she lean, darkly tanned and elegant, wearing sunglasses. The PA ladies desperately wanted to take the Scot to their collective bosom, a doctor, an eligible bachelor who would have been perfect for their English rose daughters yet he chose to consort with a Frenchwoman, whose husband was in trade, to boot! Tongues wagged.

During the holidays John took me on occasional forays into the bush, which is where I met Lady Lorna Gore-Browne, one of the WHO field workers. She was the estranged wife of Sir Stewart Gore-Brown, owner of the Shiwa Ngandu estate and baronial mansion featured in Christina Lamb's book "The Africa House". Dad knew Sir Stewart from his days in Kasama, when he would buy bananas from the estate for his workers. They would sit on the Shiwa verandah and share a beer, an unlikely pair, cockney Jack and the aristocrat transplanted in Africa.

Lorna was a clever woman, a free spirit who adored my brother. At that time she was living in a mud hut on stilts by the Luapula River.

"Ah, little John!" she cried, perched on the top step of her rondavel as we poled up in the Land Rover with fresh supplies. She ran lightly down the steps, like a young girl, and kissed my tall brother (he was 6'3") on both cheeks. To her he was always "little John". She treated us to a delicious curry lunch, with wild bananas, tiny chopped tomatoes, desiccated coconut, sultanas and homemade mango chutney as side dishes and crushed, local rock salt among the condiments. She pointed out types of local flora used for chronic ailments, including the gonorrhoea tree.

"The Africans use the bark for curing VD and malaria but, as the symptoms are so similar, they don't know which one they've got," she said languidly, with a twinkle in her eye.

A few months later, poor John knew which one he'd got, all right. He had been on tour in the Bangweulu swamps with the Scot, vaccinating villagers against smallpox. They had sat outside after supper, in the relative cool of the evening, waiting for the second doctor to arrive. The mosquitoes were out in force but no, after a few drinks Fergus was determined to sit it out to wait for his colleague. Out of politeness, John stayed. Ten days later he came down with a vicious dose of pneumonia. He continued to deteriorate as the government doctor, the same man who had dug the jiggers out of my foot, had just told John to take aspirin and promptly driven off on tour. John lay limply in bed, coughing and sneezing, with a high temperature, refusing all food. He only weighed 126lbs and was six feet tall so had no fat to sustain him. Mum was frantic. In desperation, she asked one of the Catholic mission's White Sisters to visit the house.

"He not only has double pneumonia but malaria as well," the Sister pronounced. She prescribed antibiotics and paludrine and had John admitted to the cottage hospital, a former DC's house on the opposite bank of the Mansa River.

Poor John – and poor Mum. She was worried but so relieved that John was in hospital. She knew how to treat malaria – after all, she and my father had both experienced it and it had indirectly led to the death of my grandfather. The only member of our family that had escaped it was me. To have pneumonia on top of the

266

scourge of the tropics was very bad luck indeed and John emerged from his double dose of illness looking thinner than ever. Philip, my latest flame, wrote to me at school to tell me that he'd visited John, who "hadn't looked too good". Knowing Phil's capacity for understatement, this really had me worried and I was so pleased to find my brother fully recovered on my next holiday, if paler and definitely thinner after six weeks off work. Mum made sure we took our malaria prophylactics every morning and they were put on the breakfast table, next to the salt and pepper.

Three years was a long time to stay in the bush with no respite. Sometimes Mum's lovely Scottish boss had taken her and my father on trips to local waterfalls – Musonda, or Lumangwe – and one day they decided to take some local leave and visit John Hannah, the young District Officer who had been their former neighbour. He had been transferred to Mporokoso, in the north-east of Luapula Province, where he lived in a cavernous house overlooking the airstrip.

Dad decided that John's house needed a flush toilet in addition to the long drop down the garden.

Enlisting the help of a few PA labourers, he started groundworks for the project in a small extension to the house. However, he omitted to tell my mother of this fact. Setting off for a night time expedition to the existing outdoor PK, she fell into the trench that the workers had made and broke her leg. There followed an excruciating journey on bad roads to a mission, where nuns splinted her leg, then a further 150 miles back to Fort Rosebery for the break to be set. Six weeks later the bones had not knitted properly, poor Mum's leg was re-broken and reset. Her right knee was never the same after that and she never really forgave Dad.

By this time Titus had taken a second wife, turned to drink and was pinching things in a big way. He had to go. We now employed Zebron, a tall, handsome man with a goatee beard. He was a good cook but some of his dishes tasted a little weird. We all had upset stomachs. Our consumption of gin and whisky shot up alarmingly and Dad started to mark liquor levels in the bottles. Zebron didn't last long and was given the heave-ho, when the gardener revealed that he had been putting muti into our meals "to make the bwana like him"! Even though one servant might know that another was a bad lot there would be no snitching or tale-telling while the first person was still employed.

Along with most other Europeans in town, my parents treated their staff well. The houseboy and family were given a kaya on the premises, uniforms, free water and electricity (when it arrived in the town) or a lamp plus paraffin, candles, firewood and monthly rations: mealie meal, sugar, flour, salt, soap and sometimes tea. They were usually allotted a patch of land on which to grow vegetables, given medical help and food from our own table every day. Mum sat on the Race Relations Committee and my parents helped out local people in many different, quiet and often practical ways. Unlike some do-gooders, they didn't make a song and dance about it. I particularly remember Dad teaching his PWD staff how to grow their own vegetables, make small items of furniture and collect material for compost for their gardens. He was a soft touch when they wanted to borrow money or take time off work.

"Please, bwana, I want to go to my brother's funeral."

"How many brothers do you have, for God's sake? You only went to one last month!"

"Plenty brothers, bwana."

Now, in the emancipated noughties, this behaviour would be labelled patronizing, paternalistic and racist. I am just telling it how it was to us and many other expatriates. To quote my brother John:

How racist was colonial Rhodesia? Not very, considering. The Mansa Mission folk set the tone by their great interest in the local people. There were no racial laws, like South African apartheid. There was no legal segregation. Criminals were tried in both British and tribal courts, or so I heard. On the other hand, Fort Rosebery had a little club with, as I recall, only European (i..e. white) members, but the club was very modest in its facilities: tennis courts, and a bar, basically. I don't think there was any great demand from the locals to join – nothing like the toxic situation that George Orwell wrote about so influentially in Burmese Days.

So were the Africans treated as equal to the Europeans? Well, no. The Bemba culture was pre-literate, most local Africans were completely uneducated, in a Western sense. They might well have been much cleverer about local matters but the whites had no way to see that. Superstition was rampant among the locals. One I remember was a rumour that the pathogen-filled blood samples we took from children at the study sites were being sent to England to be used by white people..... But there was little animosity – and some affection – on either side. My father was especially popular with his workers. I still have a photograph of one of our servants, Wilson Nyonyo Thole, that he was given as a token of affection.

By now I was in the first year of the Sixth Form at school and hating it. Megan, Jill and Penny, had left to go to secretarial college in Salisbury. June and Ronnie van Rensburg were at teacher training college in Bulawayo, not far from the army barracks at Heaney.

I had railed against the prospect of two more years' incarceration but Mum was adamant: I was to continue at school and get an entry to a university. She was right, of course, and I knew this, deep down. Now there were just four of us to go through to the Higher School Certificate: Joyce, Anne, Diana and me. Just two of us were boarders – Diana, in the other boarding house, Warwick, and myself, in Sherwood. It was a lonely furrow to plough but I did have the luxury of my own tiny room, at the end of a dormitory. I threw myself into school work.

Then Joyce, my great friend, fell ill. As a seven-year-old, while her parents were missionaries deep in the bush, she had contracted rheumatic fever. She had told me how she had been ferried to hospital in a machila (a hammock suspended between two poles) carried by bearers, the only possible means of transport from such a remote place.

"Just like David Livingstone," she said, "Only he didn't get better."

Now the same illness had recurred and she was flat on her back in Lusaka Hospital. I went to see her each week, begging lifts from whoever would take me, taking grapes, magazines and gossip. I had to hold magazines over her head so that she could read and be careful not to make her move, as it might weaken her heart.

"Don't make me laugh, Jude," she gasped, "It makes my sides hurt," as she lay there prostrate. Will was writing to her but she couldn't write back – that was my job.

Life was miserable and I knew that this year John would be going back to England. The immediate future looked bleak. Thank God for rock 'n' roll and the Sunday night Hit Parade from the commercial radio station at Lourenco Marques. The girls in the dormitory jammed into my tiny, airless room to listen in their pyjamas.

The Easter holidays were brightened by Diana, who came up to Fort Rosebery to stay. She and John paired up. They giggled and went for long walks together. I was pleased but their increasing closeness made me more aware of my own isolation. My old boyfriend had been transferred to another bush station. Will and I consoled ourselves with some fierce games of tennis and even more furious antics on the dance floor. Sitting on the Club verandah, he confided to me that he'd come out to Northern Rhodesia to cure a broken heart. The love of his life, a keen horsewoman, had ditched him and become engaged to someone else. He showed me photos of a pretty blonde girl standing in a cottage doorway, one graceful arm arched above her head. She looked so confident, so at ease with herself. No wonder Will had

271

sad eyes. He showed me other photos in an album and it was obvious he came from a well-off family. I don't think his family home, The Grange, could have been a 1930s semi. Our backgrounds were so different but we struck up a friendship. We walked down the road one night, after a dance. A new moon shone brightly, "lying on her back" in the words of Karen von Blixen and the sky was a velvety blue.

"Then a bloody lorry comes along and covers you in dust," said Will.

The local agricultural officer, an attractive but increasingly reclusive, sozzled bachelor, got engaged. Peter's task had been to promote schemes to introduce fish farming and pigeon breeding in an attempt to counteract severe protein deficiency in the Africans. The staple crop, cassava, was filling but not nutritious. As John said, "he went from boyish enthusiasm to becoming a regular at the bar after six months in the country. The reason was that every scheme he tried failed. The pigeons flew away, tractors were left to rust in the bush and the cassava-fed Tilapia fry in the constructed fish ponds were eaten before they could mature and breed. The Bemba were not easy to help."

We were all invited to a party to meet his betrothed, a fresh-faced young thing out from Scotland. After the food and the fast numbers, the lights were dimmed and someone put on Frank Sinatra's "Songs for Swinging Lovers".

"Shall we?" said Will.

He drew me to him and we danced. He smelled of sunshine, freshly laundered shirt and something spicy, citrusy.

They were playing "I've Got you Under My Skin". How appropriate.

Will pulled me closer and nuzzled my hair. My stomach was in meltdown and my skin was on fire where his hand rested in the small of my back. We danced slowly, languorously to the insistent heartbeat of the song. We looked at one another in the moonlight shining through the open windows. I could tell that he felt the same way as I did.

This was not supposed to happen. My befuddled brain touched briefly on all the reasons "why not". Will went through girls like a knife through butter, he was moody, he drove like a demon, he and my best friend were an item. And, and ..... I gave in and we wrapped our arms round one another. He caressed my hair and the nape of my neck. We kissed and I melted. I was falling in love and with my best friend's boyfriend. Not good news.

Mum and Dad tut-tutted over this new liaison.

"That boy, he's too old for you," said Dad. By "old" I divined that he meant "sexually experienced". "Besides, you should see the way he goes through Land Rovers. Really beats vehicles up on these roads. And his attitude – sometimes it's all hello, mate and at others you can barely get a word out of him. He can be a moody bugger – and wild. You don't know where you are with him."

Dad was quite innocent in some respects but he scented a predatory male in pursuit of his daughter, more of a threat than the boys she'd gone out with so far.

"Oh, come on, Jack, Will's all right," said Mum. "At least he and Jude can hold a decent conversation, which is more than you can say for some of the boys in town."

In private, she said to me later "And don't go getting yourself pregnant. I'm not looking after any babies while you're at university."

I said nothing to these exchanges. Mum had a fondness for handsome, intelligent men, particularly if they were well-spoken and had nice manners, so Will was ahead of the game as far as she was concerned. Little did she know that most of the sex-starved young men were wolves in sheep's clothing, hands everywhere and that one had to be energetic in defending one's honour. Public school boys were the worst, with fewer morals than the Brylcreemed farmers' sons or the Bahati miners. They were supremely confident and didn't understand the word "no". I had been chased round the kitchen table more than once in the lamplight.

I was a conventional girl, but by this stage I wasn't sure if defending one's honour was all it was cracked up to be.

My double life continued. Work without respite in term time, love in the holidays, the two linked by a chain of letters between Will and me.

After a few months Joyce came out of hospital and went on overseas leave with her family. By the time she returned, she had to repeat the year so we were no longer as close. I still felt horribly guilty but a philosophical Joyce, in characteristic fashion, forgave me.

"It's impossible to have a long-distance romance," she said. "Look at me and John."

Her last boyfriend, John, a devastatingly gorgeous man, travelled round the country with the government film unit. He was quite a bit older than Joyce and, inevitably, they had drifted apart, though she still saw him occasionally.

When he could, Will took me into the bush on his work day trips and I found out more about what it meant to work for the Provincial Administration.

By the late 1950s, the old school of District Commissioners were being superseded by the new. The first wave of officials came from the military, including our former DC, Derek Goodfellow, who had lost one arm in the war when he was with the RAF. He drove like a maniac, one-handed, of course, and managed the gear lever with his knees. Another ex-RAF man, Colin Rawlins, who had been awarded a DFC in the War, piloted his own little plane to England when he went on leave and sent his family home on Central African Airways. Our present PC (Provincial Commissioner), my friend Anne's father, was ex-Indian Army but his bristling moustache and plummy vowels concealed a sharp brain.

The new cadets were young men, most of them straight from public school though a few were graduates. The lucky few were given a thorough induction and training by their superiors but many had to sink or swim. They were given the task of touring into the bush (ulendo), by Land Rover, bike or by foot, to deal with the chiefs (the legislators in Native Authority areas), sort out legal, domestic and agricultural problems and help improve services, by building roads and bridges, clinics or schools. Being inexperienced, the young District Assistants made mistakes, such as trying to build a bridge from DDT instead of cement: the sacks looked identical and the labels had washed off. They had to learn the local language within a specified time, which guaranteed an increment in salary. Failure meant dismissal from the service, for it was essential to communicate with local people, few of whom spoke English. They had to be able to do accounts, type, fix a vehicle when it broke down miles from anywhere and organize staff in the house, office and out in the field.

The new recruits were expected to be lords of the manor and jacks of all trades rolled into one. Most relished the opportunity and the responsibility in exchange for very little pay. The youngsters had to be self-reliant but the life was lonely. It was hardly surprising that some turned to the bottle, married women or the local ladies for solace. Young men could be hurriedly repatriated or transferred because they were being chased by irate husbands, were suffering from delirium tremens or had caught venereal disease. The DC's word was law in such matters.

In previous decades the occasional DC had taken an African mistress. In the second year of the sixth form I worked with the issue of one such union. Mrs. Lane-Poole and her husband lived in the Coloured quarter of town with their family. She was a pretty, bubbly person who told me a little about her childhood.

"When the Provincial Commissioner or another bigwig called, my mum and we children were hustled out of the back door to the kaya. We had to be as quiet as mice. It didn't bother us, it was just how things were."

She was such a cheerful person, even though she must have felt socially excluded, shunned by African and European alike.

One of Will's friends, who lived upcountry, had a native, live-in girlfriend.

"He's got a sleeping dictionary," explained Will.

I was shocked, little prude.

"Why do you think his Bemba's so good? He's got an unfair advantage," he added.

Going into a village with a PA official, particularly one far from the beaten track, was a revelation. The final part of the journey to was often by foot, along a winding track through the trees, or by boat in the swamps. A cluster of huts would come into view, with a Union Jack flying. The administrative centre would be a mud hut, like the rest, marked by white-painted stones. Down would go the Africans on their knees, the women ululating, chanting and dancing, the men clapping as though they were paying obeisance. It was no wonder white people felt god-like and superior with this reception. Some of the women and children had never seen a white woman at close quarters before and they would cluster round, curiously, the children giggling and covering their mouths with their hands. If the European concerned had performed a service, such as providing a grader to level the atrocious road or killing a leopard which had menaced the population the welcome was even more enthusiastic.

"You are welcome," said the chief, the messenger, the houseboy – and they meant it. The locals were extremely courteous. They were also anxious to please. If they said "No problem", "It is not far" or "The price is small, small" you were less sure.

Chapter 18
THE WIND OF CHANGE

Dermot and friend on tour

We have seen the awakening of national consciousness in peoples who have for centuries lived in dependence of some other power. In different places it takes different forms but it is happening everywhere. A wind of change is blowing through this continent, whether we like it or not."

Harold Macmillan – Address to the Joint Assembly of the South African Parliament, 3rd February, 1960

By 1958 Harold's aforesaid wind was blowing strongly on the Copperbelt and was even beginning to affect our little corner of the bush. The big impetus for shifting perception had been provided by the Second World War, which saw many soldiers from East and West Africa glimpse what was happening in other world territories. The war also broke down class barriers and hastened the introduction of liberal, socialist policies worldwide. In Northern Rhodesia, African welfare societies had been formed in urban areas in the 1940s, where the membership comprised clerks, teachers and other professionals. From these disparate societies one association was formed which was to become the African National Congress, the ANC, two years later. In 1951 Harry Nkumbula, a short, chubby-faced man who liked his whisky, became its leader.

The ANC bitterly opposed Federation, as did most of us in Northern Rhodesia. While we felt that the North's wealth was financing the South's development, the ANC also feared that it would perpetuate the dominating position of Europeans in politics and government. By the time the Federation was established in 1953, Nkumbula had conducted a vigorous, countrywide campaign which had even affected remote rural areas like ours. However, the boycotts, strikes and protests against segregation in the towns didn't really touch the northern provinces. The locals, black and white, went to the same shops and cafés and worked together in the same office room. We didn't have a separate hatch for the Africans to buy their beer or a separate clinic for Europeans, though it was true that if I went to the clinic a nurse (black) would shove me, a European girl, ahead of a long queue of squatting women and their snotty-nosed children, a procedure I still found embarrassing. Here the influence of chiefs and native authorities was still strong and there was little in the way of a colour bar. The ethos of colonial development, adhered to by the PA, was to bring countries forward to independence but the process was to be a gradual one.

The stirrings started by the ANC were taken up by Kaunda's ZANC splinter group in 1958, which persuaded Africans not to vote in the forthcoming elections. The ANC, in contrast, encouraged its members to vote. Kaunda was a Bemba (though his father was a teacher from Nyasaland), a humanist, educated at Lubwa Mission. His party now professed to adopt a Gandhi-like policy of non-violence. In the run up to the election the ZANC began to intimidate voters and their families, so much so that the Governor declared a State of Emergency, proclaimed the ZANC an illegal organization and banished 29 of its leaders to the rural areas. However, the smoke of nationalism had been fanned into a flame and the banned ZANC was to rise like a phoenix in the form of the United Nationalist Independence Party, UNIP, in 1959. These were the years of the big copper bonus and, understandably, African migrant workers on the Copperbelt (many of whom were Bemba) wanted more pay, better working conditions and more union muscle. The next few years would witness a swift change in the political and social nature of the country which no-one could have anticipated.

Stuck in our isolated town, my parents were too busy working to give much thought to politics. When they had come out to Northern Rhodesia they had envisaged working on until they got their pensions, then buying a house or plot on the line of rail to retire. They didn't want to go back to not-so-genteel poverty in England, they loved the African climate, Dad had a relatively free rein at work and they were used to the privations of bush life. Their material wants were few. We still left our doors unlocked, walked around the town in safety and wished all and sundry mwapoleni mukwai. Our family was ostrich-like, with its head in the sand and other things on its mind.

It grew hotter and stickier as the exams approached. One evening we four were sitting in our black hole after supper, battling to embed some facts in overheated brains. I'd missed whole chunks of The Mayor of Casterbridge in Eng. Lit. but could speed-read that under the bedclothes by torchlight; ditto Miss K's ghastly purple banda'd handout sheets in history. She was getting wound up about our exams too and literally spat instructions out. We learned to avoid sitting in the front row of class or else we'd get sprayed. Flash cards compiled from the textbook might be a better bet as I'd go blind squinting at Miss K's notes. The gods had given me a photographic memory so I planned to "spot" questions and squeeze through, given a bit of luck and some last-minute cramming. Pages of text would be reproduced practically verbatim, to be forgotten the instant I left the exam room. The textbook would give me just as good a grounding, if not a better one. The sciences were more of a problem – no short cuts here for an illogical brain and I just hoped I didn't set fire to the lab in practicals.

I was struggling to copy diagrams of the reproductive system in Biology, a whole section I had missed. The drawings were Greek to me, the terminology even more so.

"What the hell's a scrotal sac?" I asked.

"Balls!" said Jean Campbell, screaming with laughter. "Jeez, Jude, you are so thick."

I was still innocent, ignorant and unaware. One of the younger girls had taken me aside to explain what "shit" meant and the f---- word hadn't yet entered my consciousness. My parents had ensured that I'd led a sheltered life, despite bawdy songs in the Club bar. Mum whisked me away when the men started on "Eskimo Nell".

The gym windows were painted white in preparation for its role as an exam hall. We sweltered on. The ceiling fan in the common room was switched to its top setting and threatened to helicopter off its moorings. There were flashes of lightning on the horizon, dust devils swirling round the playing fields and still the rain didn't come. One night the wind changed direction and we could scent damp earth on the breeze, a perfume so intoxicating that it should be put in a bottle. Suddenly, one of the little girls from Dorm 1 burst into our study.

"Quick," she gasped, "It's raining!"

Whooping with joy, we rushed into the dorm and out through the side door – goodness knows how they'd opened it. Bliss. We stripped to bra and pants and danced in the deluge, regardless of the mud and gravel splashing up our legs or the amazement of the night watchman. We lifted our heads to the heavens and drank the fresh water of the new rainy season, like a bunch of mad nymphs. We were hysterical, maddened by the heat, light-headed from sitting over books for too long, like prisoners let out after a long jail sentence.

With the first rains flying ants emerged from their holes in the baked earth and took to the sky in clouds. The Afrikaans girls caught some on their way to supper, removed their wings and ate them.

"Sis, that's disgusting!" the Pommies exclaimed.

"They're lekker, ja" said Betty. "You must try one, hey. Mind you, they taste even better fried."

Their taste buds were different to ours, that was for sure. They didn't mind the cook matron's boerewors sausages and ate sadza at home. Now I was a sixth former I had to be a head of table and watch my charges' manners. Some of the farm girls would grab at the food on serving dishes, nearly upsetting it from the waiter's hands and I had to teach Moggol, a farmer's daughter from the Eastern Province, how to use a knife and fork.

The rains didn't last and suddenly we were in there, turning over our exam papers in a baking hot gym while a mistress clacked up and down the silent rows in high heels. Diana's skin, always pale, now had the tinge of an unripe lemon. My stomach churned as I read the questions and my mind went blank. Keep calm, keep calm. I began to write.

After three weeks of hell it was over. We were free, some of us for ever. We could plan end of term celebrations and think about clothes, boys and the Christmas holidays. I didn't want to think of the next two years, when I would be back at school and most of my friends sampling the delights of fresh fields.

One year later, as a treat before we broke up, our Geography teacher had planned an excursion. We were to take a day trip to Kariba Dam, currently being constructed on the Zambezi River which formed the border between Northern and Southern Rhodesia.

The story of Kariba fascinated me and exemplified the influence of the white man in Africa, for good and ill. The construction of a huge dam, 420 feet high and 1900 feet long, blocking a cavernous gorge had taken years to complete, after all sorts of struggles and conflicts. It was to supply hydro-electric power to Northern and Southern Rhodesia, particularly the Copperbelt mines and the burgeoning population in that part of the North. We were to see it in early December, just two days after the dam wall had been sealed to contain the flow of the mighty river. It would take until 1962 to complete the entire project and the lake that would be formed by the dam would be the largest in terms of volume in the world.

Kariba gorge was a forbidding and secret place where the river flowed swiftly over a lintel of rock, plunging into a vortex of whirlpools downstream. The Africans called these rocks a trap – riwa – and they were the haunt of the river god or spirit, Nyaminyami, who caused any human being or canoe entering his domain to be sucked down into the boiling pools for ever. Thus, Kariba was associated with suspicion and fear, the legend being that it was a trap fatal for a man to enter.

In November 1877 Frederick Selous, the famous white hunter, entered the gorge. He visited the lands of the Batonga, the tribe which had to be moved when the rising waters of Kariba lake flooded their homes in 1957 and 1958. In his book "A Hunter's Wanderings in Africa", he describes the appalling cruelty of the slave raiders in this area, both Portuguese and the Chikundas, themselves freed slaves:

22nd Nov. In the afternoon we passed through a lot more burnt villages, and found the remains of two Batonkas lying in the footpath. All the bodies had been dragged into the neighbouring bush by the hyenas..... The stench was often offensive."

He graphically describes a group of women slaves:

Each had an iron ring around her neck; there were about five feet of iron chain in between each. Whilst I was here, they never loosened one from another, but every morning they were sent over to the southern shore to hoe in a cornfield all day in a row together. At night they were locked up, still all chained together in a large square sort of barn. From the verandah depended three raw-hide hippopotamus sjamboks, the lower part of each dyed black with blood."

Even in the absence of slavery, savagery was commonplace and women had a particularly hard time of it in tribal Africa. Dr. Walter Fisher's description of the events that followed the death of a local chief in the Upper Zambezi region during the early twentieth century are particularly illuminating. He tells how, within minutes of the chief's death, all his houses were destroyed, except the one in which ten of his wives were expected to sit up all night with his body on their laps! Normally, at least five of the wives would have been killed and buried with the chief; possibly another two would have had their limbs dislocated and been buried, alive, at the head and foot of the grave, there to remain until they died of starvation or be taken by hyenas.

June, Kariba 1959

In 1958, the Batonga were still a relatively primitive tribe, soon to lose their ancestral lands to the new lake. They had previously been protected by the harshness of the terrain in the Lower Zambezi valley and by the fact that they absorbed, rather than clashed with, other invaders such as the Matabele, whom they ferried across the river by canoe to conduct their raiding parties. They were hunters and cultivators, who grew two crops of millet a year, once after the rains and a second in the rich alluvium left on the banks when the Zambezi floodwaters receded. They dressed in skins, wore kilts made from bark and even in the late 1950s the women went bare-breasted, with the occasional startling addition of cotton bras in ice cream colours. This seemed sensible in such a climate, where hot season temperatures topped the 100 degrees Fahrenheit mark. For decoration, they wore earrings, bead jewellery and pieces of ivory in their noses, and daubed their faces with red ochre mixed with goat fat as a protection against fleas, lice and the sun; like the elephant and buffalo who roll in mud for the same prophylactic effect. Some of the people were gap-toothed, having had teeth removed at puberty (four incisors, two canines) to "pay" the gods for their adulthood. Like the Bemba, they practised shifting cultivation and lived in simple thatched huts, the tallest building being the granary and hen houses on stilts to keep their crop safe from rats, and the poultry from hyenas. A self-sufficient people, they demanded little from the civilised world apart from beads, cowrie shells, salt and cloth and grew their own Burley tobacco and mixed this with millet to drink from hubble pipes made from gourds.

In 1955 the Federal government had broken the news that the Batonga would have to move. The ANC opposed this, saying "It is well known that Nyaminyami is the all-powerful god of the river. He will never allow the white men to control him. With one flick of his tail he will destroy all the work in the gorge." They maintained that the river god would protect his people by allowing the water to boil, to destroy the white man's "bridge" at Kariba, and would give his subjects powerful magic to live under the water. There followed a period of insurrection and trouble, culminating in the removal of 50,000 Batonga to new villages. A huge wildlife conservation programme, Operation Noah, would also be carried out to remove animals from the rising floodwaters of the new lake.

The building of Kariba had also been a bone of contention in the European community. A gorge on the Kafue River, in Northern Rhodesia, was considered by certain factions to be closer to the Copperbelt's mines and its large population, to whom an increased supply of electricity was vital. At present, coal for the mines was sent up from Wankie, Southern Rhodesia but supplies were diminishing. Kariba gorge had first been investigated as a suitable dam site to provide hydro-electric power in 1927 and surveys continued until the early 1950s, hampered by inaccessibility, sickness and floods. At the time of Federation in 1953, the argument continued as to which site would be most suitable and cost-effective. The Prime Minister of Southern Rhodesia at the time, Sir Godfrey Huggins, convinced everyone that funding was more likely to be forthcoming for a federal project than one for Northern Rhodesia alone and secured the main tranche of money from the World Bank. The deal was done.

"Now the Europeans also realise that they cannot trust federation," was Harry Nkumbula's response.

The Zambezi valley was heavily wooded and hot, patrolled by elephants and other wild animals. In the construction of Kariba, the first task had been to build an access road into a country of crumbling ravines and tenacious thorn bush, where the sky was thick with a haze of heat and smoke from the thousand fires always burning in Africa. It was decided to make this south of the river, from Makuti, at the top of the escarpment, following the track of a migratory elephant path. The road was completed in record time and the huge construction machinery moved in. In early 1956 the townships were built, the European one 1500 feet above the river, Mahombekombe ("lakeside") in the steamy valley below.

By the time we arrived there, in early December, 1958, Kariba township, perched on a hilltop, had a cosmopolitan, almost Mediterranean air and its signs were bilingual, for an Italian consortium were building the dam. It even had its own Catholic church, St. Barbara, where masses were said for workers who had died constructing the dam (an average on one per week). Many had fallen into the emerging towers of the dam wall and remain there, encased in concrete. In contrast, Mahombekombe was reputed to be a rackety place, a hotbed of beer drinking, gambling, prostitution and political agitation.

We were hot and dusty after our long drive down from Lusaka. We had crossed the steep, switchback roads of the Zambezi, down one side and up the other, then hit the final 50 miles of dirt road to Kariba. How different the landscape looked to the flat, high veld savannah around our school. Ranges of purple hills framed the horizon, mopane trees had burst into vivid colour and grotesque baobabs were etched against a hazy sky, as though they had been planted upside down with their twisted roots showing. Baobabs were drought-resistant and stored water in their immense trunks; their smooth, grey bark resembled an elephant's hide and it was easy to imagine these huge beasts moving between them. We didn't see any, to our disappointment, though there were piles of dung on the road but we caught a glimpse of leaping impala and vervet monkeys in the dense bush.

We sipped a cool drink in an air-conditioned café in Kariba and prepared to go down to the observation point above the dam wall. Miss Wilson, our teacher, mopped her brow. Phew, it was hot. June fanned herself with her straw hat, which looked like a thatched rondavel roof.

"Jeez, I wish we'd worn shorts," she said. "My pedal pushers are sticking to my bum."

"It's your bottom, not your bum," admonished Miss Wilson, "or your derrière."

No description or photograph had prepared us for the first sight of the gorge or the vast scale of the rising pillars of the dam wall. The gorge was deep, cast in shadow, and the waters of the mighty Zambezi crashed through it still. From our elevated viewpoint we could see an endless, forested floodplain through which the river wound its way, like a silver snake. It was hard to believe that this expanse of wilderness would soon be underwater. No wonder the Batonga revered their river god. Our eyes glazed over as the guide giving us the inspection tour droned on in the heat.

Men on cradles worked on the wall – they looked like ants from this distance. The previous year 17 had died when one of these cradles broke, sending the men to a cement grave within the dam wall. The noise of compressors, drills and other machinery assaulted our ears, along with the roaring river.

Our guide drove us down to the base of the dam wall, whose uncompleted towers reared above us. Some bare-chested Italian workers stood on the bank, fishing. They were pulling some whoppers out of the spillway flume which had been left open. They were deeply tanned and muscular.

"Talent! At last," breathed June, who had been dozing off. She glanced sideways under her sun-hat and dimpled at the hunks.

"You'd better watch it, Miss W's going to give you a test in the car on the way home."

I think Kariba and the Zambezi valley made such an impression on me because of its still untamed vastness. We had stood on the hill above the dam wall and seen the whole of Africa spread below our feet. The Batonga people had scratched out an existence and survived in this difficult but beautiful natural world but all this would change in the name of progress. This was years away from the question of regulating water flow and the Mozambique floods or the knotty problem of the dam's maintenance by two cash-strapped, different political entities in the new millennium.

Home for the Christmas break followed. I had a new friend, Anne, the Provincial Commissioner's daughter. She had been at a ballet school in Camberley but she had stopped growing so was judged to be too short to make this a career. She had left with perfect posture and her feet turned out at ten to two and was great fun, with a wicked sense of humour. She was a good cook and was derisory about my hopeless efforts in the kitchen. We made the most of the holidays and enjoyed bumping down the dusty road to our special lake, Bangweulu.

Chapter 19
STORM WARNING

Chameleon

I had relished the challenge of Higher School Certificate work in the fifth form (or lower sixth) and made the most of my friends still left at Jean Rennie. One plus was that we took lessons with the Gilbert Rennie boys for History, one of my subsidiary subjects. Our teacher was excellent – Mr Stevens. It also exposed us to male company.

"Talent!" June exclaimed once more.

Joyce fell sick in the second term and lay in Lusaka Hospital. Betty had gone and was running a café in Chingola, a Copperbelt town. At least Megan and Jill, in the class below me, were still students and we had the Matric girls in our class. To qualify for entry to a South African university, most girls stayed on for an extra matriculation year, although if you had passed well enough in the fourth form you could enter university straight away. Many of our fifth form were to go on to teacher training college near Bulawayo at the end of the year, including one June Finley-Bissett.

We giggled our way through lessons, went round in a rowdy posse and mercilessly teased poor Candy. The lower sixth was given a small common room where we were supposed to revise during the school day but spent it drinking cups of coffee, penning silly jokes, composing love letters to our boyfriends and stroking one another's necks to relieve exam tension. We were like a troop of monkeys, in more ways than one. We listened to Elvis, Little Richard, Tom Lehrer and Flanders and Swann and thought we were the crème de la crème. In fact, we were a witches' coven, the bane of our teachers' lives. Some of us were made prefects so had to set some sort of example by being punctual (a real difficulty for me) and issuing orders.

"Walk, don't run down the corridors."

"Are you smoking in that toilet?"

"Where's your hat? You have to wear your hat to go on the bus to town."

"You'll have to take off that necklace, Nicole, you know it's forbidden to wear jewellery to school. Only sleeper earrings allowed."

We wouldn't have dreamt of having our ears pierced. Only common girls did that, like Esme, who was pretty, confident, sang like a dream, cheeked the teachers and taught me the words of "Let There be Love." She was the essence of cool before the word had even been invented.

We were finding Diana annoying. She had a boring boyfriend with a big ego who eventually got the push. The other thing that irritated us was her lack of confidence, real or imagined, in her academic ability. She worked like a demon but secretively. You know the sort of thing.....

Left: *Fetching water*
Below: *Children playing*

"I haven't done enough revision, no honestly, true as Bob, I can't remember a thing," just before the exam then coming out with top marks.

The boarders were given a little more freedom in the lower sixth. On Saturday mornings we were allowed to walk up to the shopping centre in Woodlands, at the top of the hill, and have coffee with our friends who lived in the suburb, provided you gave the mistress on duty details of the relevant address. We could buy ourselves supplies – cosmetics and items for "feminine hygiene" and drink a milkshake. Wow. We were taken to the cinema in town to see the odd film deemed suitable and educational for young ladies – Julius Caesar, Moby Dick, The Student Prince – or to the local theatre for musicals and visiting thespians, usually one-man shows for professional actors fancying a spot of winter sunshine in the tropics. I was allowed out to Scottish Country Dancing at the Methodist church on Friday nights with Miss Macleod, where I was taught the finer points of the pas-de-bas and the strathspey ("very good for the calf muscles"). If we were exceptionally well-behaved we were allowed to Friday hops run by the Anglican church, where we could admire the sophisticates of Lusaka at play. We wrote, painted scenery, sewed for and starred in revues which were acted out with the boys' school sixth form and performed Shakespeare and Gilbert and Sullivan. Nothing modern or remotely racy was allowed.

Under the pastoral eye of Miss Wilson we were taken to practise surveying, standing knee deep in the mud round Kabulonga Dam. It's a wonder we didn't catch bilharzia. I concentrated on the four subjects I had decided to take for my Higher School Cert plus General Paper.

Weekends were definitely more interesting in the lower sixth. Joyce came out of hospital and was at home convalescing. Her family took us to farms on the Kafue Road, where we swam in cattle water tanks. June's family were out at Makeni and she introduced us to the delights of the Blue Boar, a road house with a swimming pool. A new drive-in cinema opened, which we thought the height of cool. If you wanted a Coke or a burger it was brought to you in your car and put on a tray which clipped on to the door. If we were really lucky, we could hang out in Moggie's Milk Bar, on Cairo Road, treat ourselves to a Coke Special and eye up the boys.

In the midst of the dry season John left to go back to university in London. I was bereft, so pleased to have Will around in the holidays and the thought of him during term-time.

The rumblings of political discontent were developing into a muted roar. The Copperbelt and other towns had seen boycotts of the coronation, municipal beerhalls, clinics and hospitals since the early 1950s. So far we had not been much affected in our corner of the bush but this started to change in 1959, when a wave of violence and intimidation swept through much of the country and a State of Emergency was declared.

We had known little about this in the Luapula Province, where there was no colour bar. The government was attempting to conserve natural resources and improve the standard of farming, something the ANC and the ZANC saw as a trick. They told their followers that once the land was improved the Europeans would take it over. Kaunda was imprisoned for subversion in May, 1959 and UNIP was created under Mainza Chona.

A general election was in the offing and the cry of "One man, one vote" was raised, a rallying call which was spreading throughout the entire continent. African nationalism and discontent was bubbling under a tranquil surface and the local population in Luapula Province became sullen and uncooperative. As we swept down the Samfya road, hordes of children would yell "Freedom!" and "Kwacha!" (the ZANC slogan, meaning "dawn" – the dawn of the independence movement) instead of giving us a cheery wave. It was well known that ZANC was intimidating potential voters and their families in the run up to the election. Our staff were afraid to go home to the township in the dark and there were riots in the densely-populated Luapula valley and shores of Lake Bangweulu.

Philip came to our house for a beer one afternoon. He looked shaken and pale under his deep tan, his normal grinning face now creased into a weary frown.

"The last riot was terrible. We were attacked by a mob with spears and the Police had to fire into the crowd. Four men were killed and I've just had to bring the bodies back to the mortuary. The smell in the back of the Land Rover..... None of my boys would touch it. I've just had to wash it down myself and it still smells."

Dealing with dead bodies had probably not been part of Phil's job description, nor Dad's, but they both dealt with it. Dad had been a male nurse in the early years of the war and had overcome any squeamishness then.

When a European died in town, no African would touch the body or go anywhere near the graveyard. They had their own graveyards, sometimes set in dense, beautiful forest called mushitu. Initiation and circumcision of both sexes was also carried out in the deep, secret bush.

In Fort Rosebery, the practice of laying out a body, grave-digging and conducting a funeral all fell to the expatriate community and my father's carpentry workshop made the coffins. One of John's card-playing pals died suddenly after a dose of malaria. He had one toddler and his lovely wife was pregnant with a second child. We buried Alan on a hot day but the msasa trees in the tiny European cemetery gave us some respite.

Even death sometimes had its funny side.

"You know, Dulce," Dad said at lunch one day, "That road foreman died – you know, the big Danish bloke with red hair. Big boozer. Cirrhosis of the liver, I reckon. His wife left him. Anyway, we had to get him into the coffin for the funeral. Helluva job – he must have been six foot six – he was too tall! And rigor mortis had set in."

"What did you do?" I asked, goggle-eyed.

"I says to Fred – we'll have to get him in, there's no time to make another coffin before the funeral. Well, I put my arm under his knees, like this....." Dad illustrated the point, helpless with laughter. "And bent them, so he fitted in. Blimey, what a job."

I started to laugh until Mum shut me up.

The sequel to this came later on in the week.

"You know they buried The Great Dane on Monday. Well, on Wednesday his wife pitches up, doesn't she, and

wants to know where his pay packet is. We'd buried him
with the bloomin' thing in his pocket."

Chapter 20
BUSH BABY

Bush Baby

See hope, beauty and potential in our unfinished states. Be patient. Be like the budding flame lily on the vine.

Juliana Clegg

The final year at school was hard all round. I flung myself into academic work for the Higher School Cert, lonely in the boarding house because most of my friends had left. They visited periodically, dressed in fashionable clothes, wearing high heels ("Winkle pickers!" said Dad) and make up and were full of stories about their new, exciting lives. Megs was in a secretarial college in Salisbury but she was worried about her dad. He was ill but uncommunicative, not telling anybody what was wrong. June was doing her teacher training, Joyce was in the class below me because of her time off school and Joey, my Afrikaner friend, was working in Lusaka, buzzing around town in a new Volkswagen Beetle. Periodically, I railed at my poor parents about being stuck in Jean Rennie. There I was, stuck in a gym-slip and short socks while they were seeing the world.

"Listen, Jude, you know I had to leave school at fourteen. I just wish I'd had your opportunities, young lady," Dad urged.

"You have a good brain and you must use it. Of course, you could go to Cape Town – it's got a beautiful university," said Mum, wistfully. "Or there's the new university in Salisbury." I had been offered a place at the new University College of Rhodesia in what is now Harare but I wanted something more cosmopolitan.

I couldn't contemplate studying under an apartheid regime. No, it was back to England or bust for me and I would just have to put up with Jean Rennie, with all its limitations. Deep down, I knew my parents were right and that I was being a pain. I must put up and shut up.

As we bumped down a bush road in a Land Rover one afternoon, one of my friends said to me "You'll miss all this, you know, when you go back to the UK."

"What? Dirt roads and dust and boring conversations at sundowners? Seeing the same old people all the time? You must be joking!"

In retrospect, he was right. We were a motley crowd of people in the bush but we rubbed along together and there was a degree of tolerance and easygoing friendship that I have found nowhere else. And the wonderful climate – almost perfect..... But then nowhere is.

Letters from friends helped to keep me going at school. Megan was the main correspondent but one appeared in the post box from June Finley-Bissett:

Teacher Training College
Private Bag T 333
Bulawayo, SR

Hail my friend –

Bissett greeteth thee in forlorn tones this morning. The news you gave me last night was indeed a great shock. I did expect to pass French this go. You can spare what deah Valma had to say about me ploughing it..... Now follows three pages of chat, mainly about various boys!

Now, who are you romancing with? And how is my old flame Hindscratch?..... (Eric Hindmarsh, an occasional dance partner who used to call me Napoleon, Boney, get it?)

There are only 30 chaps let in the barracks here. Most dismal, my dear. The atmosphere is rather tense here in SR. This Nyasaland trouble is awful. The 450 chaps, Terriers, from Brady Barracks left on 15 minutes' warning by road for Nyasa on Friday. They have kicked Stonehouse out of the FRN (June's father was the person who punched him on the nose at Lusaka airport). *So it goes on!*

No, Woofie (one of our plainer, more strait-laced friends) *hasn't had her teeth straightened. She has lost her half-crown heels but will not even wear lipstick. I have tried everything in my power to induce her to do so. She condescends to a dusting of powder sometimes and has blossomed quite a bit – seems to get on quite well with the chaps. I am glad, actually as it does her good.*

303

Well it seems as if I have exhausted my supply of blah.

Much love
June, alias The Terror

During the holidays I had found a job at Kathy's Bakery and Tea Room, to save up for university. Kathy and Jack Pretorius were an industrious couple, he the gentle giant, she the more vociferous of the two who wore the pants in more ways than one. Her tanned, deeply lined face was always fully made up and surrounded by a cloud of blonde, peroxide curls but she dressed in khaki shirt and trousers, with veldschoen on her feet. She was an older, tougher version of Michaela Denis, the wildlife TV presenter.

"I'm telling you, Jack (she pronounced it "check"), we should run this country. You Poms haven't a clue. We were the first ones to go into the bush and we can live like the muntus, man," she told Dad.

It was true that Kathy could bake a wedding cake in a pit bush oven and ice it like a dream, with sugar wickerwork and rosebuds. She could make clothes, shoot, ride a horse, drive a span of oxen and service a Land Rover, but was very precise in her running of the bakery and tea room and kept it spotless, ruling her staff with a rod of iron. I served behind the counter and scuttled in and out of the kitchen to wait at tables with Mrs. Lane-Poole's delicious scones and cakes, being careful not to tip a trayful into a customer's lap. I was still clumsy.

"Come on, Judy, you must learn to wrap up bread a bit faster than that. And you pack ("peck") the paper bags like so," she demonstrated, filling them at high speed, twirling them round and twisting the tops neatly, with two little bunny ears at each corner. If I tried to work as fast as her I spilled half the contents as I was twisting. Still, it was doing wonders for my mental arithmetic and assertiveness skills. I soon learned which customers came back regularly, which ladies were awkward, complaining about this and that or demanding a refund, or bonselas (discounts) like bread reduced in price at the end of the day. The locals couldn't afford much but liked to treat themselves to an iced bun or a cigarette or two. These were sold singly as well as in packets ("you give me one one Life fwaka, dona"). Dad liked Life and Matinee cigarettes, Mum preferred Benson & Hedges or Vogue. Clerks from nearby offices would come in to buy fags for their bosses before they suffered from nicotine withdrawal symptoms. Cigarettes were cheap and their consumption was prodigious by black and white people. There were moments of excitement. One day a ragged, red-eyed man drew out his change from his pocket, together with a bundle of dried leaves. He abandoned his purchases and rushed out of the door.

"He's been smoking dagga," Kathy remarked. "He knew I'd ring the police."

We had light-fingered customers, of course, and tragedy, too. Mrs. L. was a frequent customer, along with two pale-faced, waif-like children. She and her family were staying in a caravan in the grounds of the Mansa Hotel while her husband did contract work around town. He was a drinker and a gambler and his pregnant wife walked around town during the day, too bored to stay in the hot tin box that was their home. One night she and her husband were drinking in the bar when their caravan caught fire. The couple could afford to buy beer but not paraffin lamps. A candle had blown over in the breeze and the nanny, who was babysitting, ran away when the blaze started. People rushed out of the bar to stop the blaze but by now the caravan was a ball of flame. Strong arms restrained Mr. L. as he struggled to break free to rescue his children, tears streaming down his face. The older two children escaped but the baby died. I felt so sorry for the mother, sitting listlessly with her cup of coffee, and slipped buns to the children when Kathy wasn't looking. She was a beautiful woman, with deep blue eyes and a cloud of black, shoulder-length hair. Now her features were pale and raddled and she wouldn't look you in the face. Everyone in town, including the gossips who didn't have a good word to say for the family, had made a collection to help the homeless, bereaved parents.

Kathy was the manageress but kind Jack came in to cash up, after his regular job at PWD. He was so hairy he sported an all-day five o'clock shadow and had black curls repulsively erupting from the V neck of his work shirt, a sight to which my eyes were irresistibly drawn.

From the bakery I had a panoramic view of the main road into town down towards the Boma and could spot Will walking up the road to the mess, always a thrill. He and his pet Alsatian were both slightly knock-kneed, which I found endearing. One day a column of black smoke rose up above the trees on the opposite side of the valley. A siren wailed and two or three blue Police Land Rovers shot down the hill.

"What's up?" I asked.

Dave Ward, one of the young policemen, rushed into the shop.

"Mansa Mission is on fire! What is it with these people? Lance Mee has done nothing but help them."

Lancelot Mee was in charge of the Mission. He was a quiet soul with an African wife, very scholarly, and had translated the Bible into the Bemba language. He was devoted to helping and educating the local people. His more famous brother, Arthur, had edited the Children's Encyclopaedia, the source of much of my childhood general knowledge. Mum sometimes went to the Mission to play the wheezy harmonium for weddings or services and I played carols on this instrument when it was wheeled on the back of a truck to the school at Christmas time. Its pedals were remarkably noisy and tended to override the softer tunes. "Silent Night" would forever be associated with the sound of pumping pedals in my mind.

The fire was one manifestation of rumblings of discontent. By the time it was put out, all the Reverend Mee's archives had been destroyed. Luckily, no one was hurt – this time.

I also had plenty of school work to do in the holidays and lugged bags of books on to the plane at the end of each term, along with the old grey suitcase ("no more than 44lbs", Dad noted as he hoisted it up with the portable scales with a hook). Luckily, the pilot turned a blind eye to excess hand luggage and stowed it under the net at the back of the aircraft, with suitcases, boxes and mailbags. We were studying the Romantic poets in both English and French literature, which suited my moonstruck frame of mind and Father Claude, one of the White Fathers, was helping me with French conversation. The priests had got their name from the white cassocks they wore. Twice a week I walked up the hill from Kathy's to the grandly named Bishop's Palace for my tuition, which stood close to Will's bachelor quarters. It was a splendid place, with a porticoed walk around the cloisters, and was reputed to have the best wine cellar in town. The Anglicans made do with services at the Club and were only now having a church built on the corner where the market had stood. The construction proceeded in fits and starts and the building was still roofless. I felt sad that they had been obliged to cut down the big fig tree to make way for the church.

In the middle of the year Will was transferred to Samfya. Plans were being made to expand the Boma workforce there and it was also developing as a trouble-spot. Kaunda's rustication in prison provided the spur for more intense nationalist activity. In June, the United National Independence Party, now led by Chona, quickly gained support along the line-of-rail and in the Northern and Luapula Provinces. The incineration of Mansa Mission was part of the protest against European dominance.

In January, Kaunda was released from prison. He now adopted a moderate approach, with a policy of non-violence and peaceful negotiation – as did Nelson Mandela in South Africa, many years later. The end of the year would see a situation of uneasy calm and in 1964 UNIP, led by Kenneth Kaunda, would form the first Zambian government after Independence.

I missed Anne, who had gone to a posh secretarial college in Cheltenham. We kept in touch. It was a time of change.....

Will's transfer was a bitter blow but his frequent letters to me at school kept the flame alive. During the holidays it was no longer possible to stay with Bill and Freda because she had cancer. She refused to have treatment – typical Freda – and looked amazingly well and immaculate.

"Yes, isn't it surprising, I still look well even though I have a crumbling body," she told us, in her direct way. I didn't know what to say. Her thick brown hair was still curled up into its chignon and her complexion was as fine as ever, even if her cheeks looked a little flushed.

Will asked the DC for permission to allow me to stay in his Samfya house at weekends, with a crowd that sometimes included my parents. After a long day of swimming, sailing and tennis Will cooked vast quantities of spaghetti Bolognese in the little kitchen, which we washed down with beer. We had rare moments of private time together, where we could snuggle up on the sofa, books and drinks at the ready, to listen to records and talk. One evening we walked down a secret path to the next beach, deserted in the week, and went skinny dipping. We walked into the sandy water and swam through the reeds, which caressed our naked bodies like silk. Sometimes we rose in the pre-dawn chill to go hunting, walking through the forestry reserve in search of kwale (partridge) or buck for the pot. One day Will and Alan, the fisheries guy, shot a large reedbuck and skinned it on

Alan's lawn. He slit the stomach and removed its entrails, then peeled off the skin in one piece. He shoved a haunch at Blondie, who sniffed it and shied away nervously.

"Call yourself a dog?!" he exclaimed. "She's a proper Pommie mutt, that one."

For the last term I persuaded Mum and Dad to let me board with some of their friends in Woodlands. I had no classmates with me and had to discipline my dormitory of fifteen nubile girls, all of whom were older than me and physically much more mature. As I struggled to revise in my little room, I was interrupted by trips into the dorm to quell a bunch of restless teenagers. The matrons and house teachers had retired to their rooms by now and gave me no support. When I told the housemistress I would not be staying there for the final term I could tell that she was disappointed in my lack of leadership qualities. Be that as it may, my main aim was to pass exams, not keep a bunch of stroppy girls in order.

At the end of the school day I now cycled up the long hill to Woodlands, sweating under the wretched two layers of blouse and gym-slip. The leafy suburb was studded with beautiful msasa trees as the town council forbade householders from chopping down native trees. It was a pity other councils hadn't had such foresight. Suicide month coincided with peak revision time and I sat in a cold bath each afternoon with my books propped up on the bath tidy. The house was small and airless and I had to keep the bedroom door closed at all times, which made it even hotter. I felt like screaming, along with the Christmas beetles shrilling like a train in the feathery tree canopy. The couple were kind and the husband was a honey. The lady of the house was German with good intentions but easygoing she was not, her rules being almost as rigid as those of the matrons. She taught me how to make marble cake, lay out a dress pattern properly and play gin rummy. She was what would be called nowadays a helicopter mother. Occasionally I babysat for the two little boys, holy terrors. I am afraid I also incurred my hostess's wrath for carelessly spraying ink over a lampshade as I was shaking out my fountain pen. Still, the weekends were my own and it was wonderful to have the freedom to visit friends in town whenever I liked. Megan and June came to visit, Megan in tears because her father had died. He had been suffering from silicosis, a lung disease he must have contracted years earlier, working in the Roan Antelope mine, Luanshya.

The exams came and went and the year drew to a close. I had won the Eng. Lit. prize and a Federal scholarship which would help with university expenses. Mum and Dad were proud and sent a telegram to Gran. I left school, feeling numb and apprehensive about my results, which would arrive in the new year.

I went back to my holiday job at Kathy's, now run by Mr. Patel, who had taken over Zlotnik's, the grocery store, as well. Mrs. Lane-Poole was still in the kitchen but our boss was now Mr. Bhakta, a middle-aged, shy Indian. His greasy, thinning hair was combed flat and he smelled of garlic. In his grey worsted trousers, I thought that his portly, retreating rear resembled that of an elephant. Our mid-morning tea was now laced with spices. Mr. Bhakta was just as hard a taskmaster as Kathy and watched us like a hawk. One day he caught me turning away a customer as there were no tinned tomatoes left on the shelves.

"Never refuse a customer, Miss. You can get it round the backside."

I applied for a job that was better paid and got it, to my surprise. I was to be the secretary to the Fort Rosebery Management Board. The previous incumbent, a bossy PA wife swiftly followed by McLulu, had left the books in a mess. I took the huge ledgers home each night and pored over them by the dim electric ceiling light because an inspection by auditors was imminent. As I waded through pages of pencil corrections I was amazed to see how far back the mistakes went. It taught me that confidence didn't mean efficiency and eventually I balanced the books.

Willy nilly, my maths was being given a workout. Apart from taking notes and minutes (in as rapid a longhand as I could manage), typing for my boss, filing and keeping the accounts in order, I received customers' utility payments and paid the labourers' wages, a weekly chore. Piles of the exact money were set out on the desk and the capitao would lead the men in one at a time. I counted out the person's coins in pounds, shillings and pence, placed them in a packet and took a signature or, more usually, his thumbprint, placing his finger on the inky stamp pad then on the list, next to his name, which I read out. This was embarrassing for both of us but it was the only way: they couldn't read or write and I couldn't speak much Bemba.

People rolled up to the Management Board office to pay their water and electricity bills. One day I noticed a flat-bed lorry outside with several stern-looking Africans standing in the back, holding branches.

"Who are they?" I asked Bill, the accountant.

"They're Kenneth Kaunda's lot. Come to see the DC. Mind you, it's me they should be seeing – they owe a packet on their electricity bills!"

My 18th birthday came and went in December, celebrated with a party and a curry supper cooked by my parents, poppadums supplied by Mr. Patel from Zlotnik's. They were delicious. Otherwise, it was a do-it-yourself affair. On the day of the party, I walked into the bush with Blondie to find some flowers and came upon a huge clump of flame lilies almost hidden in the long grass. They looked like glittering crowns, their iridescent crimson petals edged with gold. I picked a bunch for the house to fill Mum's copper bowl.

I had sewn a dress of glazed cotton sprigged with carnations and handed out invitations. Anne helped me to decorate the house and choose the records. It was hard work for my mother as, now, our cook/houseboy was a teenager she had trained herself. She was fed up with older, experienced servants who ended up thieving food, drink, clothes and the little jewellery she had left, the latest casualty being a Burmese jade ring given to her by Gran. Young Domino was a lovely chap, always smiling and helpful. He helped to shift furniture round while my parents cooked for the party. A crowd of 40 people filled our house, we danced until we dropped and changed record players halfway through as ours packed up. The food ran out so Mum supplied bacon, eggs and filled rolls; when she collapsed the remaining guests took over. It was the rainy season and Dad's lawn looked like a ploughed field by the time everyone had departed, many the worse for wear, at 4.00am the following day. At least nobody had passed out, been involved in a punch-up or ended up in a storm drain.

We enjoyed the usual wet Christmas. The harmonium's pedals still made a racket as we played it for carols in the tiny school and for the Christmas Day Morning Service held in the Club. This was conducted by the Welsh trade school teacher who happened to be a lay preacher; afterwards he proceeded to the bar and got roaring drunk. On Boxing Day Dad took us to Samfya, bless him, where we watched Roy Williams shoot the murderous crocodile.

In January Anne left to go to England and secretarial college and I knew I would miss her dreadfully. Diana had started at the new University College in Salisbury, June was working in Lusaka and so was Megan. Joyce was back at school, to repeat the year she had missed through illness. Things were changing.

In February my results came out. They were not as good as I had hoped and I couldn't get in to London University, unless I wanted to read English. I decided I couldn't spend the next three years just poring over books and could read enough throughout life to satisfy my needs. I wanted to travel and be out in the fresh air. I was no longer the Pommie bookworm. I decided to read Geography at Liverpool, a university recommended by a graduate who was conducting an anthropological survey in the surrounding villages. Liverpool. I knew nothing about the place but its School of Geography had a good reputation and specialised in African studies. Besides, nothing could be worse than Jean Rennie.

My mother wrote to Gran:

Wednesday, 6th April, 1960

Judy had a day off work last week – the usual. She is just as I used to be, very irregular and of course the inevitable pain. She started last Friday and she scratched her name off the list of players in the tennis tournament on Sunday. However, Stan Young came round looking for a partner so she decided to play – I think it did her good to get out in the open and she quite enjoyed it, really. The night before, all the young got together and went to one bachelor's house for a party, the lads taking the drinks and the girls the food.

Judy is booked to leave here the first week in September..... Her friend Will comes in from Samfya today for his Bemba exam and will be here for two days. We tease her a great deal about him and his big feet (Will took size 13 shoes!) *He is 6'3" tall and quite well made, although he has lost a lot of weight since he first came out. He has asked us all out to Samfya at Easter.....*

Tell John that his bête noire, F, is back in NR, near Ndola. We learned that while he was here he lost £100 in wages which he left in an unlocked drawer. This will make John smile. The mistakes of the PA are always very tactfully hushed up.

Poor old Blondie doesn't get a morning walk now Judy is working.

Much love from us all
Dulce

Mum had also learned the Bemba language but had no confidence in her ability. She and Dad took the exam on 16th and 17th April, written and oral. Mum knew she would be especially nervous in the oral..... But she passed and he didn't. John said he would never say another word of Chibemba once his exams were over!

The two Scots girls I had been friendly with left for pastures new and found jobs in Bulawayo. One of them, Jean, later married one of our policeman (NRP) friends Mike Mylod, a lovely, funny guy.

Jean wrote from Bulawayo:

Rhodes House, 35 Ninth Avenue,
Bulawayo, Southern Rhodesia.

22nd July, 1960

Dear Judy

Thanks a ton for your letter. I was beginning to wonder if anyone in Fort Rosebery still loved me (a short kick in the pants to Ernie Greig etc.) As usual, it fell into the comedienne category and Betty and I had a hearty laugh (har! har!).

Fort Rosebery hasn't been out of the news very much at all. We heard about the caravan fire tragedy..... We also heard reports over the radio about the refugees, approximately 600 of 'em arriving in Fort Rosebery so I bet you were kept on the hop.

Life has become very towny now and we are thoroughly civilised upstanding young citizens. One thing about the place is that clothing is about half the

price it is up there and I've refitted my wardrobe with
some very pretty dresses, woollens, shoes, blouses,
the lot. I always try to get British-made clothes and
Italian accessories – for the frills I love to go all I-tie.
You should see me hurtling around in three and a
half inch heels – little miss débutante. Honestly they
kill my feet but pride knows no pain. The teenagers
around here have their petticoats sticking out so far
you almost get one in the eye when you pass them.

Betty and I have moved into a double room and
we have made it very comfortable. Transistor radio
and our own little bed-lights and what not..... plenty
of cupboard space. We do our own washing and
ironing and after 18 months of having Banda doing
it for me the first time I held an iron in my hand, it
felt like a lead weight but now – not a crease.

This place gets worse and worse as far as the
political situation is concerned and I want to get out
in one piece to see all my friends again..... Methinks
I'm a trifle homesick to see all the folks.

It won't be long now before you become a Varsity
Student and the complete rag of the Liverpudlians.....

Love,
Jean

I spent as much time as I could in Samfya. I was a
reasonable sailor now and was even allowed to take the
dinghy's helm. Will took me on the government launch,
the "Mwaiseni", a fine clinker-built boat built from local

mahogany, over to the swamps. I stood at the wheel, learned how to take a bearing and stay on course.

We had our fair share of mishaps, to the anxiety of my parents. One day Will and I took a little speedboat with twin outboard engines to drop off the DC at a village on a lagoon, Lake Chifunabuli, down the shore. The lake was rough and even the lagoon was choppy. We coasted in towards the shore, where the DC waded in to see the headman, shoes and socks in his hands. We turned around and headed for the lake.

"Crikey," said Will, "If it's as bouncy as this in the lagoon I wonder what it's going to be like on the lake out there."

We passed the sandbar and plunged into the white horses of the Bangweulu proper. One of the twin Perkins engines sputtered and died.

"Bloody hell," shouted Will. "That's all we need."

He pulled and pulled but couldn't start the engine. There was nothing for it but to run the one good engine at idling speed and steer the little boat broadside to the waves. Any faster and we would have been flipped over. We had no lifebelts on board, of course. It was a strange experience, to be in stormy waters under a cloudless sky. The strong winds were trying to push us offshore and it was hard work, coaxing the boat along. We took it in turns to man the tiller and inched along the coast, little by little, fighting not to be taken out into the middle of the lake. Our journey home took us hours.

It was dark by the time we pulled into the little harbour. Our faces and arms were burnt to a crisp and we must have looked like savages as we walked into Will's house, where my frantic parents were waiting.

Top: *Afternoon sail, Samfya*
Bottom: *Late afternoon on the beach, Samfya*

"For God's sake, where have you been?" thundered Dad, furious. He ranted on in this vein but we were too exhausted to answer.

"Shut up, Jack. I thought you'd drowned," Mum said quietly. She was calm but her face looked grey and her eyes were moist.

Yes, drowning had crossed my mind. Will muttered his apologies and said he must go to tell the DC we had returned. Thank God he'd been such a competent sailor or we'd have be at the bottom of Lake Bangweulu, food for the crocodiles. That was what I loved about him – he was rock solid in a crisis.

By Easter Will had been forgiven – sort of – and I was allowed back to Samfya. He had a lot of work to do and went into the office on Easter Sunday for radio duty. He sat crouched over it, twiddling knobs and listening intently to whatever was coming into the earphones.

"Jesus, the Congo's blown up. There's big trouble in Katanga," he breathed. "Riots and shootings. They want to send over some refugees. I'd better go and tell the DC. Here," he said, handing me the headphones, "Put these on and make notes of what you hear."

I grabbed the headphones, sat in front of the radio and listened to the chilling news of what was happening just over our border. Some nuns had been killed on a mission and the European families at Kashiba Mwense, one of the border posts on the Luapula, feared for their lives. I had never been there but John said the bar served fantastic fillet steak and played cool jazz.

"It's hardly surprising," Will said later. "After all, old King Leopold used to run the Congo like his own private country and the Belgian government hasn't done much for the Africans."

In 1877 Henry Morton Stanley, the same man who had said "Dr Livingstone, I presume" at Ujiji, had discovered that the Lualaba was not the source of the Nile but of the Congo River, which flowed into the Atlantic Ocean. He reported the tremendous potential of the Congo Basin to the Belgian king for extracting wood, ivory, palm oil and rubber. Leopold instructed Stanley to establish trading stations along the river and then annexed the Congo. He personally received 50% of the trading concessions' income from considerable natural resources, not least of which were minerals. Brutality and corruption were rife. The Force Publique used the chicotte (the sjambok), the gallows and mass executions to subdue the populace and exterminate races deemed inferior. In the early 20th century, it is estimated that 10 million people had died or fled the region. After all, this was the country so well documented in Joseph Conrad's "Heart of Darkness."

In 1908 the Belgian government took over and, by the 1950s, the country had a modern infrastructure, including more hospital beds than all the other African countries combined (with the exception of South Africa). However, for the Africans, daily life resembled that under the South African system of apartheid. The government worked on the principle of "pas d'élites, pas d'ennemis", thinking that an educated African middle class would be subversive. The Belgian Congo's mineral wealth was huge and part of it lay close by, where the Copperbelt extended in an arc over the border into Katanga.

The Belgians were complacent, even in the late 1950s and thought they had at least another hundred years of rule. The riots and killings were the first wave of a deluge of violence that would see the colonial power relinquish the reins with indecent haste in June, 1960, a few months after that Easter morning. White refugees poured into Fort Rosebery and were billeted in the Club. There were many horror stories, the worst being about the couple who had put their children in the well of the car, out of sight, when escaping from Elisabethville down the Pedicle road. They were ambushed and the children were killed. Somebody had seen the bullet holes in the car door.

All this news was unsettling. It was dangerous to drive on our roads now after dark. I was already in my parents' bad books as Will and I had broken down in the Land Rover coming home from Samfya one night, losing all power and lights, and had to wait until morning to be rescued. We had tried to find help in a couple of villages but the locals' erstwhile friendship had been replaced with wariness, if not downright hostility. Refugees from the Congo flooded into town and were billeted everywhere, including the Club. The prim PA matrons looked askance at the glamorous young Belgian girls, walking round in low-cut tops and short shorts. The Rhodesian Air Force paid us a visit. They arrived late in the day and, as our airstrip had no night time landing facilities, everyone drove their cars and Land Rovers out to the airstrip and positioned themselves alongside with their headlights blazing to help the aircraft find our tiny airstrip.

It was ironic that, during this period, my father was finally given permanent and pensionable (P and P) status by Her Majesty's Government Overseas Aid Scheme (OSAS), with a pension of between £30 and £40 a month at the age of 55. He was so proud! This news came just as the movement to achieve independence intensified. African nationalism had been given a kick start by the Conservative Ian Macleod, Secretary of State for the Colonies, who promoted and speeded up the process of decolonisation. Civil servants were beginning to wonder how much time they had left in Northern Rhodesia.

There was song doing the rounds at this time, to the tune of My Old Man's a Dustman, which was written by the DC at Abercorn (Mbala):

Oh, my old man's a DC, he wears an OBE,
He works down at the Boma and lives in an AK3.
He tours around the district with carriers at his back,
And a cook and clerks and messengers, and a great big Union Jack.

He's a very important person, one of the elite.
He graces every function and sits in a front row seat.
To live in a state of greatness affords him lots of joy,
But when he unbends, he condescends to speak to the hoi polloi.

He came straight here from Oxbridge, thought he was here to stay,
But there's no doubt he'll be thrown out on Independence Day.
He hasn't saved a penny since he was a Cadet,
And what sort of employment can a surplus DC get?

So if you are in London, and you should chance to meet

A ladies' undies salesman who stops you in the street,
Remember please the story of the good Sa–mar–i–tan
Don't kick him in the gutter, he – might – be – my –
old – man!

An AK3 was the design of a type of government bungalow. The architect was the father of one of my Jean Rennie contemporaries, Ann Akeroyd.

This little ditty resonated with ex-pats, my father included.

My parents would have put a stop to my relationship with Will if they had known anything about our latest adventure.

I was staying with Brian and Hazel, a young policeman and his new wife, in their little bungalow in Samfya for a few days. I spent every spare moment with Will, to Hazel's annoyance. I think she felt a little jealous. In any event, she was almost as vigilant a chaperone as my Mum.

One sparkling, windy morning Will turned up in high spirits at Brian's door.

"Come on, time for a sail, old girl," he grinned.

"Less of the old. What, in this wind? You've got to be joking." I could barely stand up on the cliff top near the back door.

"It'll be great. Just think, we can be belting under Brian's window with the sheets hauled in tight when he comes home for his tea break. He'll be mad as hell he's not with us."

It was hard to counter Will's enthusiasm but I wondered if he was having second thoughts as we struggled to rig the boat in the wind. With difficulty, we launched the boat into the teeth of the gale and fought our way offshore. We tacked at high speed and surged along the coastline in the direction of Mwamfuli and the lagoon. I whipped from one side of the dinghy to the other, hauling in sheets hard, as the boom whipped round. My hands were still blue with cold and the ropes were making white indentations in my fingers and palms. I glanced at Will, in his element, hair flying, a broad smile on his features. I had total trust in him. We picked up speed and soon were miles down the lake, running parallel to the shore.

Suddenly there was a tremendous crash. The boom flew across towards me, cracking my nose with such force that I thought it would knock me overboard, breaking my spectacles on the bridge. The two lenses flew apart and disappeared into the water just as the boat capsized. I sank heavily into the water and came up after what seemed like eternity, floundering in my heavy sweater and gulping gallons of lake. Will surfaced beside me, spluttering.

"What happened?" I gurgled.

"Centre board broke – just couldn't hold us."

Coughing, we hung on to our disabled boat, lying helpless on her side, the sails spread-eagled in the water, and trying to pull her towards the lagoon. Thank God, we passed the sandbar and paddled into calmer waters. With my blurred vision I could make out a group of excited villagers gathering on the shore and wondered if we would get a hostile reception. I realized they were all women. Three of them waded out towards us, laughing, and helped us bring the boat on to the beach. One lady, heavily pregnant, hugged me to her bosom and indicated a thatched shelter.

As we staggered up the beach, shivering, Will said "She says we must rest in her hut. Come on, Jude." I was glad Will's Bemba was fluent.

We stripped off to our underclothes and spread our shirts and shorts on the grass to dry, then hugged one another to keep warm. Will's head and arm were bleeding and I felt dizzy, with a throbbing nose. He chafed my hands and kissed me, saying "I'll go and get help. We're not far from the main road." I lay down, my head spinning and listened to the women chattering outside. We had been lucky, this time. I fell asleep.

Will was as good as his word and came back with his Land Rover. It was later, much later. He hugged me and said "Well done, bush baby."

Both my parents had been unwell and Mum had been forced to take a couple of days off work – most unlike her. Dad had lost a lot of weight. Being made permanent and pensionable had given him a boost but he still felt low. Being a typical teenager, self-absorbed and largely unaware of their problems, I nevertheless did realize that they desperately needed to take a break, some local leave.

Chapter 21
ALL CHANGE

Victoria Falls Hotel

It says a lot for Mum and Dad that they planned a trip down to Victoria Falls for all of us before my departure to university, given that I might not see my parents for at least two years. Despite blotting his copybook in Dad's eyes by driving too fast, nearly drowning his daughter on at least two occasions and, Dad guessed, making repeated assaults on her virginity, Will was included in the invitation.

The next ten days were unreal, dreamlike. Our trip was mundane enough, long stretches of dirt and tar road in the dust of the late dry season interspersed with night stops at government rest houses.

We had tea with Megan, now working in Lusaka, and her mother on the balcony of Woodgate House on Cairo

Top: *Dad*
Bottom: *Mum*

Top and centre: *Evening at Samfya*
Bottom: *Last sundowner on the stoep*

Road. I knew from a letter she had written that there was a new man in her life.

"I've met this guy," she said. "He's a lot older than me and a farmer – a farmer! But he's good fun and is very go-ahead. He's taught me how to sail"

"Hmm, don't know if that's a good thing!" I answered, shooting a glance at Will. "Is it serious?"

She tapped her nose and laughed.

"I think I can nab him."

I didn't know if I envied her or not. She was so intelligent and pretty, Megan could have had the pick of all the boys. Besides, she had lost her father and was so young to be thinking of marriage.

Despite Dad's misgivings, he allowed Will to drive for most of the long journey to Livingstone. On one stretch of strip tarmac, where it was case of holding your wheels on to the strips until dropping on to corrugated dirt if you met another vehicle, we blew a tyre. There was a tremendous bang but Will kept control of the Consul, something I doubted Dad would have been able to cope with.

The Falls were impressive, even at the end of the dry season. We passed through the town of Livingstone and drove straight there, seeing the cloud of spray from Mosi oa Tunya (the smoke that thunders) from miles away. The Zambezi flowed lazily between lushly forested banks before tipping into a deep basalt gorge a mile wide.

Will woke me early one morning to see the Falls at daybreak. We drove the ten miles out of town on a deserted road and parked the car near the big baobab tree and David Livingstone's statue on the south bank, where he still gazes at the Devil's Cataract. He wrote that "scenes so lovely must have been gazed upon by angels in their flight." The river flowed slowly, fringed by palm trees silhouetted against the sky and everything was peaceful, with just the muffled roar of the falls nearby. We walked into the rainforest and found a bushbuck and her fawn browsing there, their spotted coats well camouflaged in the dappled sunlight filtering down through massive trees festooned with creepers. Our view was no different to how it must have looked a century before, when the famous explorer had first seen the spectacle. How things have changed these days, with tarmac paths, fences, a border post, bungee jumping and river rafting.

I wrote to Gran – an embarrassing sample of a teenager's purple prose:

P O Box 3
Fort Rosebery

24th August, 1960

Dear Gran,

We've been having a lovely time, loafing a good deal (Mum looks very well on it, which is a good thing) and enjoying all the sightseeing, especially around Victoria Falls, which are simply amazing. The wedding went off very well (I had been a bridesmaid to a friend who was marrying a policeman) *and I had a gorgeous hangover after all the pink champagne consumed. Actually, I only had one glass but some furtive character kept on filling it up, unbeknown to me! The church had no roof, only rafters, but all the same it looked very effective and everyone was all*

331

togged up to kill. There was a police guard of honour outside the church for everyone to walk under..... I will be able to show you the photos when I arrive in London, which will be four weeks tomorrow as I leave on 21st September.

We were thrilled with Livingstone and the Falls..... Of course, the Falls are quite breathtaking. Our first sight of them was really wonderful – a mass of thundering power, a foaming wall of water surging over a sharp edge into a fantastic fissure full of the loveliest colours. There is a rainbow at the bottom of the gorge and it is reflected in the falling water. The palms, tall trees and creepers are tropical Africa at its best and set off the Falls beautifully. We spent ages just looking and got absolutely soaked in the rainforest – but we came at the best time of year, apparently, as there is still a lot of water coming over but not so much spray that you can't see properly. We also took a trip upriver and saw quite a bit of game on the banks – elephant, buck, monkeys, baboons, plus hippos and crocodiles in the water and a multitude of bird life. There are some lovely drives along the banks of the Zambezi.....

I'll be seeing you soon!

All my love
Judy

I had omitted to mention my most important piece of news.

The valley was hot and steamy, like Kariba but the evenings were the best time of day, with glorious sunsets over the river. I felt as though we were living in a fantasy world and wished this escape would never end.

On our last night, Will took me to the Victoria Falls Hotel, on the Southern Rhodesia side, an elegant colonial building. He put on a proper shirt, tie and slacks and I wore the yellow cotton bridesmaid's dress I had made for Les and Wendy's wedding. Will always liked me in yellow. We couldn't afford a meal but sat quietly on the verandah, sipping our drinks and watching the shadows play over the lawns down to the gorge. The falls rumbled in the distance. Will was very quiet and I felt sad, as in less than a month I would be flying to England, with this as a distant memory. The Theme from a Summer Place was playing in the bar and Will extravagantly bought me a second brandy and ginger ale. The fiery glow of an African dusk suddenly descended into night and we heard the whine of a mosquito round our legs.

"Time to go," Will said.

We drove slowly back over the bridge and stopped by one of our favourite places, a little café overlooking the river. The air was filled with the scent of wild jasmine and we could hear the river beyond the grove of trees around our parked car. Crickets chirruped and tree frogs piped "tink, tink" in the darkened bush outside the car, for there was no moon that night.

Will asked me to marry him and I said yes.

My mind is a blank as to what happened next but I do remember creeping in to wake Mum when we got back to the rest house and telling her our news. She was delighted but wrote in a letter to Gran that we hadn't told my father. Will and I had decided to keep this revelation a secret but he knew I had wanted to tell my mother. Dad didn't know for ages and I imagined what his reaction might be.

My memory of those last few weeks at home is hazy. Will's proposal had blown my mind. The days passed in a whirl and I hugged the warm feeling of our wonderful secret to myself, immune from harsh reality. I was torn between wanting to fulfil my parents' hopes, looking forward to my new life at university, the culmination of years of study and incarceration, and the alternative – remaining in Africa with Will. We could not afford to marry and deep down we realized that a wedding might be a few years away..... Our backgrounds were so different..... Will's mother was ill with what would prove to be a fatal cancer and he knew he might have to fly home to Yorkshire soon..... The country's future was uncertain and so was ours. I had found love a few years too soon. And Africa had also sneaked up and stealthily stolen my heart.

A lot of things were left unsaid.

Will came into town to say goodbye. He gave me a beautiful Oxford Atlas to take to university, the best one I have, lovingly inscribed.

We kissed and clung to each other – how could I bear to apart from him? I thought my heart would break. Will stood back.

"You must go. You owe it to yourself – and your parents. I'll still be here," he said. "I shall think of you all the time."

I went, excited at this new phase of my life but with a heavy heart. Another journey, another separation. Who knew what the future would hold?

PART THREE

LATER

Chapter 22
A FAR OFF PLACE

Royal Liver Building, 1960

Some months later I am sitting in the refectory of a rather grim students' union building at university. A group of us sits eating an unappetizing but cheap lunch of brown Windsor soup and ham rolls, here called barm cakes. The air is thick with steam and cigarette smoke, while outside a grey sky weeps rain on to the soot-blackened buildings of a northern city.

"So where are you from, again?" asks one of the boys.

"Well, from London originally, but my home now is in Africa."

"Where in Africa, exactly?"

I wade into my standard description of where Northern Rhodesia is when a blond boy wearing horn-rimmed specs and a tweed jacket interrupts.

"So you're one of those posh neo-colonialist fascists who exploit the downtrodden natives, then," he drawls.

My hackles rise and I am about to take the bait when I realize it's pointless arguing with him. He has no idea..... He is later to become an unsuccessful Labour parliamentary candidate for Basingstoke. I don't trust any politicians now and have become apolitical.

"So, what are you?" he continues.

He is definitely a boy, not a man. I am disappointed to find that all first year students are boys – I have been spoilt. I don't pursue the argument.

The question remains, unanswered, in the air. Am I English or am I a white African? Or a bit of both, a hybrid, or neither? I don't know.

A far off place is what Africans used to call the next village, a town 50 miles away, another country, overseas. It was all the same to them.

What happened to my family and friends?

My parents returned to the U.K. just before Zambian Independence in 1964. They tried to settle in England but kept returning to Africa, tried the USA and eventually retired in Hampshire. Their long married life of 58 years was happy, for the most part.

My brother John went to the USA and has lived there for 55 years. He is an eminent professor of psychology and neuroscience, specializing in animal behaviour, but has retained his sense of humour and an appreciation of the absurd.

Juliet was a Zionist in her teenage years, went to the USA and lived in a hippie commune in the seventies, I believe! She is now an academic and journalist, married with one daughter and lives in Boulder, Colorado.

Betty got married quite young and was a pretty bride. She ran a café in Chingola, then moved to South Africa.

Diana graduated from the University College of Rhodesia and Nyasaland, Salisbury, married and emigrated to New Zealand.

My great friend Joyce became a secretary. She married a policeman and lived in Papua New Guinea, then moved to Australia, where she knew her two children "would never be kicked out." Sadly, her husband couldn't settle and they are now divorced.

Dear Joey was driving her VW Beetle in Lusaka when she was hit at a crossroads by another car. She died instantly.

Another sixth form classmate, Anne Black, lives in Brisbane, Australia, not far from Joyce.

Darling Megan married her farmer and they had a long and happy life together in Zambia until Ron's death in 2007. She has a son living in Holland and a daughter in Cape Town. She still runs the Chisamba farm and is responsible for the employment, welfare, health and education of 500 people – as well as her livestock, crops, machinery and tribe of dogs.

June Finley-Bissett became a teacher in Zimbabwe but I lost touch with her.

Anne Middleton married a journalist and lived in Uganda, where she too was killed in a car accident.

Top: *Jono and lion cub*
Bottom: *Michael and family visit Victoria Falls*

Many years roll by and I am at an agricultural show in North Yorkshire with my husband. We are invited for a drink by our solicitor, who turns to me saying "Here's someone I think you know."

I see a tall man staring at me behind sunglasses and a sun-hat – something about him is vaguely familiar. It is Will.

More years pass and Will invites four of us – my brother John and his American wife, me and my husband – to dinner at his house. His new girlfriend is there and we are introduced. It's freezing outside and his comfortable house is chilly. Still, he gives us a warm welcome and introduces us to his two obedient gundogs. We sit in his tidy living room, sip our drinks and talk. I notice wedding photos, in silver frames, of Will's sole surviving son on a side table. Will is now a stockbroker, twice married and divorced, and has single-handedly cooked a full roast dinner with all the trimmings. He always was good at entertaining. He talks too much, a sure sign that he is nervous, and I feel ill at ease.

To my amazement, he announces that he's put his old cine films of Africa on video and wants to show them to us. They have been cobbled inexpertly together and the print is faded and jumpy in parts but there it all is. The lake, Samfya and its white beach, the sandy roads, Victoria Falls, canoes threading slowly through the Bangweulu swamp, their boatmen gracefully polling the makoros through the tall reeds.

And there we are. I am shy and won't face the camera, willowy, with long chestnut hair (was it really that colour?), he is laughing in his blue shirt and shorts.

Memories crowd in. The smell of parched earth drinking in the first rains, so distinctive that I wish I could bottle it. Scents of curling wood smoke and my father's moonflowers opening at dusk. The beat of drums across a valley and rain hammering on a tin roof. Antelope moving in a dawn mist through the bush, the exuberant colours of msasa leaves as they unfurl, the roar and spray of huge waterfalls, the sound of African laughter and song. A land of space, big skies and big rivers, vast lakes and burnt orange sunsets, which once was my home. And dust, bush fires and violence and flame lilies, too.

Now Will flashes me a look and smiles. It was a long time ago, in a far off place.

A TEENAGE SOUNDTRACK

Lloyd Price	Personality
Boyd Bennett & The Rockets	Seventeen
Buddy Holly	That'll Be the Day
Guy Mitchell	Singing the Blues
Frank Sinatra	I've Got You Under My Skin
	Swinging Down The Lane
Frankie Vaughan	Green Door
Erroll Garner	Misty
Elvis Presley	Heartbreak Hotel
	All Shook Up
	Blue Moon of Kentucky
Doris Day	Que Sera Sera
Jerry Lee Lewis	Whole Lotta Shaking Goin' On
The Platters	Smoke Gets in Your Eyes
Nat King Cole	Let There Be Love
Cliff Richard	Living Doll
Hugh Masekela	Kwela Claude
Yma Sumac	Wimoweh (The Lion Sleeps Tonight)
The Modern Jazz Quartet	God Rest Ye Merry Gentlemen
Julie London	Cry Me A River
Percy Faith and orchestra	Theme from a Summer Place
Bill Haley and the Comets	See you Later, Alligator!

GLOSSARY

I apologise for the length of this glossary. Central Africa certainly teaches you how to become a linguist: there were 45 dialects in Northern Rhodesia in the 1950s, perhaps fewer now.

agh	oh
aina	ouch
ANC	African National Congress
azeko	finished
Bangweulu	where the water meets the sky
baobab	Andansonia digitata, monkey bread tree; stores water in its trunk to withstand drought
bhatcha	darling
bilharzia	schistosomiasis, a liver fluke
bioscope	cinema
blackjack	a hooked seed
blueskop	blue-headed agama lizard
boerwors	coarse sausage, lit. farmer's sausage
boma	thorny stockade for animals; provincial administration offices
bonsela	tip, gift
braaivleis, braai	barbecue (lit. burnt meat)
broekies	knickers
bulala	kill
bundu	bush
Chembe	fish eagle
Chibemba	Bemba language
Chilapalapa	lingua franca spoken throughout Southern Africa on mines and farms, also Chikabanga
chinlone	a type of football/martial art played in Burma
Chinyanja	Nyanja language

chitemene	slash and burn agriculture, shifting cultivation
chitenge	brightly patterned cloth
craic	gossip, chat, fun
DA	District Assistant
DC	District Commissioner
DO	District Officer
Dacoit	bandit
dambo	marshy area which drains in the dry season
dona	madam, housewife
dorp	small town
dwaal	daze, dream
eeish	wow, tut tut
e (pronounced eh)	yes
ena lo	like this
fanaga lo	like that
fulwe	tortoise
fwaka	cigarette
gogo	(pronounced with a guttural g) insect
guti	mountain or moorland mist
hairyback	South African
highveld	high plateau savannah
houtie	derogatory term for African, from hout – wood
indaba	meeting, conference (azeko indaba – no problem)
iwe	hey, you!
iyo	no
jigger	burrowing worm which penetrates through eggs picked up on soles of feet, usually
kalimba	hand piano, also called mbira

kapasu	district messenger, rural policeman
kapenta	small sardine-like fish, dried fish
kopje	hill, often topped with rocks or boulders
koeksisters	type of plaited doughnut drenched in syrup
kwashiorkor	disease caused by malnutrition
leguaan	monitor lizard
lekker	good, lovely, delicious
longyi	type of sarong worn by Burmese people
lowveld	low-lying savannah, such as occurs in the Luangwa and Zambezi valleys
machila	hammock slung between two poles
mafuta	fat
mailo	tomorrow
Makishi mask	headdress worn at ritual ceremonies, e.g. circumcision, NW Province
makoro	dugout canoe
ma we	goodness me
mealies	sweetcorn, maize
miombo	type of woodland found in Luapula Province, of Brachystegia-Isoberlinia species
monkey bread	fruit of the baobab tree
mopane	Brachystegia speciformis, tree found in low veld areas such as the Zambezi and Luangwa valleys with distinctive camel's foot leaves
mosi	smoke
msasa	miombo woodland
mukwai	sir
muntu	man
mushi	delicious, excellent
mushitu	virgin forest, deep bush
muti	medicine
mwaiseni	welcome!
mwapoleni mukwai	good morning
mwashibukeni mukwai	good morning (very early)

nahpoo	lit. il n'y a plus, there is no more, World War I slang
ndeshya	hurry up
ndita mukwai	thank you
ngandu	crocodile
ni shani?	How much?
nshima	mealie or cassava porridge
nyama	meat
Ouma	grandmother
Oupa	grandfather
PC	Provincial Commissioner
Pommie	English man or woman
piccanin	African child
PK	piccanin kaya (lit. small room – toilet)
pootsie	fly which lays eggs on skin which develop into burrowing subcutaneous worms
punda	shout
PWD	Public Works Department
riem	strip of animal hide
rooinek	redneck, Englishman
sadza	mealie porridge
safari	expedition, tour
salwar kameez	long top and loose trousers worn by Indian and Pakistani women
shiwa	lake
simba	lion
sis	yuk (expression of disgust)
situpa	pass, certificate of employment
sjambok	stock whip made from hippo hide
soutie	Englishman (from soutiepiel – salt penis)
sterek	strong
stoep	step, verandah

tackies	plimsolls, gym shoes
takuli	finished
tickey	threepenny bit
Tilapia	type of cichlid, commonly called bream
tunya	thunder
ulendo	safari, tour
umupila	ball
UNIP	United National Independence Party
veld	lit. field, savannah
veldschoen	soft nubuck or suede walking shoes or boots
voetsek	lit. "forth say I", go away
vlei	marsh
vrek	die
ZNAC	Zambian National African Congress

BIBLIOGRAPHY and FURTHER READING

Charles Allen (ed) (1975) *Plain Tales from the Raj*
Charles Allen (ed) (1979) *Tales from the Dark Continent: Images of British Colonial Africa in the Twentieth Century*
Sue Arnold (1996) *A Burmese Legacy*
David Bennun (2004) *Tick Bite Fever*
Karen Blixen (1937) *Out of Africa*
Barbara Carr (1963) *Not for Me The Wilds*
Frank Clements (1959) *Kariba*
Barbara Crossette (1998) *The Great Hill Stations of Asia*
Michelle Frost (2014 and YouTube undated) *Illuminations*
James Fox (1982) *White Mischief*
Alexandra Fuller (2003) *Don't Let's Go to the Dogs Tonight*
Alexandra Fuller (2012) *Cocktail Hour Under the Tree of Forgetfulness*
Alexandra Fuller (2015) *Leaving Before the Rains Come*
Susan Gibbs (2011) *Call of the Litany Bird*
Peter Godwin (1997) Mukiwa: *A White Boy in Africa*
Peter Godwin (2006) *When A Crocodile eats the Sun*
Vic Guhrs (2010) *The Trouble with Africa*
Elspeth Huxley (1959) *The Flame Trees of Thika*
Elspeth Huxley (1985) *Out in the Midday Sun*
George Kay (1960) *A Social and Economic Study of Fort Rosebery*
David Kynaston (2008) *Austerity Britain 1945-51*
David Kynaston (2009) *Family Britain 1951-57*
David Le Breton (ed) (2012) *I Remember It Well: Fifty Years of Colonial Service Personal Reminiscences*
Christina Lamb (1999) *The Africa House*
Doris Lessing (1983) *African Laughter*
Doris Lessing (1950) *The Grass Is Singing*
Chris McIntyre (2004) Zambia: *The Bradt Travel Guide*
Jan Morris (1968) *Pax Britannica*
Northern Rhodesia and Nyasaland Publications Bureau (1960) *A Brief Guide to Northern Rhodesia*
George Orwell (1934) *Burmese Days*

Robin Page (1989) *Dust in a Dark Continent*
Jeremy Paxman (2011) *Empire: What the Ruling the World Did to the British*
Ruth Prawer Jhabvala (1975) *Heat and Dust*
Douglas Rogers (2010) *The Last Resort*
Katharine Rukavina (1951) *Jungle Pathfinder: The Biography of Chirupula Stevenson*
Dominic Sandbrook (2005) *Never Had It So Good*
Paul Scott (1981) *Staying On*
Robyn Scott (2009) *Twenty Chickens for a Saddle*
Pamela Shurmer-Smith (2014) *Remnants of Empire*
Stephen Taylor (2000) *Livingstone's Tribe: A Journey from Zanzibar to the Cape*
Barbara Trapido (2003) *Frankie and Stankie*
Paul Theroux (2002) *Dark Star Safari*
Laurens van der Post (1952) *Venture to the Interior*
N. Wainama (2005) *How to Write About Africa*
Evelyn Waugh (1937) *Journey Without Maps*
Michela Wrong (2000) *In the Footsteps of Mr. Kurtz*

BLOGS AND WEBSITES

www.spanglefish.com/robinclay
www.lowdownzambia.com
www.zambiaworldwide.org
www.remnantsofempire.com
www.greatnorthroad.org

ACKNOWLEDGEMENTS

I consider myself very lucky. So many people have helped me in the course of writing this book and I give them my heartfelt thanks.

Firstly, my family: my late husband Bob, with me in spirit; my sons Jono and Michael; my remarkable grandmother and parents, for their love, sacrifice and support; my brother John and his wife Cindy.

Secondly, Bob's family, for all their help in recent years, particularly Annie and Ed.

Thirdly, the writers: The Egton Bridge Writers' Group, who encouraged me to resume writing at a difficult time; Laurel Goldman and her writing class, in Chapel Hill, North Carolina, for the pleasure of their company and useful criticism.

Thanks to all those friends who helped me in providing material for the book, including Juliet Wittman, Megan Landless, June Finley-Bissett, Joyce Nelson, Jean Mylod; dear Melanie Bousfield, photographer extraordinaire, who has worked with me on other projects and now this; Bob Butterworth, raconteur extraordinaire and a good friend; Alan Kitching, for his help and friendship, and to his wife Audrey for lending him to me. Love to you all.

I am grateful to those inspirational people I feel I know but have never met: Heather Chalcraft of The Lowdown and creator of the NRZ website (NRZ) on Facebook; Daphne Weaving of the Chingola website and Pamela Shurmer-Smith, writer.

Thanks to my friend Viv for cake and companionship, Richard for his technical support, Kate for the miracle Chinese needles and Rosie with her massages, for healing an aching back after too many hours spent at the computer. And finally, my dog Truffles, who sat patiently waiting for walks while I spent hours writing this book then gave me a comforting lick whenever I needed it.

I am so grateful to Arthur Cunynghame, of Loose Chippings, for his all-embracing talent, expertise and encouragement.

ABOUT THE AUTHOR

After studying Geography at university, Judy has spent many years in various parts of Africa with her husband. She worked as a town planner, private secretary, medical and arts administrator, tutor and lecturer and has now "retired" to concentrate on writing, painting, travel and a social life. She has two sons and three grandchildren, her finest productions. She lives in the North Cotswolds, Gloucestershire with her dog, a stone's throw from her family.

PREVIOUS PUBLICATIONS

A Farthing a Box
Egton Bridge Parish Map for the Millennium
Bilberry Pie (editor and contributor)
He Longed for a Drink of Cool Water from the Long Well (contributor)
Remnants of Empire (contributor)